DANIEL RADCLIFFE

THE BIOGRAPHY

DANIEL RADCLIFFE

THE BIOGRAPHY

Sue Blackhall

JOHN BLAKE

Published by John Blake Publishing Ltd,
3 Bramber Court, 2 Bramber Road,
London W14 9PB, England

www.johnblakepublishing.co.uk

www.facebook.com/Johnblakepub
twitter.com/johnblakepub

This edition published in 2014

ISBN: 978-1-78219-989-2

British Library Cataloguing-in-Publication Data:

A catalogue record for this book is available from the British Library.

Design by www.envydesign.co.uk

Printed in Great Britain by CPI Group (UK) Ltd

1 3 5 7 9 10 8 6 4 2

Papers used by John Blake Publishing are natural, recyclable products made from
wood grown in sustainable forests. The manufacturing processes conform to the
environmental regulations of the country of origin.

Every attempt has been made to contact the relevant copyright-holders,
but some were unobtainable. We would be grateful if the appropriate
people could contact us.

CONTENTS

INTRODUCTION

The little boy peered through his glasses, overwhelmed at the crowd, the cameras and the questions. Just yesterday no one had known his name. Now he was big news. He was no doubt wondering where all this was to lead, for himself and the other two children sitting alongside him. What he could never have imagined was that this trio would become a global phenomenon. It was literally as if a magic wand had been waved, casting a spell on ten-year-old Daniel Radcliffe who would soon be the most famous boy wizard and child star in the world, his life overtaken by fantasy, fiends and the feisty orphan who is Harry Potter.

It might never have happened at all. For Daniel had so very nearly been the subject of another kind of well-meaning sorcery by his parents. To say Marcia Gresham and Alan Radcliffe were wary of their son becoming Harry Potter and all it could entail is an understatement. So anxious were they about the huge change it would make to his life that they initially wouldn't even let him audition for the part. One could understand their concerns, for, unlike his debut starring part in a television drama production of *David Copperfield*, this was not to be a one-off role. Whoever won the coveted part would be committing to seven films shot in America, such a long way from home, and becoming the 'property' of the mighty Warner Bros. empire. With the deal changed and with agreement from Daniel's parents, the role was finally his. The rest, as they say, is history. Daniel would go on to become a worldwide star with the hugely successful Harry Potter films leading to a diverse and equally renowned stage and film career, as well as incredible wealth. Like all great stories, however, this young actor's has its ups and downs but he has never, quite rightly, ever lost his own magical appeal.

CHAPTER 1

THE MAGIC BEGINS

Daniel has used the word 'lucky' many times in reference to his getting the iconic role. He has also said that by chance he happened to be in the right place at the right time. He was on a night out in 1999 with his parents in the London audience at the play *Stones in His Pockets*, where Potter producer David Heyman and screenwriter Steve Kloves were sitting several rows in front. Heyman was already known to Daniel's parents, as his mother, Norma Heyman, was a client of literary agent Alan Radcliffe. During the interlude, Heyman introduced himself, omitting any mention of the new project, a film adaptation of J. K. Rowling's hugely successful series of boy wizard books that was already in pre-production in October 1999. Or so the story goes.

In fact, upon seeing Daniel at the theatre, Heyman had made a surreptitious call to director Chris Columbus, who was now panicking because the perfect Potter had still not been found so close to the start of filming, to tell him that by amazing coincidence he had stumbled across the boy who had made such an impression in the BBC two-part drama *David Copperfield*. Columbus urged Heyman to make contact, leaving Daniel bemused at the garbled conversations between the grown-ups. 'I had this feeling that my parents were keeping me out of the loop, somehow,' he said. 'All I could think about was why this guy had been staring at me.'

At one point, Daniel was ushered behind a theatre column with his parents seemingly talking in some secret code about something he knew nothing about. In fact, the complete story is that, when the casting crew were looking around for their Harry Potter, Columbus had watched Daniel in a video of *David Copperfield*. He has always been irked about the myth of David Heyman seeing Daniel at the theatre, turning round and happening upon Harry Potter. Columbus said: 'That story drives me crazy. It's only part of it. We had a casting director who would bring in hundreds and hundreds of kids every week and I'd look at all these videotapes submitted from all over England but we never really found the right boy.'

The search lasted for nine months and around sixteen thousand children were seen. There are reports that one casting director actually lost their job amid the desperation to find the right boy. It was watching the *Copperfield* video that made Columbus think that at last they had the perfect Potter child actor. 'I became enchanted with the kid and told the casting director that we had to see him. He had that haunted quality we were looking for. I couldn't get his image out of my mind.' The immediate response he received was that because of the reluctance of Daniel's parents it would never happen. The casting search continued until one day a frustrated Columbus threw the video on his desk and demanded in frustration, 'This is what I want! This is the kid. Just bring him to me.'

With a new two-film contract in place, Daniel's parents eventually relented and let him audition. 'To the Radcliffes' credit,' said Columbus, 'they were totally aware of the enormity of the project and were not going to make this decision lightly. We made it very clear to them that we would protect their son.'

It was the experience Columbus had had with child actors that secured him the directing role in the first place. He had not been first choice. The job was originally offered to Steven Spielberg who actually worked for a few months on the project with Steve Kloves but later withdrew after disagreeing with Jo Rowling's insistence on an all-British cast. Spielberg was later to say, 'I just felt I wasn't ready to make an all-kids movie and my kids thought I was crazy. And the books were by that time popular so, when I dropped out, I knew it was going to be a phenomenon. But you know, I don't make films because they're gonna be a phenomenon.'

In another interview, he was to go even further, saying, 'I purposely didn't do the Harry Potter movie because, for me, that was shooting ducks in a barrel. It's just a slam dunk. It's just like withdrawing a billion dollars and putting it into your personal bank accounts. There's no challenge.'

Fate, it seemed, was to play a huge part in Daniel's future, for Spielberg had also wanted to hire young American actor Haley Joel Osment, who already had a number of films behind him including *Forrest Gump* and *The Sixth Sense*, as Harry Potter.

Another American boy star, Liam Aiken from *Stepmom*, was also said at one time to be up for the part.

Other names for the director's job included Terry Gilliam of *Monty Python* fame, Jonathan Demme who directed *The Silence of the Lambs* and *Philadelphia*, and Brad Silberling (*City of Angels* and *Casper*). But fortunately for Daniel, Columbus was taken on – and Columbus knew exactly who he wanted, despite what he described as an 'intense' process. 'There were times when we felt we would never find an individual who embodied the complex spirit and depth of Harry Potter. Then Dan walked into the room and we all knew we had found Harry.'

And there was someone else who also thought Daniel would be perfect for the part and had recommended him – Maggie Smith, who had been greatly impressed by him when she acted alongside him as Aunt Betsey Trotwood in *Copperfield*. 'I owe her big,' Daniel was to say many years later. So it was a kind of staged fate – the meeting at the theatre that night combined with a series of fortuitous events – that was to turn Daniel into one of the world's most famous stars.

Daniel got the call for a more formal meeting followed by three auditions and a series of screen tests. He said he entered them all with little confidence but a lot of hope. 'My parents told me to believe in myself but they also said not to get my hopes up too much because I could end up really disappointed.'

He had every reason to be cautious because the cast hunt for Harry Potter was hugely publicised, with new names in the frame for the title role being mooted every day. But he was slowly getting there. In one crucial five-minute screen test he had to express a range of emotions from pleasure to gravity including performing a poignant Harry Potter speech

– 'Do you know what I hear? I can hear my mum screaming and pleading with Voldemort and if you heard your mum screaming about to be killed you wouldn't forget in a hurry' – being one of the lines from it.

Columbus put Daniel on the spot by deliberately fumbling his own lines to see how he would cope. In the clip, at the time of writing still on YouTube (under 'Daniel's Radcliffe's first audition'), Daniel is still literally very much the hesitant and natural blue-eyed boy. (He was to remain just that, as he developed an allergy to the green contact lenses he was initially asked to wear to match the eye colour of Rowling's wizard. The idea of digitally altering the colour was brought up but it would have been a time-consuming process and so, with Rowling's agreement, the screen Harry Potter had blue eyes.) A shy Daniel is seen donning several pairs of dark-rimmed owlish spectacles handed to him before Columbus announces 'perfect' to the pair that were to become the Potter trademark.

Another enchanting screen test has Daniel talking about a dragon's egg and after one false start the play-acting going well. The films were shown to Jo Rowling who, some ten years later, was to admit to Daniel that she found it very moving. 'At the time I didn't have a son of my own and watching you made me feel like I did.' She was also to admit that initially she wasn't happy with the three child stars being so good looking, expecting the roles to go to more 'geekish' kids 'But then I just thought to myself, "Well, this is film",' she added.

Daniel has said he was in the bath one night a week or so later, musing about how he stood little chance against the thousands of kids who had made a bid for this major role when the phone rang. 'I heard my dad say, "Hello, David". David

Heyman was the only David I knew at the time so I was pretty sure it was him. Dad came upstairs and I thought it was going to be a let-down call to say I didn't get the part. But he came upstairs and told me. I just sat there for a while to let it sink in. It never really did. Then I just started to cry because I was so happy. There are no words for it really. I just sat there, wiped out for a while.' It was he said a 'life-defining moment'.

As a special treat that night, Daniel was allowed to stay up a bit longer than normal and watch an episode of *Fawlty Towers*. But it was anything but a normal night for him. 'I tried to sleep but woke up at 2am and then woke Mum and Dad too. I asked them, "Is it real? Am I dreaming?"' It was no dream and, as was to be said at the time, 'Daniel Radcliffe is about to embark on the ride of a lifetime.' Harry Potter was about to be launched on the world.

But Daniel and his young co-stars, Emma Watson and Rupert Grint, were at this time just kids who had been chosen for a film, which might or might not be successful. The world did not even know their names but, within twenty minutes of the cast announcement, Daniel had a large press gathering outside his house. And Daniel's friends only found out about his major new role after seeing him on the news – he was too shy to telephone any of them and tell them himself. Daniel recalled of their first-ever photo-shoot with top photographer Terry O'Neill: 'I was referred to as "the boy with glasses", Rupert as "the other boy" and Emma as "the girl" throughout the whole thing. But that was fair enough. Why should anyone have known our names?'

The result of the session was a selection of charming photographs of three what now seem such very young and innocent children – Emma and Rupert were both aged eleven – almost bewildered by being shot into the spotlight. The captions listed their names and added they were 'best friends at Hogwarts School of Witchcraft and Wizardry'. Making an 'official' statement about the new stars, Lorenzo di Bonaventura, then the president of worldwide theatrical production at Warner Bros. said, 'We searched through all Muggle and Wizard households to find just the right young people to play Harry, Ron and Hermione and we have found them in Dan, Rupert and Emma. These are magical roles, the kind that come around once in a lifetime and they required talented children who can bring magic to the screen.'

Daniel, Emma and Rupert were hidden away at London's Landmark Hotel for three days before a press conference on 23 August 2000. It was only really when he attended this that Daniel realised 'this was going to be quite a big deal really'. He looks back now and calls it a 'mad day'. There was a plea to the gathered press to remember that 'these are considerably younger than the actors you normally fire questions at so please respect that'. The three children were introduced as they walked through the door, the last time anyone would ever need to introduce them: 'This is Rupert, this is Daniel and this is Emma,' and then the cameras flashed as they sat together on the arm of a chair. David Heyman read out a statement from Jo Rowling: 'Having seen Daniel Radcliffe's screen test I don't think Chris Columbus could have found a better Harry.'

From that day on, Heyman was to be like a proud father of the trio. He still has a photograph that he took in 2000 of a little Daniel and a little Rupert walking together and getting to know one another. It was taken on the day the boys met for the very first time – the day that Heyman knew it was all going to work out. 'While we were alternatively amused and bemused by the rumours about what we were doing,' he said, 'we were overjoyed to finally put them to rest. They were tremendously talented British kids who would bring so much to the film.'

Now, on press conference day, looking cute and very, very young, Daniel, wearing those trademark glasses, was facing his first press throng and answering questions. Soon the world would know his name, but on this debut appearance he was wrongly captioned as Daniel Radford in BBC coverage of the conference. In reference to Harry's pet snowy owl Hedwig, Daniel said, 'I think I am a tiny, tiny bit like Harry – because I'd like to have an owl.' He was not 'top of the form at school' and said neither was he a 'goody two-shoes'. He had no idea what he would do with the money he earned from this film.

Rather unkind journalists wanted to make the point that a little boy who had probably never even read *Harry Potter* had won such a role. Daniel had to admit he had read the first two books 'a long time ago' but had forgotten the stories. He later confessed, 'I found it really hard to get into them. I couldn't get into any books when I was that age. A lot of the other boys in my class know I've read the first one or two and they've read all of them and they're a bit angry because I have read the least *Harry Potter* books.' He was put on the spot as to just how much he knew about the books when asked if he knew the real name of Voldemort. 'Rupert was trying to help me and wrote the answer down on a bit of paper and slid it to me. We thought we were being really subtle and clever but of course we were seen. It was then I realised I had to read the books.'

In fact, by the time filming began, Daniel was on his fourth *Harry Potter* book. 'There was a lot of swotting up,' he confessed. He admitted that initially he wasn't quite sure whether he could get to grips with 'this poor kid' Harry but became obsessed with him after reading the books, one straight after the other. Then there was no stopping him and by the time filming began he was well into the character. 'Despite having been filming as him all day I would charge around my hotel room in Newcastle where we were filming the scenes with the broom; the shot where it leaps into my hand. We would be doing all that stuff and I would be going back to my hotel room at night and having hand fights with nobody. I could have done with a brother to play with.'

Daniel is self-effacing about being chosen as the famous boy wizard. He believed that he, pretty Emma, who would play Hermione Granger, and ginger-haired Rupert, Ron Weasley, the three kids who would be become eternally linked with Harry Potter, were chosen because they had the right look more than for their acting potential. 'I still feel that because they were so close to starting filming that I was chosen out of a mix of desperation too.'

Daniel was the last of the child star trio to be chosen for the role. It is incredible now to know that he had very nearly missed out at the last minute. For young actor Tom Felton was screen tested too and got so close to being Harry Potter that he was told to dye his blond hair dark, put on Potter glasses and read for the part. But it was seeing the chemistry between Dan, Emma and Rupert together in their screen test – despite Daniel later saying he sounded like he was on helium – that had convinced Columbus he now had the perfect line-up.

Relegated from the lead role, Tom won the part of Harry's schoolboy rival Draco Malfoy.

For Columbus, directing three school kids in such a major project could have been daunting, although he had worked with children before on *Home Alone* and *Mrs Doubtfire*. He now had to get a fresh batch through the two twelve-month shoots involved in the first two Potter films he directed before being succeeded by Alfonso Cuarón (though he was to work as a producer on the 2004 *Harry Potter and the Prisoner of Azkaban*).

Daniel later praised Columbus, saying, 'I don't think anybody but Chris with his indefatigable enthusiasm and zeal could have done that job; zeal which he passed on to me. And he made every day fun so I never felt that sense of pressure.'

There were always, of course, Daniel's parents keeping a close watch in the background. They instilled in him that, having been given such a golden opportunity at such a young age, he had to deal with it in a mature way, not be the little boy with the big I am attitude. 'My parents said to me that if I did start acting up on set another boy could always be found,' Daniel explained. 'It wasn't harsh; it was the truth. Any actor who thinks he is irreplaceable is wrong. You are not. I was aware that getting a part like that at my age also meant they could get someone else to take over. It is something anyone going into the profession needs to know.'

And so shooting for *Harry Potter and the Philosopher's Stone* began, complete with its full cast. 'The most nerve-wracking thing was the first day, because before that it had just been me, Rupert, Emma and Chris Columbus rehearsing in Chris's office. I got the call sheet for the first day, I looked under the cast and it said: "Daniel Radcliffe, Emma Watson and Rupert

Grint". So I thought, "Fine, I'm used to that." Then I turned over the page and it said: "Extras, 150." At that moment, I got quite scared.'

One of the things that impressed David Heyman most was that, although the green contact lenses to which Daniel was to develop an allergy were causing him pain right from the very first day of shooting, he never complained. 'There are people who have nowhere near his talent or celebrity who don't show that commitment,' remarked Heyman. But Daniel's main concern was that he not be seen as a stereotype child actor. 'You're sort of worrying. Are these guys going to have preconceived ideas of what I'm like? And one actress did tell me later she'd been expecting a total nightmare! But we quickly became friends.'

This first film set the scene of Harry Potter's life – not that the millions who had already read Rowling's books needed it. Harry is the little wizard boy whose parents Lily and James were killed by the monstrous Voldemort. He is packed off to live with his bullying aunt, uncle and cousin, the Dursleys. Harry's lucky break comes when he is whisked off to Hogwarts, the boarding school for trainee wizards. The headmaster of Hogwarts, Professor Albus Dumbledore, is played by Richard Harris, Uncle Vernon Dursley by Richard Griffiths, Rubeus Hagrid by Robbie Coltrane, Molly Weasley by Julie Walters, with Ian Hart as Professor Quirrell, Alan Rickman as the sinister Severus Snape and John Hurt as Mr Ollivander. It was quite a starry cast for a debut film. Harris, who had originally turned down the role, later accepted after his granddaughter Ella said she would never talk to him again if he refused. Daniel was also reunited with his *David Copperfield* co-star Maggie Smith who was to play Professor Minerva McGonagall.

He was always to be in awe of such big names being involved with the Harry Potter films, saying, 'It was amazing. We wanted to be actors and were suddenly surrounded by wonderful actors … even smaller parts were played by the most amazing actors … I think we pretty much collected the whole set by the end (of the Harry Potter series).'

Daniel still recalls what he describes as one of his proudest moments as a schoolboy actor. And it involved legendary actor Richard Harris who was one day having difficulty learning his lines. With a subtle tact beyond his years, Daniel approached him to offer support. He described his actions as 'a moment I can only describe as political genius' and asked Harris for help with *his* lines in the scenes. 'I said, "Mr Harris, I am having trouble doing my lines." I felt like I peaked that moment.'

Locations ranged from Berkshire (for the Dursleys' home) and North Yorkshire to London, including London Zoo and King's Cross Station where the famous Platform Nine and Three-Quarters was filmed. The hub was Leavesden Studios, a former aerodrome, just outside Watford, which had been hired for the project by Warner Bros. It was here that the very first day of shooting took place on 29 September 2000. Initially, Daniel has said, creating the Potter character was all about 'the costume and the look'. In those early days, the important thing was simply to learn his lines – the more skilful art of acting would come later.

Daniel was soon to become accustomed to having each day clearly defined. A car would come and pick him up at 7.30am and return him home at 8.30pm. It was a schedule he was to follow for the next ten years or so. There were rules to follow, too. He couldn't change or grow his hair or get involved in sports such as skiing in case Warner Bros. had their star put out of action through injury. You can understand why, just for fun, he one day arrived for filming with bloody-looking sticking plasters on his face and claimed he'd been fighting. Another time he put a fake blood capsule in his mouth, pretended to trip on the stairs and let the blood pour out. 'They really fell for it, then they chased after me with a water pistol.' He was also always getting into trouble for scratching his forehead and knocking his fake scar off.

Daniel has always refuted the suggestion that he lost out on being a child. 'People always say to me, "Do you feel like you missed out on a childhood? Do you feel like you had your childhood taken away?" And I'm like, "No, ridiculous … kids who are abused have their childhoods taken away from them."' But it was certainly no longer what you would call a normal time for the young Daniel. His schooling involved between three and five hours' tuition each day on set, and at the end of a long session of filming he found a haven in his room at home listening to music – the likes of the Sex Pistols and the New York Dolls; weekends were reserved for homework. He rarely ventured out because he felt his newfound fame would cause problems for his friends and that his parents would be worried about him. 'I didn't have that normal teenage period when you build up friends in your area and you have a social circle,' he said.

For the child stars on set, it was all one big adventure; Columbus had his hands full. It was later claimed that Daniel had broken more than eighty wands during the Potter films because he used them as drumsticks. And during a scene in which Harry and Ron meet for the first time in a train carriage,

Daniel and Rupert had such a fit of giggles they had to shoot the scene separately. There were childish pranks such as Emma and Rupert writing 'kick me', 'pull my hair' and 'I'm thick' signs, which they stuck on Daniel's back without his knowing – 'and I *did* get kicked,' said Daniel ruefully. Daniel, in turn teased fellow actor Robbie Coltrane with such pranks as setting his mobile phone to Turkish and putting frogs in his car. In all, the kids could be a bit of a handful. Coltrane recalled: 'They'd throw things at each other and play their Game Boys. They liked to get the make-up people to give them gashes. Daniel got one to give him a black eye, and he came in the morning and the other ones said, "OMIGOD! What happened?" ... Columbus was wonderfully patient. He should be sainted. The trouble with children is that they don't have the same emotional memory adults have. I'd have been like, "C'mon, you little shit. I want to sleep. I haven't slept for four weeks."'

But when it came to being Harry Potter Daniel could not be faulted, said Coltrane: 'He holds the film together. He's in almost every frame. Dan is an eleven-year-old with a thirty-five-year-old heart. There is so much going on behind his eyes you realise this is a kid who has lived a life. This is a kid who can appear haunted and troubled by his past. Yet he's charming. That kind of maturity is hard to find in an eleven-year-old.'

Daniel was later to admit that he would steal Coltrane's jokes to repeat to everyone else.

There were also behind-the-scenes dramas, including Daniel developing another allergy, this time to the nickel in his iconic wizard's glasses. Little rings and whiteheads around his eyes were not a good look, but it took a week before they worked out what was causing them and he was provided with spectacles made from hypoallergenic metal (which for many scenes contained no glass to avoid reflection, and as Daniel's head grew as he aged during the years of filming, his Potter spectacles got bigger too!).

But most of the time, recalled Daniel, it was a case of having fun every day, getting to ride on things and being allowed to go wild in one giant playground – except when it came to actually performing. Then he took it seriously. 'I was only eleven and the other kids would say, "Let's do something funny on this take,"' he once recalled. 'I'd think, "No, why don't we just do our fucking jobs?" The crew don't fuck about, do they? They don't do one take where they all fucking shake the cameras. So why should the actors do it?'

For Daniel, it was a welcome break from what he has described as the 'middle-class' school he was attending at the time. 'Suddenly I was taken out of that and put in an environment with people from a thousand different backgrounds. When I was on set I was exposed to this whole other world and it was brilliant. I also feel incredibly lucky because there is no more amazing place for a child to be than a film set.'

While filming Harry Potter, Daniel was conscious that a much less-publicised project of his filmed the year before had slipped somewhat more quietly into American cinemas earlier that year on 30 March 2001. *The Tailor of Panama*, based on the book by John le Carré, centred around a tailor, Harry Pendel, in Panama, who reluctantly becomes a spy for a British agent. The main stars were Pierce Brosnan, Geoffrey Rush and Jamie Lee Curtis, with Daniel taking the minor role of Pendel's son Mark. The screenplay was by Andrew Davies and John Boorman, who was also the director. The film, with some graphic, very non-Potter scenes was to be described as 'a moderate commercial success', although it did not break even at the box office. Daniel's role was very minor with just a handful of lines and an appearance at the breakfast table, and he barely got a mention in reviews. If only the critics had known what direction his later acting career would take.

Then came a welcome break for the new child star, with Daniel managing a holiday in Spain where he celebrated his twelfth birthday in July 2001. Revealing just how ordinary he was despite being thrown into the spotlight, Daniel told how he had opened most of his presents before he went away 'so I had a chance to play with them a bit'. He was still bemused by his newfound fame and, incredibly, was unsure whether it was something he wanted to carry on with, admitting, 'I haven't really decided what I want to be yet … I'm definitely interested in it [acting], but there are a number of other things I'm very interested in as well – music, writing … scripts and things.' He also, rather naively, told one interviewer that he was interested in the issues of autism and would perhaps go to university when he was older to study it. But this was, of course, before the whole Harry Potter phenomenon took over.

The London premiere of the year's 'most highly anticipated film' took place on 4 November 2001 in Leicester Square with a gathering of around ten thousand people. Warner Bros. had launched one of the biggest publicity campaigns in history, which included having huge posters of Daniel put up in London, New York and other major cities. It was a very nervous and anxious Daniel who walked the red carpet, totally overwhelmed by the hundreds of fans calling his name. 'Surreal' was how he described it. When asked if Harry Potter had changed his life, Daniel replied, 'I think if it was going to change, it would have changed by now.' But he has admitted that he cried when he watched the finished film and saw his name among the credits. And it was the 'wall of noise' that hit him when he got out of the car for that very first premiere that made him realise life would never be the same again. 'That was the moment it rammed home to me. I thought that perhaps people are going to be interested in me from now on.'

The New York premiere was on 11 November, but, as happened when the book had been released there, the title was changed to *Harry Potter and the Sorcerer's Stone* because it was thought the word 'Philosopher' sounded too boring for the American market. It was a marketing decision made by Jo Rowling and Scholastic, the publishing house that released her novels in the USA. The rather intense explanation given for the change was that, in the USA, 'a philosopher connotes a scholar of philosophy, ethics, metaphysics, logic and other related fields. Philosopher does not typically connote an alchemist or magician, and magic is essential to the *Harry Potter* books. Consequently, the publisher suggested another word with a more magical connotation.' Rowling came up with the word 'Sorcerer' after discussions with her American editor, Arthur Levine. This meant that every scene that included the word 'Philosopher' for the British market had to be shot twice to accommodate the change to 'Sorcerer' for the American market. This didn't meet with approval with some fans; one commented: 'Apparently we Americans are the only ones in need of a special title so that the word "philosopher" doesn't frighten us.' Rowling was later to say she wished she had been more forceful in keeping her original title.

Another major press conference was held that November, at Knebworth House, Hertfordshire. The stars had to answer questions over two days. One journalist caught up in all the hype recalled: 'After seeing the film and spending a night in a posh London hotel, film writers from around the world boarded coaches for a mystery trip "somewhere outside London". We ended up at Knebworth House for a press conference with the stars and the gift of a Harry Potter leather satchel (a sturdy bag that now carries the laptop on which I'm writing this).'

Daniel was this time a little better prepared with his Harry Potter answers. 'It makes me feel very privileged to be playing him. It's exciting because he has such an interesting life. Cool.' He wasn't bothered too much about what he was getting paid, he said, because 'getting the role was reward enough'. The event was not without its controversy, however, with complaints that it was 'carefully controlled' and that journalists were stopped from speaking to some of the cast, including Richard Harris – no doubt because he had previously announced when asked why he'd taken the role of Dumbledore: 'Who knows? It's a job. I don't go to movies. I hate movies. They're a waste of time. I could be in a pub having more fun talking to idiots rather than watching idiots perform … all I know is that they kept offering me the role and the more I turned it down the more money they offered me.'

And actress Zoë Wanamaker, who played Hogwarts' game mistress Madam Gooch, said Warner Bros. were 'notoriously mean' when it came to payment and that she was so insulted by what she termed 'crap money' that she declined a deal for three Potter films. 'If they want me for a second, they'll have to up their rates.' It seemed not everyone was as happy as Daniel to be part of the mighty Warner Bros. franchise.

The first-ever Harry Potter film was released in America and the UK on 18 November 2001 and then worldwide throughout that month and December. It would appear in 131 different countries and in 40 languages. Daniel made his first trip to New York to publicise the film and was very much the shy and unconfident schoolboy in his interviews, but he handled the repetitive questions well, reiterating again and again how he was chosen as Harry Potter, what similarities there were between him and the character and his favourite scenes.

As his *David Copperfield* producer, Rebecca Eaton, was to note: 'There would be 250 people asking questions and there's Daniel, his feet literally not touching the floor.'

He delighted the audience of the David Letterman show by declaring New York was 'so much cooler than London', and, although obviously cripplingly shy, he cleverly fought off a question in one of his very first interviews with *Access Hollywood*. When asked how the Quidditch scenes were filmed, little Daniel answered: 'I can't tell you because it would ruin the magic for everyone.'

But Daniel was not prepared for the massive fan following he had already attracted. An interview with MTV was interrupted when someone spotted a girl outside the building. She was naked apart from a Harry Potter towel and carried a sign saying: 'Nothing comes between me and Harry Potter.' The girl was invited into the studio but Daniel's main concern was that she was inadequately dressed for a bitterly cold day. 'It was freezing!' he exclaimed.

In its opening US weekend, this first Potter film took £55m

and, in Britain, nearly £16.5m. It made Letterman's closing good wishes to Daniel – 'I hope you have a long and lovely career' – something of an understatement. And as Daniel himself was later to admit, 'We did not have *any* kind of concept of how big it was going to be, but my parents had the right attitude and always kept the right attitude with me, which was that it was all just fun. You know, going to a premiere was fun. Doing interviews was fun. You found ways of making it into a game. So I never felt pressure as a young kid, I never was really stressed out by it, and I never felt daunted by what was ahead.'

The critics were pretty sure Daniel was going to succeed as Harry Potter. Bob Graham of the *San Francisco Chronicle* wrote: 'Radcliffe is the embodiment of every reader's imagination. It is wonderful to see a young hero who is so scholarly looking and filled with curiosity, who connects with very real emotions, from solemn intelligence and the delight of discovery to deep family longing.'

Elvis Mitchell in the *New York Times* commented: 'Mr Radcliffe has an unthinkably difficult role for a child actor; all he gets to do is look sheepish when everyone turns to him and intones that he may be the greatest wizard ever. He could have been hobbled by being cast because he resembles the Harry of the book cover illustrations. It's a horrible burden to place on a kid, but it helps that Mr Radcliffe does have the long-faced mournfulness of a 60s pop star. He also possesses a watchful gravity and, shockingly, the large, authoritative hands of a real wizard.'

Back in the UK, too, the film – and Daniel – mostly won acclaim. Peter Bradshaw in *The Guardian* wrote: 'The young prince of light himself is played by Daniel Radcliffe, who has charm and a lovely, open face, though he is subtly but distinctly outclassed by his pals. They are somehow a touch more lively than Harry himself, who accepts his destiny and heroism with a kind of evenness bordering on insouciance, and is never troubled with any doubts or reversals that are not swiftly erased.'

The *Daily Mail* (establishing itself as a long-time adversary of Daniel's), meanwhile, got it slightly wrong when it said that the next Harry Potter film 'won't be greeted by the same level of Potter-mania', adding, 'Meanwhile the clock is ticking for the film's three stars. Radcliffe is now 13, Grint 14, and Emma who plays bossy, bushy-haired Hermione Granger is 12 … by the time the third Harry Potter adventure comes out they will be well into their teens and surely too old to be believable, bombing about on their broomsticks. I suspect they won't make a fourth…'

The Philosopher's Stone won many nominations and awards, including nominations for Best Performance by a Younger Actor by the Academy of Science Fiction, Fantasy & Horror Films, and Best Young Actor/Actress at the Critics' Choice Awards. Daniel's first-ever Hollywood award was as Male Youth Discovery of the Year from the Hollywood Women's Press Club. He was also awarded the MTV Movie Award for Breakthrough Male Performance, Best Young Actor by the Broadcast Film Critics Association Awards, the Sir James Carreras Award for Outstanding New Talent and Italy's prestigious David di Donatello Award. He was also voted Person of the Year 2002 by *Time For Kids* magazine. It was an extremely nervous little Daniel who in February 2002 was to receive a Variety Club Award for Best Newcomer and make an acceptance speech. He said: 'Wow! I'd like to obviously thank the Variety Club for this honour. Also I'd like to thank Christopher Columbus and David Heyman and everyone at Warner Brothers for their guidance and support and J.K. Rowling for writing these amazing books in the first place. Also the cast and crew especially my good friends Emma Watson and Rupert Grint.'

By now, with his son in such high demand, Daniel's father Alan had given up his job to accompany him full-time wherever he went. 'My dad works incredibly hard as my chaperone. He looks after me and all those kinds of things. I always hesitate to use the word manager because it brings up horrible images. I've met some managers in my life. I don't think of him as a manager because he's a dad doing what any dad would do for his son if he were in this position – organising and helping.'

It all pretty much showed that Daniel's life would never be the same again. 'What's interesting is that there was, like, a year when there was nothing. That first year we were announced and then we were filming so nobody recognised us, so we had, kind of, a year…' It was perhaps being so young at the time that saved Daniel from fully realising what was going on, as he himself admitted: 'If I'd been older and slightly more self-aware about the following that Harry had, I would have been slightly more intimidated. Ignorance and confidence of youth – it's enough to transcend that.' But Daniel was to make the Harry Potter part his very own by growing into it and by simply growing up.

CHAPTER 2

SCHOOLDAYS TO STARDOM

A tiny Daniel stood at the back of the school stage dressed as a monkey. He had no speaking part in the production and could only watch and listen as fellow pupils performed in front of proud parents. Daniel was just five years old. He could never have envisaged how, in around five years' time, he would be taking not only centre stage but the world stage too.

No one could have predicted what was in store for the little boy born on 23 July 1989 at Queen Charlotte's Hospital in Fulham, west London. Daniel is the only child of Alan George Radcliffe and casting agent Marcia Jeannine Gresham (née Marcia Gresham Jacobson). There are some South African roots in Daniel's family – as well as Polish, Jewish and Northern Irish roots (his father was born in Northern Ireland) – as his maternal grandfather was South African but it is believed his maternal grandmother left the country for

England in 1960, bringing the then two-year-old Marcia with her. Originally having some aspirations to become actors themselves, Daniel's parents later changed course and they are now both closely involved in their son's career. Both parents hoped they would pass on some of their natural dancing abilities as Alan is a former ballroom-dancing champion and Marcia was a talented ballerina, having won ten trophies and several medals when still a young girl.

Daniel's very early schooldays passed relatively normally with only the occasional hint that he might follow the acting route, although he created a bit of drama when, aged five, he thought it would be funny to call 999 ('I learned that was wrong very quickly!'). When he was about seven, he was diagnosed with dyspraxia – 'like dyslexia but with coordination' – and, although tests showed that verbally he was quite ahead of his years, his motor skills were below average. There are still times when Daniel finds his dyspraxia frustrating. He still can't ride a bike or swim very well and often has 'easy' shoelaces because he has difficulty tying normal ones.

He attended the prestigious all-boys private school Sussex House, an independent day school for boys aged eight to thirteen. Although the school can boast of having an 'outstanding record' for exam results, it was here that he was to encounter problems, and he can still recall when he was eight one deputy head teacher telling him that he was stupid. It was to have a marked effect on Daniel – as it would on any child who feels they are written off before they have even started – and, if there was one memory for which he held a grudge, then that was it.

Daniel said: 'At the time I just believed him. I thought, "I probably am stupid," but when you grow up you think that's outrageous for a teacher to say that to a small child … I was probably just talking to somebody or asking for something. I was a very disorganised, talkative boy. And there are some people who just don't do well at school. I am not somebody who will learn best when you tell me to sit down and be quiet and sit still. I learn by talking back and engaging in conversation and walking around.'

After Daniel told his mother what the deputy head had said, she marched straight up to the school and had a word with him. Because of his hyper-personality, Daniel still wonders if he might have been diagnosed with ADHD (Attention Deficit Hyperactivity Disorder) had he been born a few years later. It appears he had some of the symptoms such as a short attention span and being easily distracted. The diagnosis is usually made between the ages of three and seven, although sometimes older, and is most common in boys. Daniel said he 'missed the boat' on any potential medical reason for his general inattentiveness. And it was to mean unhappy schooldays for him and lead to some bitterness: 'I always feel sorry for people when they say school is the best days of your life. It really isn't. If it was, you must have a terrible life.'

Sometime later, Daniel was to air an even stronger dislike of his schooldays. 'I fucking hated school,' he remarked, 'because if you are not very athletic or intellectual you are made to feel pretty mediocre. I mean intellectual in the academic sense. You take in information and regurgitate it. I was never any good at that. As a consequence, I struggled at school and was very slow at reading and writing, but if I could talk and have the information told to me, then I'd take it in entirely differently.'

Before being catapulted to Harry Potter stardom, Daniel, as already mentioned, was in the BBC drama *David Copperfield*. The role had come via Sue Latimer, the woman who would become his agent and who was an acquaintance of the Radcliffes. Aware that Daniel was going through a particularly bad time at school, she felt that perhaps getting involved in an outside interest would help his confidence. 'She knew I was having a crappy time at school, so she just asked my mum to let me audition and that it would be an experience none of the other kids in my class would have had,' said Daniel of his role as the boy Copperfield. Up until then, Daniel had only had his 'bit part' as the silent monkey in his school production of Nellie the Elephant where, he said, 'I had to wear floppy ears and orange make-up and I had to wear tights. I think I went on and danced around for about forty seconds or something. I hope nobody ever digs up a picture of me like that because it was so embarrassing.'

His parents were so protective of his embarking on an acting career that they had previously refused to let him audition for a production of *Oliver Twist* because of his young age. By the time Daniel's pleadings had won them over, the film's cast had already been chosen. So there were obviously reservations about his auditioning for anything at all in case he was left bitterly disappointed. And for a boy with no real experience, getting the lead role of Copperfield on mainstream television seemed way out of his league anyway. Daniel said, 'I don't think anybody expected me to get the part, and then I did.' It all started when his mother sent a Polaroid photo of Daniel to the BBC and he caught the eye of those involved with *Copperfield*, especially producer Kate Harwood who was also a friend of the family.

She said of Daniel, 'He has a particular quality of naturalness and innocence. The camera loves him and other children don't feel threatened by him. One normally dreads working with child actors but in his case he was wonderful. We cast him for his special qualities of gentleness and watchfulness. He has those in spades. He has a great deal of charm and simplicity.'

Daniel had also grabbed the attention of director Simon Curtis who later recalled he fitted the bill perfectly as the young Copperfield: 'I wanted a boy in the first half who I found personally appealing. A director friend of mine told me, "If you're casting a kid, cast a kid you like." As the casting director walked Dan across the room in preparation, he winked at me, which made me laugh. I think that was the hundred-million-dollar link, considering where he went next.' The recollection appeared in a book, *Making Masterpiece*, by series producer Rebecca Eaton, and when she later quizzed Daniel about his early audition antics, he confessed, 'I wouldn't have the confidence to wink at a director now, even one I know well. I was just so full of youthful hopes that hadn't quite been knocked out of me by puberty yet … It's kind of wonderful that it all started with something like that.'

After his read-through, Daniel returned to school, excited that he had something to tell the other kids in the playground. He wasn't at all concerned about being successful or not because he had nothing to lose, nothing at stake, and his parents remained laid back about it all. But after about five callbacks he *was* successful and the part in Charles Dickens's classic was to be his first-ever appearance on screen – and the first of three roles as an orphan (including one in particular for which he was to become the most famous). Daniel was nine when filming started, turning ten four days later, but he was already showing a childlike charisma on screen.

The televised drama was shown in two parts, the first airing on Christmas Day 1999 and the second on Boxing Day. Fresh-faced Daniel as the young Copperfield (Ciarán McMenamin played him as an adult) was one of an illustrious cast including Maggie Smith (neither she nor Daniel was aware at the time how their working together was to play a massive hand of fate), Emilia Fox, Ian McKellen, Bob Hoskins, Zoë Wanamaker, Pauline Quirke, Dawn French, Imelda Staunton and Paul Whitehouse – and several of these big names would also become part of Daniel's Harry Potter family. There were moments when it didn't all go smoothly of course, with Daniel confessing that the scene when Mr Creakle, played by Ian McKellen, tells Copperfield his mother is dead reduced him to nervous laughter time and time again during shooting. 'I didn't really know who Ian McKellen was then but I knew he was famous because we only had that day with him for the scene. I just got nervous. Luckily by the end of the day when we shot that scene again, I was so tired, so worn out that I was just an exhausted little boy standing there, which was just what they wanted.'

In fact, Daniel had found it hard to contain his natural high energy while filming. At one point, he was playfully tied up by some of the crew after he shot his water pistol at them. There still exists a photograph of a very remorseful Daniel wrapped up in plastic, and you can't help feeling sorry for him.

Aged nine, and shortly before he got the *David Copperfield* role, Daniel was going through what he described as 'a particularly bad trot' at school. As already seen, he was not popular with his teachers because of his disruptive attitude. It didn't get much better when he landed the prized Harry Potter role and went on to find such amazing fame. Some of his fellow pupils turned against him and Daniel has admitted some simply didn't like him. It was no wonder that in one interview when he was still young Daniel said that, when he got into trouble at school, he wished he could don an invisibility cloak, 'drape it over me and sneak out the door' or perhaps have a three-headed dog, 'because then no one would argue with me'.

But Daniel has also confessed that he later 'ended up getting cocky' at the height of Potter fame, and that after five years on film sets among adults he had developed a sharp tongue and was quick with a sharp retort. It was a lot for a little boy to handle. The constant requests for autographs were demanding (when first asked, he made the mistake of signing in full and now feels he shouldn't shorten it), but they were nothing compared to his having to sort out who wanted to know him for himself from the hangers-on and the fickle. 'It is weird when people stake a claim to knowing you more than your friends do. I feel they must be disappointed when they meet me,' he once remarked. 'I think people have an image that we are really cool when we are not. I am a geek. I am happy in my own company. I am not what people want when they meet a movie star. I've met movie stars and have sometimes been disappointed and hope people aren't like that with me too much.'

Daniel has said that, although the common belief is that he always wanted to be an actor, it wasn't until the *David Copperfield* role came along that he was sure that was what he wanted to do – despite being impressed by a pantomime of *Aladdin* he'd seen at Salisbury Theatre aged five: 'Yes, I might have said I wanted to act when I was five but I certainly had no real aspirations to do so. At six I wanted to be in the army and at seven I wanted to be an astronaut. It changed every day. I just had dreams about not going to school the next day – which did eventually come true.'

But even at a very young age, Daniel was part of the acting world. He was only eight or nine when he worked alongside his literary agent father at the ICM theatrical agency run by Duncan Heath. 'I had a sort of holiday job,' recalled Daniel, and it was certainly a more interesting one than most kids get. He answered the telephone to the likes of Michael Caine, Rupert Everett, Anthony Hopkins and Michael Crawford. 'Once Rupert Everett asked – because my voice was so high – who the new girl on reception was,' he recalled. His mother Marcia, a casting agent, also put him to work. 'I'd sit in her office and go through *Spotlight*. She'd give me a description and I would pick the actor. I remember for [the part of] Buttons in York I picked Jude Law and Mum said, "Hmm. He's probably a lot beyond that now, Dan, but good thought."' But the experience was Daniel's first taste of earning – he got £10 for the day – 'I was like, "this is more money than I've seen in my life. This is incredible!"' At the time maybe, but he could never have envisaged just how his fortunes would change.

There were some comfortable reviews for the charming little boy actor. One critic, Bob Wake, wrote: 'Daniel Radcliffe has a naturalistic presence – rare enough in child actors – and he seems like a real boy, which is all that's really required. David Copperfield is not meant to be an exceptional child. He is an ordinary child to whom extraordinary things happen.' 'Daniel Radcliffe is engaging in the role of young David, exhibiting innocence and vulnerability,' wrote Mike Cumming for msn entertainment.

It could have all ended there for Daniel or he could have become a jobbing actor or known in the future for other diverse appearances. For, as already stated, after learning about his next proposed project – Harry Potter – Marcia and Alan felt the original filming commitments in America would be 'too big a shift' in their young son's life. They even kept the offer of the part secret. Then they said a firm 'no' – all of which of course would have changed the whole Harry Potter history. Daniel knew nothing of this at the time, but he was later to say he realised his parents were right to be so hesitant. It was only when the deal was changed to commit to just two films, both to be made in Britain, that his parents consented. Daniel said: 'I think my mother just thought, "OK, well, you know, maybe we should let him audition" and everything sort of went from there … everything was going to become pretty crazy.'

Finding such early fame as Harry Potter didn't help with Daniel's popularity at school. There was a bit of name-calling, he recalled. 'A few kids in school thought it would be funny not to like me – and I'm sure some of them didn't like me. Some say it was jealousy, but I don't think so. I think it's just people being people – that's what we do.' Daniel has also admitted to feeling 'socially awkward' and feeling like he didn't fit in at school. 'But at some point, self-preservation kicks in and you can call yourself a misfit and say, "I'm different for a reason, and I will pursue that path…"'

It didn't get any better when he started at the City of London School. 'Because I'd been on set with some genuinely witty people over the years, I could turn round to these idiots and at least try and tear them apart. They didn't like that. I'm not saying I was Oscar Wilde at fourteen, but I had a line for anything they could throw at me. I'd never been one of the cool kids but you realise that all the kids who were really cool at your school were actually scuzzy and horrible and boring. The nerds are the ones that make the films and do loads of other really cool stuff in their life.'

Life for Daniel was not helped by the bad acne he suffered, which made him even more self-conscious. One time Daniel found himself in a fight with an 'incredibly unpleasant' boy five years older than him. 'There had been a bit of animosity between us already and he was being really horrible to a kid I knew, so I pulled him off this other bloke and he threw me into the lockers. Then I think I said something to him and he punched me in the face. Then I punched him back. In films it always looks really cool, but I was hair pulling, biting – there was nothing elegant or macho about the whole affair. I thought, "You know what? If you're quick enough to run away, then that's what you should do."'

Daniel was to have a miraculous escape from all this of course when Harry Potter took him away from the classroom and he was tutored on the film set, and today he insists he wasn't bullied in the real sense of the word. 'It wasn't, by any stretch of the imagination, in any way traumatic or has affected me. It wasn't even bullying. It was the fact that I was not particularly liked or I didn't get on with a lot of people, and sometimes it had to do with the Harry Potter thing. I wouldn't say that I was bullied in any real way – not to the extent of people who've really been bullied. I don't compare to them.'

Daniel gave a fuller account of this time to paste.com, the

online music and entertainment site. 'It wasn't bullying so much in the "beaten up" sense, as being picked on and a bit of targeted aggression. I never went home with cuts and bruises and scars as some unfortunate kids do. Just a bit … humiliated, I suppose. Jostled. And it was all to do with "being Harry Potter", and other contemporaries not being able to cope with that.'

He continued, 'I suppose that a lot of young actors who get some sort of prominence go through the same thing. I just endured it and got on with it. It helped that I got out of school a lot (which the bullies clearly resented) and I was tutored on film sets for much of the time. So I was given a great deal of freedom – as they saw it – and anyone who didn't conform to their narrow-mindedness got in their way. All very silly really.'

The one-to-one tuition while filming was to benefit him greatly as he learned to focus and pay more attention. 'It kind of takes you back to a purer form of learning, when it was one student who hasn't got twenty other people to deal with.

He is no doubt miffed that Sussex House, the school he attended between eight and thirteen, after its treatment of him, is now so proud to record him as one of their past pupils and he should perhaps feel that at the end of the day he 'won'. 'Being on a film set was a much more varied life than at school, age-wise, background-wise. I was very much a product of the public-school system. There was only one other kid in my class who had parents not involved in the stock market or law.'

Daniel has also said that he did find early fame difficult to handle, and that until he was fourteen he avoided looking at any press reports about himself at all. Then one day he went on the Internet and googled his name. He still does not know if it was a good idea or not. 'Obviously there were a lot of people saying nice things but you don't see them, you only see the people who are just vile about you,' he explained. 'There's a line in *The Thick of It*, which is one of my favourite programmes, when they say that googling yourself is like opening a door to people telling you how shitty you are. It comes from a place of sadomasochistic egomania. "OK, I'll write my name in and see what comes up." Because all you're going on the Internet for is to hear nice things about yourself. And all you find are terrible things, generally speaking. And it doesn't matter if there's a list of twenty comments, and there can be nineteen of them that can be fantastic, and the one that's bad eats you up. Since then, I stopped googling myself.'

But like many other high-profile names he understandably does not get why people feel they have the right to be vile about someone they do not know.

It was while in Australia, shortly before Daniel started work on the 2007 production of *Equus* that the decision was made that he would not return to school and he left a year early. His parents decided that rehearsal hours and the general commitment would rule out any normal school days. He did continue to see a language teacher twice a week but mostly he had private tutoring. 'We just sat and discussed ideas … I was so happy. I got the most amazing teacher and there's a lot you can do in one-to-one tuition that you just can't do in a class. That's the reality. If you've got a classroom full of people, you can spend a little time with all of them and you'll just about get through the lesson plan. On set, we had things to get through for the year, but if I found something really interesting, we'd just go off and learn about that. It's a much truer way of learning that encourages knowledge for its own sake, not an exam. Exams are why a lot of people stop learning when they leave school … It's a wonderful way of working. I imagine it's how Roman children were schooled.'

This form of education meant life was now much happier for Daniel and he felt really ready to continue with his acting. He was fine about Harry Potter being such a huge part of his life. At the time he said: 'Far too many people my age seem to be young and jaded already. These aren't people who've had tough lives – they've had great lives and educations. And you just think, "What have you got to be jaded about?" I know it's not cool to be enthusiastic about things, but I can't help it. I was never particularly good at anything at school. I got by. I was rubbish at sports. But I found something I'm good at and I enjoy and so few people find that. I haven't got anything to be unenthusiastic about.'

CHAPTER 3

GROWING UP WITH HARRY POTTER

Despite the huge success of his debut as Harry Potter, Daniel's parents insisted that he take some time off before filming the sequel, *Harry Potter and the Chamber of Secrets*. They wanted him to resume normal schooling but it must have been a difficult time for Daniel who, as we've seen, had already experienced problems feeling academically poor, and now had to cope with the sometimes negative reaction from fellow pupils to his fame. Daniel just tried to deal with all the attention. Life hadn't really changed that much, he said at the time. 'People come up to me on the street and they see my face on 50ft-high billboards. I know they sound like big changes but they're really not as big as could have happened.'

Meanwhile, behind the scenes, there were some negotiations going on over Daniel's payment for this second film. It is believed he was initially offered around £125,000 – until actors' union Equity stepped in and got him the better deal they felt he deserved. After a short break, and just three days after the release of the first Harry Potter film, Daniel was on set filming the second. Now aged twelve, nearly thirteen (as the *Daily Mail* had rather made a negative point of), the adolescent Daniel was beginning to show. In one scene he had to hitch up his trousers to prove he wasn't wearing socks – and revealed rather hairy adolescent legs. 'They said, "Nobody is going to believe any twelve-year-old would have that much hair", so they had to shave two inches up from my ankle.'

Rather intrusively, there were reports that Daniel was among the child stars who had to have their heads checked by nurses for head lice every day. As every parent knows, wherever you have a large group of children, there is the chance of the itchy critters. A crew member was quoted as saying: 'All the kids are given a thorough head examination every day while they are in make-up before any filming can go ahead. The producers wish Harry could perform some real wizardry on this one. But in the absence of any magic, bosses were forced to put their heads together and decide on some rigorous daily checks. If and when problems occur they are dealt with then and there so they don't get out of hand.'

A spokesman for Warner Bros. commented: 'The health and safety of children involved on any production is of paramount importance.'

Daniel's voice was also breaking during filming, so getting the continuity right was important. Warner Bros.' take on it was 'we will cross that bridge when we come to it'. There was much press speculation about how this would be dealt with, with *The Sun* running a story with the headline 'Harry

Potter and the Broken Voice' and reporting that a 'sound-alike schoolboy', Joe Sowerbutts, who had provided the voice for PlayStation and Nintendo games, was to have his voice dubbed over Harry's. The newspaper said there had been a 'desperate hunt' for Potter impersonators and that it would be thirteen-year-old Sowerbutts's voice heard replacing Daniel's in the final broomstick and forest scenes. Joe was quoted as saying, 'I couldn't believe it when they told me I was going to be in the film. I was really surprised that Daniel's voice broke because he's younger than me. But you could say it was a lucky break for me.'

There were quotes from 'a child who worked on the film' – 'Daniel was already starting to wobble when they were filming in February and they were getting worried about it then' – and an 'insider' – 'They're terrified he will look too old to play Harry in the next movie if there is any delay in production. It's a race against time.'

Warner Bros. were to deny any voice other than Daniel's was used and, in an interview with Oprah Winfrey, a still shy Daniel sitting alongside Emma and Rupert said that he had not had to suffer the teenage boy's experience of his voice alternating between upper and lower. 'It just went down immediately.'

None of this would soften the growing hysteria that followed the approach of a new Potter film release. In June 2002, there were reports that Potter fans were freezing the Internet as they tried to download sneak pictures from the film.

This second instalment called for Daniel to approach his character in a different way. It was much darker, he said, funnier and with more emotional depth. 'Harry has developed and I have had to develop, too. I have two instincts now, mine and Harry's. I ask myself what would Harry do in a situation and I bring that to the screen.' He said that he was aware that the girls at Hogwarts loved Harry Potter while the boys hated him. 'He's a real show-off and cringeworthy. They are very edgy around him,' said Daniel. In the film Harry had to talk in 'parcel tongue' to snakes, giving Daniel the chance to learn an invented language courtesy of a professor at Kent University.

One challenging scene called for Daniel to fight an 80ft serpent called a basilisk. 'It was hard to fight. I kept kicking its teeth out.' The crew had to keep doing repair jobs and the scene was shot over and over again. In another scene, Daniel acted opposite an orange ball – a stand-in for the house elf Dobby – and he had to really focus on looking at the ball at the eye level where Dobby would be. Computers were later used to fill in the animated character. Daniel explained, 'It was kind of hard knowing what kind of facial expression an orange ball is making.'

He thrived on the action scenes, including hanging out of a car window – 'I was hanging 25ft to 30ft in the air and it was just really cool' – and a duelling scene. He may have still been young but Daniel was beginning to feel more comfortable in the role and all the demands that acting in a fantasy film made of him. He started to put ideas to Chris Columbus, something he said he would never have dreamed of doing in the first Potter movie. 'But I have more confidence now. It has all been a bit more of a challenge, but hopefully I have met that challenge,' he said at the time.

The relationship between Daniel and Columbus grew, with the 'kind and generous' director being credited by Daniel with giving him a love of film in general. 'He told me about so many different films and I felt I had wasted so much time. I should have watched them years ago,' Daniel enthused. And despite the big differences in age and experience, Daniel said they got their energy from each other: 'If I am soaked up then he will be too.'

Columbus was again made aware of the issues involved in working with children rather than adults – and changed the final scene when Emma Watson became embarrassed about Hermione having to hug both Harry and Ron in front of the entire cast. It was altered to her just hugging Harry and awkwardly shaking hands with Ron instead.

Harry Potter and the Chamber of Secrets premiered in Britain on 3 November 2002 and in America on 14 November. It went on general UK and American release on 15 November and initially hit the screens of around fifteen countries worldwide. This time, the story sees Harry, staying with his grim relatives, receiving a surprise visit from Dobby the house elf who warns him not to return to Hogwarts as terrible things are going to happen. He does return, of course, only to discover that The Chamber of Secrets has been opened. The starry line-up again included Richard Griffiths as Dursley, Maggie Smith as Professor McGonagall, Robbie Coltrane as Rubeus Hagrid and Alan Rickman as Severus Snape, along with Kenneth Branagh as Professor Gilderoy Lockhart, Warwick Davis as Professor Flitwick and John Cleese as Nearly Headless Nick.

Sadly, it would be the last time Richard Harris would appear as Dumbledore. The seventy-two-year-old actor had lost his fight against cancer in October. He was not to fulfil his wishes to work on the third film. Commenting on Harris's death, Daniel said, 'It was awful. I have what I think is the kind of supreme, amazing honour of being able to say that I was in the last scene that he ever shot. I don't think Richard is the kind of guy who would've wanted us to mourn over him. He would've wanted us to be happy and just remember him for all the times he made us smile and just laugh … we got on really, really well. He was just fantastic to have on set because he was, as one might expect, an amazing storyteller – and he had a lot of stories to tell. You never quite knew how much to believe because some fiction was drafted in. But he was just fantastic to be around and obviously he's missed by everybody.'

Daniel took part in Harris's colourful farewell tribute at The Strand – which was not without its quirky moments. Theatrical publication *The Stage* was scathing about Harris's own poems being read. 'Unfortunately he was no Seamus Heaney and even when luminaries such as Liam Neeson and Daniel Radcliffe were wheeled on to read his ghastly stuff (to the sounds of a 30-piece orchestra) it couldn't light up what turned out to be a spectacularly dull evening.'

Chamber of Secrets was a long-awaited sequel, which even the critics, on the whole, admitted was worth the wait. The review in *Empire* magazine singled out Daniel's new maturity: 'The teachers – even Alan Rickman and Robbie Coltrane, who as Snape and Hagrid provided much of the first film's fun – are relegated to the background, which places even more responsibility on the shoulders of young Daniel Radcliffe. No longer has he simply to gape in wonder at the magic around him: this time the kid's got to act and, during the final encounter with Tom Riddle, Harry's fierce loyalty and bravery finds a determined Radcliffe hitting all the right dramatic notes.

'Harry, as a character, is beginning to come of age; this

movie nudges towards a darker good-versus-evil thread for later movies. Radcliffe, too, is making the move from boy to teenager. His voice has broken and, if it keeps deepening at the present rate, he'll be out-rumbling Vin Diesel before they've even got to *Goblet of Fire*.'

A review in the *New York Times* also commented on Daniel's voice change. 'For the audience, a similar shock arrives much earlier, the very first time Daniel Radcliffe, the young English actor who plays everybody's favourite English schoolboy wizard, opens his mouth. Though Mr Radcliffe remains smooth-faced and wide-eyed, his voice (like that of Rupert Grint, who plays Harry's pal Ron Weasley, and Tom Felton, as the odious Draco Malfoy), has begun to break, and he speaks in the unmistakable, awkward tongue of adolescence.'

And in London, Sukhdev Sandhu in *The Telegraph* commented: 'He may still look like a New Labour policy wonk, but his voice has deepened, his brow is a little more furrowed. He seems troubled, as if he'd rather be at home staring at his bedroom ceiling and punching his fist to a Raging Speedhorn album, than be called upon to save the day again for his Hogwarts chums.'

Despite a warning from Columbus that this latest Harry Potter movie might be too scary for children, and parents should think about whether they should ignore the PG rating – 'If you have a seven-year-old or under and you are thinking about taking them to the movie then talk to them about it' – no one seemed put off. *The Chamber of Secrets* went on to make £54.8m in the UK. More impressively, it took around £600m worldwide, appearing on more than eight thousand screens in thirty-two different countries. In France alone, the film sold a record 631,400 tickets on its first day, the best opening for an American film in French box-office history. It was released on 1,007 screens in France. One reviewer's description of it as a 'cinematic cash cow' was decidedly accurate.

It was to be another huge all-round success, with thirty-one nominations including, for Daniel, for the second year, the Saturn Award for Best Performance by a Younger Actor, and it won the year's Best Live Action Family Film at the Phoenix Film Critics Society Awards. But despite the accolades, Daniel still had doubts about his early acting abilities. 'When I look at child actors like Dakota Fanning [an American star in the *Twilight* film series] and the work she did when I was a kid I go, "Wow, that is so amazing." I was not that as a child actor. Absolutely not. I was really enthusiastic and cute looking, I guess, and I had some good instincts.' It was only much later in his career that he felt able to admit he had managed to 'put together performances that I am consistently pleased with'.

Filming for *Harry Potter and the Prisoner of Azkaban* began at the end of 2002, its original start date allegedly postponed to enable Daniel to have some time back in the classroom. His mother Marcia told journalists, 'Honestly Warner Bros. make our lives easy. They even delayed filming this latest film so Daniel could start at his new school and have one term of being normal.'

The story centred on Sirius Black, a mass murderer believed to have been a supporter of Voldemort, escaping from wizard prison and rumoured to be out to kill Harry. Dementors – the 'non-beings' and 'dark creatures' – were sent to Hogwarts to guard him. Harry was now having to face up to the violent death of his parents and being pursued himself. Daniel watched the films of French New Wave director François Truffaut and Italian director Vittorio De Sica in order to understand Harry's feelings of hopelessness. 'The thing about this film is that not only is Harry angry but he also has to deal with some truly, horrific things,' Daniel explained. 'He actually hears his mother screaming as she is murdered and it doesn't really get much worse than that, so there was a lot of preparing to be done.'

Part of this preparation involved a disturbing conversation with his father who recalled how aged just eight he heard the wife of a man being murdered by the UDA (Ulster Defence Association) during the Northern Ireland Troubles. 'I just had a really, really long discussion with my dad about it. He helped me so much with all the stuff with the Dementors particularly.'

The regular cast were there, only this time Michael Gambon took the role of Dumbledore following the death of Richard Harris. The part was initially offered to Sir Ian McKellen but he turned it down for two reasons, he said: one because he felt his role of wizard Gandalf in the *Lord of the Rings* trilogy was 'far superior' and because Harris had harshly criticised his acting ability. 'People said to me, "Didn't you wish you'd played Dumbledore?" I say no! And seeing as how one of the last things Harris did was say what a dreadful actor he thought I was, it would not have been appropriate for me to take over his part. It would have been unfair.'

Other new actors in the line-up included David Thewlis as Professor Lupin, Timothy Spall as Peter Pettigrew, Emma Thompson as Professor Sybil Trelawney and Lenny Henry as Shrunken Head. To Daniel's delight Gary Oldman took the part of dangerous wizard Sirius Black. 'Ever since I've been acting I have loved his movies,' he said of Oldman. 'He was just the nicest guy. I was really worried because if you really, really like someone and they aren't as nice as you hoped you are heartbroken. But Gary was awesome.' The two shared an interest in music and were to become close friends. Oldman bought Daniel a bass guitar as a gift and gave him lessons. Daniel has said that, with Oldman around, he himself 'upped his game'. Above all, the respect Daniel held for Oldman was reciprocated: 'Dan has really matured and is a very good actor, very disciplined. He certainly does his homework on what's required of him.'

Chris Columbus, the man who had so successfully steered the first two Potter films, dropped out of working on this one, saying he wanted to spend more time with his family. His place was taken by Mexican film-maker Alfonso Cuarón (later to shine spectacularly at the 2014 Oscars for his film *Gravity*) who took a deeper approach than Columbus. He asked the three young stars to write essays on how their characters had developed and what caused them to act in a certain way. 'That was the most important piece of acting work that we did on *Azkaban*,' the director explained. 'Everything they put in those essays was going to be the pillars they were going to hold on to for the rest of the process.' Emma, Rupert and Daniel had, he said, reached new 'emotional territory', had matured greatly since the first Potter film and were greatly improving their craft.

Daniel saw it as a chance to expand on what they had been taught by Columbus. 'Basically I think everything that we learned with Chris we were now able to put into practice with a different director,' he explained. 'I think the reason Alfonso was able to do longer takes and was able to do more complicated shots was because, with Chris, we just didn't have

46

the experience or the focus to do that kind of stuff. And so, with Alfonso, we were kind of just getting the shot. And it is harder, it's more challenging – which is good because, if we're getting older and we're not being challenged, well then there's no point in doing it, really … and it helped us a lot to evolve or develop just making the transition.'

In this Potter instalment, most of the action took place during the school holidays, so Daniel, Emma and Rupert got to wear normal clothes for many scenes. Akin to the real age of the young stars, the characters were now in their teens. This prompted a lot of empathy from Daniel: 'Harry being a teenager has the same feelings as any other teenager … but because of his past I think he feels anger or loneliness more strongly, so I think that was kind of hard for me, but because I obviously am feeling the same things as him I guess I just kind of took what I was feeling, basically just exaggerated them, and, like, listened to music or anything to get me in the right state of mind for the filming – and then just kind of hoped for the best.'

In fact, there was much made of how both Harry Potter and Daniel were making the transition into their teenage years. During his publicity appearances, he was quizzed about whether he had a girlfriend now that he was that much older, and whether he thought he and his character had changed. By the time *Prisoner of Azkaban* was released, Daniel was fourteen. He admitted, 'hormones are interesting things', but added, 'I don't have a girlfriend, no. I'm sorry to disappoint you. I'm sure we have noticed members of the opposite sex now but we are just going through what every person our age goes through. I'm not complaining about the extra attention…' He was, he told one interviewer, 'going through what every teenager goes through except with posters…'

Now under the direction of Cuarón, the Potter story atmosphere was a lot darker than the one that Columbus had created. Daniel was determined to meet the challenge of tackling scenes he would have found impossible when starting out on the Potter trail. One of the Dementor scenes with Sirius called for Harry to have his soul sucked out. Daniel was so intent on making the shot work that he lost control of his breathing and started to hyperventilate. 'He was so into it that he almost fainted,' remarked Emma Watson.

Nevertheless, there was still time for jokes on set. Alan Rickman set up a 'fart machine' in Harry's sleeping bag in one scene in the Great Hall and activated it on the ninth and final take, breaking the silence of the shot. The Great Hall was also where Robbie Coltrane would dance the cancan and the Macarena on a table in between takes. The kids would play pool or crazy golf on a course Daniel had created out of broken electrical fans. Other ways to make the challenges – and sometimes boredom – of time spent on the film set more interesting included placing bets, often on really trivial things. 'With Harry Potter ten months will go by,' said Daniel, 'and you can bet on anything all the time, such as "50p the sun comes up in the next half an hour and we get the shot". Everything becomes fair game and now we all have an aptitude for finding wagers anywhere.' Daniel also whiled away the time on the Potter set by playing table tennis, computer games or simply reading. But, he said, 'Most of the time, I'm on set. There is not a huge amount of downtime.'

There were also a few production dramas. In February 2003,

a blaze broke out during filming near Fort William, Scotland, and more than a hundred acres of heathland caught fire. Four fire crews worked for nearly twenty hours to put it out, including dropping water bombs from a helicopter. It was thought that the Hogwarts Express steam train might have been the cause.

Prisoner of Azkaban was to be both the most controversial film in the series and acclaimed as one of the best. In *The Washington Post*, Ann Hornaday wrote about the new approach: 'Stephen King meets Charles Dickens … the franchise's eponymous hero, a teen who attends a boarding school for witches and wizards, is a winsome, bespectacled orphan who uses his powers only to fight evil – a cross between Carrie and David Copperfield…' Hornaday saved most of her praise for Emma Watson as Hermione. Her closing comment about the new director's work was: 'the school's giant clock, one of Cuarón's frequent and wistfully effective allusions to times passing, will no doubt serve as a bittersweet reminder that their beloved hero is growing up and his story must eventually come to an end.'

This was quite an incisive comment, for Daniel himself had started to have doubts about Potter, wondering if he should even film the third instalment. He confessed, 'I thought if there's a time to get out, it's now while there's still enough time for another actor to come in and establish himself. For a while I thought, "If I do all of them, will I be able to move on to other stuff or should I start doing other stuff now?" But in the end I decided I was having way too much fun. And actually there aren't many great parts out there for teenage boys, certainly not as good as Harry Potter.'

And he was still improving his acting skills, which was important to him. There could be no better way than to learn from the host of professional and acclaimed actors he was encountering. 'I learned from people around me. They are people who haven't worked on as much as I have but have done it in another way, like drama school, so I am always looking around to learn. That is the advice I would give anyone. You can learn as much about how you don't want to be as what you do want to be.'

There was a welcome break from his work schedule in December 2003 when Daniel and his family spent Christmas in Australia. The holiday was a gift from Warner Bros. to thank Daniel for his press tour of Japan earlier that year, which had of course been a triumph, if not overwhelming, for the young lad. 'I can't tell you how far this phenomenon stretches because I'm so at the centre of it,' he was later to recall. 'I can't see the edges. I'm aware of it being a phenomenon because you can hardly not when you disembark a plane in Japan and there are 5,000 people waiting for you. Sometimes I look back and wonder how I coped with it, but I suppose you have more energy.'

Daniel was delighted with his well-earned gift from the mighty Warner Bros. 'They said they would send us anywhere we wanted to go and we [Daniel and his family] said, "Australia please", so we arrived on Christmas Day and went to the hotel where Christmas lunch was being served.' The Radcliffe family were to make lifelong friends with an Aussie family they met on that visit. 'They invited us to their house to finish Christmas lunch. It was either that or the hotel room. So we experienced the meaning of Australian hospitality. They were really, really sweet. They even nipped out to get us presents. We made some really, really good friends and, to this day, my mum and dad are still in contact with them.' A friend of Daniel's father from drama school also lives in the country. In short, 'we just got on with the place really, really well and so we just love it there,' said Daniel.

Daniel was also fully aware of how it could all end one day – no more Warner Bros. treats, no more adulation, no more Potter: 'You laugh off a lot of it. You have to dismiss it as being ridiculous. And realise the fans are not there for you; they're there because you play this character. If I play another role, there won't be five thousand people to greet me at an airport. It's Harry more than me. And as long as you make that distinction, it's easier to cope with it. It's only when you start to believe you're as good as they think you are, and you're somehow above the rest of humanity, that things go badly wrong.'

Prisoner of Azkaban had its American premiere on 23 May 2004. Another frenzied throng were waiting, with many fans arriving at nine that morning. Daniel said to E! News: 'You can't take it in all at once. You forget how huge it is.' He was back on television talk shows speaking about Harry's new 'teenage angst'. On one show, accompanied by Emma Watson, he was put on the spot after a Harry Potter quiz was set for four fans. One got all the answers right, but Daniel – and Emma – had to admit that, no, they couldn't recall the registration number of the Dursleys' car.

The London premiere was on 30 May and, again, despite the *Daily Mail*'s earlier pessimistic forecast, there *was* another hysterical crowd. *Harry Potter and the Prisoner of Azkaban* went on general release on 6 June 2004. It was to be placed among *Empire*'s top 500 greatest films and grossed $796.6m worldwide. Daniel received two nominations for *Prisoner of Azkaban*: once again, the Saturn Award for Best Performance by a Younger Actor and the Critics' Choice Award for Best Young Actor. However, he still didn't feel he could rest on his laurels and that there would come a time when there would be no more Harry Potter – and he would have to show the world he was capable of diversifying.

Filming for *Harry Potter and the Goblet of Fire* started in July 2004. In this latest Potter saga, Harry was about to start his fourth year at Hogwarts. Contestants for a magical tournament are selected by a Goblet of Fire. Among the new members of the cast were Ralph Fiennes as Voldemort, *Dr Who* star David Tennant as Bartemius Crouch Junior and Robert Pattinson as Cedric Diggory. *Twilight* star Pattinson was later to be involved in a 'Who is most fanciable?' competition, with Pattinson saying that Daniel would win every time. Daniel vehemently disagreed, claiming, 'He is much prettier and can be more charming. And he can do that thing of being sultry and sexy. Rob can just stand there and look at something and start to smoulder. I just can't do that. I'm a natural fidget.'

This was the first Potter film with a British director, Mike Newell, best known for *Four Weddings and a Funeral*. With an increasing feeling of involvement, Daniel, Emma and Rupert felt confident enough to talk some of the scenes through with Newell. It was another indication of just how far they had all come from the early days. 'We made suggestions and spoke up,' said Daniel. 'We are older now, so it is good for us to feel like we're not child actors anymore. We've grown up and are now able to make our own acting decisions, obviously in collaboration with Mike.'

Newell himself was happy enough with all this for he was aware of how established the whole Potter franchise was before he came along. And he had praise for the first director, Chris Columbus. 'People didn't know how to throw a spell before Chris. There weren't characters before Chris came along; there was just the book. And he left us with this tremendous legacy. He cast the children and the children were marvellous. Then what happened was that the characters grew into the children and the children grew into the characters until they're indivisible.'

To prepare for the water scenes in which Harry rescues Ron, Hermione and Cho Chang, Daniel took a six-month course of scuba-diving lessons. He wanted to prove that he was capable of performing some stunts himself. 'Usually we have a stuntman and I always felt a bit cheated when they shouted "cut" and someone else took over. But this time I can honestly say, "it's me".' There was a lot of work involved, he said. 'I had the most amazing stunt team who I trained with and who were down there in the tank with me. I was sharing somebody else's air from their scuba-diving tank and we both had regulators. They'd say, "Three, two, one," and on the "three" I'd blow all the air out of my lungs, and on the "one" I'd take in a very big gulp of air and then it's all about how much action you can do with that amount of breath in your body. The hard thing was not just holding my breath, but I wasn't actually allowed to let any of the air out because Harry is supposed to become a fish with gills; there's not supposed to be bubbles going around. So, if I look at all pained, you know why.'

Daniel won praise for his efforts from stunt director and co-producer Peter MacDonald, who agreed that it wasn't an easy task having to swim like a fish and 'remember to be Harry Potter too'. Filmed in a huge purpose-built tank measuring

20ft by 60ft square and containing over half a million gallons of water, it was to remain one of Daniel's favourite scenes, even though he was underwater for a taxing forty-one hours over five weeks of filming. 'The sequence meant three or four minutes for just eight seconds a day. But I will never film that way again. It was pretty cool.'

Just how these scenes should be shot had been quite a difficult decision to make, and producer David Heyman said it was one of the film's greatest challenges: 'Filming in an actual loch would have been too cold and impractical. We looked into doing a process called "dry for wet", where you suspend an actor and blow wind on them to give the illusion they are underwater but the hair didn't undulate convincingly.'

Daniel's insistence on doing this scene himself was not without its own 'hairy' moments. He suffered a couple of ear infections after spending so long in water and at one point during rehearsals he accidentally signalled that he was in trouble, sending the crew into a massive panic to bring him back to the surface. Daniel recalled, 'I got the signs wrong. I thought I was signalling everything is fine but in fact I was signalling, "I'm running out of air, get me to the surface". I said the wrong thing and they all thought that I was drowning and got me up to the surface very, very fast.'

Daniel made sure he had a memento of the water scenes by organising a cast line-up and using the photograph as that year's Christmas card. Proving himself as a real action hero, Daniel was also hurled around and dangled from rooftops in *Goblet of Fire* during Harry's battle with the Horntail – a 40ft-long beast. 'The dragon battle was very physical and terrifying at times.' Daniel said. 'When we were doing the stunt where

Harry falls down the roof, I found myself literally dangled by my ankles, hanging upside down 40 feet in the air. Then I was dropped suddenly and hurtled head first to the ground. I knew it was safe because our stunt team is so brilliant. But I did feel my life flashing before my eyes for a second.'

Daniel probably would have liked some kind of stunt person, though, for the dance scenes he found so embarrassing to act. He had to take to the floor with Emma Watson and Shefali Chowdhury, who played Parvati Patil, Harry's partner at the Yule Ball. Daniel described rehearsals as 'My Big Dance Day'. The camera work was clever, never focusing on some of the less than competent footwork. But to be fair, while the other kids had around three weeks of dance practice to learn the waltz, Daniel only got four days or so because his presence was required in all the other scenes. 'You'll notice that Mike kindly didn't show anything below my waist. It's dancing from the waist up so you never see my feet move, which is quite a good thing.'

One particular testing scene was when Harry loses a classmate and has to tell the boy's father he is dead. 'I had to tap into emotions that I had personally never felt,' he said. However, Daniel was aware that he had come a long way since the very first Potter film and said that he and his two young co-stars had different things to offer. 'I think we were all good at different things,' he later said. 'Rupert was the most outgoing of the three of us; he had this confidence when it came to comedy, and he still does. My tendency is to underplay stuff and sometimes I look at the films and I know I thought I was being subtle at the time, but actually I'm just doing bugger all. That's a learning curve. You can't dwell on the things you're not happy with, though; you've got to move forward and get better.'

The Potter cast set off once again on their publicity tours and press conferences for *Goblet of Fire*. Asked to compare himself with the now older Harry Potter, Daniel replied, 'It is much easier to act him now but it's different to the other films because I have struggled through all the things like hormones, just like Harry. It's all still fresh in my mind as it doesn't stop when you reach fourteen.'

He was no doubt being asked about the whole teenage angst thing because in this fourth Potter film Harry starts to notice girls – well, Cho Chang anyway. There was a scene where he asked her out, the words tumbling forth, and she has to ask him to repeat himself. 'What I like about Harry is that he's pathetic when it comes to the whole romance thing,' Daniel said. 'And I know what it feels like to stand there and not know what to say.'

The London premiere took place on the rainy night of 6 November 2005 and the New York premiere on 12 November. Daniel was to again experience the madness of Harry Potter fans when one day his limousine stopped at traffic lights in Manhattan and another car drew up alongside. The female occupant tried to climb out and into Daniel's car through a passenger window. Another girl had held up a banner reading 'Mrs Radcliffe is here' with the obvious meaning that Daniel should look no further for a wife. But it did confuse Daniel's mum who was accompanying him!

Some reviewers were unsure about the more mature nature and scarier scenes of this latest Potter film. In Britain, it was given its first 12A rating, whereas the previous ones had been PG. A spokeswoman for the British Board of Film Classification said viewers should be 'prepared for a very different film to the first three'. In America, it was given its first PG-13 rating. *Empire* commented: 'New to the mix is the embarrassing reality of tortured adolescence, with sexual awakenings and brooding mood swings exacerbated by the added distraction of glamorous foreign-exchange students. Making quite the grand entrance are the chic girls of Beauxbatons Academy and the hunky boys of Durmstrang Institute. Welcome to Harry Potter and the Rampaging Hormones.'

Another added: 'Harry was just turning 13 in the previous movie, *Harry Potter and the Prisoner of Azkaban*, and the Potter series turns PG-13 with this instalment. There is still at least a mail-owl, and what looks like a mail-raven (it may represent FedEx), but many of the twee touches of the earlier films have gone missing to make room for a brawnier, scarier plot. Is it fair to wonder if the series will continue to grow up with Harry, earning the R rating [age 17 or over in the US] as he turns 17?'

The film was to gross $869.9m. Daniel was nominated at the MTV Movie Awards for Best Hero and as one of the Best On-Screen Team with Emma and Rupert. There were again nominations for the Saturn Award for Best Performance by a Younger Actor and the Critics' Choice Award for Best Young Actor. On 13 March 2006, at London's Sony Ericsson *Empire* Awards, Daniel, Emma and Rupert received Empire Outstanding Contribution Awards for the four Potter films.

It was a great honour of course, but Daniel knew he had to keep his feet firmly on the ground. He didn't want to become big headed and was well aware that fans were still seeing him as the boy wizard rather than the real person: 'Early on in your career you have to be able to separate the person they are cheering for from the person you actually are. They are cheering for a perception they have of you, which is a famous person, an actor and this particular character. So if you start to think that they are cheering for you as a real person then that's when you get big headed and you become an awful human being.'

In April 2006, aged sixteen, Daniel was the youngest non-royal ever to have an individual portrait – drawn by Stuart Pearson Wright – in the National Portrait Gallery. It was a pretty fine way for him to celebrate the first of his landmark birthdays. But Daniel was to be a little more forthright when asked about the big day. 'I'd say it's a pretty big deal being sixteen in England because you can have sex. Yeah, and in England you can get married with parental consent. I don't plan on getting married though. You can have sex and play the Lottery. And I couldn't wait to play the Lottery!'

Harry Potter and the Order of the Phoenix, the fifth instalment in the series, started filming at Leavesden Studios on 4 February 2006. The director this time was David Yates, who was then best known for his direction of Richard Curtis's script in the 2005 television film *The Girl in the Café* starring Bill Nighy. The film won three awards including the Primetime Emmy Award for Outstanding Made for Television Movie. Yates's credentials also included the acclaimed 2003 six-part thriller *State of Play* for which he won a Directors Guild of Great Britain Award for Outstanding Directorial Achievement and a nomination for a BAFTA TV award. Now he faced a new challenge with the world watching. Yates said one of his main difficulties was depicting the boy wizard who in the book is meant to be fifteen when Daniel was now obviously older. 'The key things of this movie are really about identity, about discovering who you are as a person, at that very difficult and often dramatic age between about fourteen and seventeen,' he said.

Daniel was simply miffed that his co-stars were now all taller than him. He joked he was going to have a 'complex series' of trenches dug so that 'all my cast mates can walk in them when they're doing a scene with me'.

New members of the cast included Helena Bonham Carter as Bellatrix Lestrange, the sadistic cousin of Sirius Black, Imelda Staunton as Dolores Umbridge, as well as fourteen-year-old newcomer Evanna Lynch who had beaten 15,000 other girls to the role of Luna Lovegood. Daniel was later to say that Staunton, together with Gary Oldman, had been the greatest influence on him during the series. 'I could spend weeks talking about how much I learned from her [Staunton],' he said, and one of the best pieces of advice was given to him by Oldman: 'Don't be afraid to use your own emotions and your own sadness, because even if you're using your own thoughts, you've got your glasses on. You've got the scar on. People will see Harry being sad, rather than Dan *acting* Harry being sad.'

There was a scene when Harry hears of the death of his mentor, Sirius Black, played by Oldman. The older actor demanded Daniel 'got physical' to prepare for it, Daniel recalled: 'We'd been doing a few takes, we'd been going at it for about two hours we were probably doing the scene and then he said to me, "Dan, do you mind if I do something a little bit more physical with you this time?" I sort of said, "Yeah, fine", thinking maybe he was gonna give me a hug or something like that. But actually he took me by the shoulders and shook me incredibly hard for about thirty seconds and shouted at me. The bizarre phenomenon is you sort of regress very quickly into this childlike state and I just started crying ... I think it really worked for the scene.'

Oldman was to remain Daniel's inspiration long after, giving him support in his future projects: 'I hope always – that's what my career will be about, pushing yourself, seeing what you can do. And what you can't do – seeing what you screw up at. That's the thing I learned from Gary Oldman. Be fearless and damn the consequences. You might be crap, but at least you've tried.'

In *Order of the Phoenix*, Harry was returning to his fifth year at Hogwarts and a complex plot involving Voldemort and a newly founded Dumbledore's Army. This Potter sequel was something of a landmark in both Daniel's career and his life. For he had now left school and was able to commit more time to filming, meaning the actual production process was the shortest ever. Daniel was more than happy to have yet another new director – 'It keeps the films fresh and stops us all getting complacent,' he said, adding that, although all the cast were established, there was still 'so much room for growth and improvement'.

One landmark area of growth was that Daniel had his first Harry Potter kiss with character Cho Chang, played by Katie Leung. 'I think we were both a bit nervous because we did know everyone was talking about it and there was the knowledge that this was a highly anticipated scene and that everybody had been waiting for this scene in some ways,' he recalled. 'We were a bit nervous but after the first few takes it was fine and we started thoroughly enjoying ourselves!' Contrary to rumour, it didn't take thirty takes before the screen kiss was perfected. 'What I meant was that there were thirty takes spanned over six different camera setups – I didn't request all those takes myself!' Daniel said by way of clarification.

Katie said that, when it came to the scene, Daniel was 'great', adding, 'I'm sure everyone wants to know if he was a good kisser. He definitely was.'

The scene was to be nominated for Best Kiss at the MTV Movie Awards. The Cinelinx website voted it one of the 'Brightest and most Visceral Moments' of the Harry Potter films: 'This was Harry's first kiss, and everyone's first kiss is a very big deal. Harry's first kiss was the kiss heard [sic] – and debated – around the world.'

With ever-growing confidence, Daniel felt he was able to discuss Harry's character with director David Yates and came up with the suggestion that as a sign of respect he would wear clothes similar to those worn by Professor Remus Lupin who had been killed in the previous Potter film. Yates liked the idea and Daniel's suggestion was accepted. Yates also said that Daniel and his two co-stars were now evolving and felt more able to add comedy to their roles. 'Daniel can play comedy really well but his natural inclination is to be drawn to the darker, more intense stuff.'

By now Daniel and Yates had developed an understanding of each other. 'I have nothing but great things to say about David,' Daniel said. 'We get closer every year. We get on very, very well off set. We have a very good relationship not only professionally but personally as well. As we go on in the films, we become more in tune with each other to the point that he can say, "Cut", and I will know immediately, without having to see or hear him, if whether what I've just done is what he wanted, simply because I know what he's looking for in a performance. Well, I think I do. I can't always get there, but he's always very good at being honest with me and saying, "You can do better than that." And that's a wonderful thing, to have that kind of trust and relationship in a director.'

Daniel was now a star in his own right, a fact acknowledged by his guest appearance on 28 September 2006 in an episode of television's *Extras* created by Ricky Gervais. 'Ricky basically said, "Look, we've got an idea of something to do with you, would you be happy to do it?" I said yes. I hadn't seen the script, I had no idea what was happening, but when Ricky Gervais says, "Do you wanna work with me?" you say yes, you don't think about it. When we did get the script, it was fantastic – I had a real laugh doing it.' The guest slot couldn't help but allude to the boyishness of Harry Potter – as well as making Daniel out to be so much different in real life. He was dressed as a scout and wearing the Potter spectacles for a scene with Gervais as Andy Millman, the lead character in the series, and Ashley Jensen as Maggie Jacobs. The three meet in the catering wagon with Daniel having such lines as, 'Get me a Bourbon, would you, babe?' He then tells Andy he is 'ready for action' and stretches a condom, which then jumps out of his hand on to the head of actress Diana Rigg behind him.

The exchange, faithfully re-created by fans on the Internet, went thus:

Dan: 'Can I have my johnny back?'

Diana: 'MAY I have my johnny back?'

Daniel: 'May I have my johnny back?'

Diana: 'Please.'

Daniel: 'Yeah.'

Diana: 'Not called a johnny, though, is it?'

Daniel: 'Durex?'

Diana: 'No, that's a brand name. May I have back my prophylactic, or sheath?'

Daniel: 'May I have my prophylac...'

Diana: 'Tic.'

Daniel: 'Prophylactic. Can I have it please?

Diana: 'Yes.'

Diana: 'Excuse me. Haven't you forgotten something?'

Dan: 'Oh ... Thank you, Dame Diana.'

Andy: 'Still going to use it then?'

Dan: 'Yeah, it'll be fine.'

Andy: 'Lucky girl.'

Another exchange with Maggie has Daniel saying he's 'done it with a girl' and taking off his Potter glasses with the words: 'Oh, God, I've still got these on. I ... I don't need these. They're just for the character. Even if I did need glasses in real life, you know, I never read.'

There were some who weren't that happy with seeing their boy star in the risqué sketch. Today.com reported: 'Daniel Radcliffe isn't the squeaky clean boy wizard some Harry Potter fans think he is. The star of the flicks based on the wildly successful fantasy books appeared in an off-colour skit, dressed as a Boy Scout, propositioning an older woman (played by Dame Diana Rigg) and playing with a condom. The skit has been picked up by YouTube, where it's drawing some outrage, but mostly amusement. "[Oh my God], when I was watching it was like … I've never seen that side of Dan," exclaimed one fan. "Normally I just see the sweet sort of well-mannered quirky Dan, not THAT!"'

Other comments included: 'I may have to tear my eyes out now, but it was pretty good in a making-me-feel-extremely-uncomfortable kind of way' and 'I seriously doubt he'd have input into the show as to his portrayal, and if he had, I doubt he would cast himself as a pervy, illiterate virgin. It was also very funny…'

Daniel enjoyed the controversy because it proved he didn't take himself too seriously. He told Moviefone.com, 'It's very important to show that you have a sense of humour about yourself. Particularly for me early on, to show that I had a sense of humour about the whole child star thing, and that I was aware of that stereotype … The reason I jumped at the chance to do it was because I was so aware that that's the image people had of child stars. So the fact that I was being given a chance to hint at the fact that I wasn't like that – though people could still watch the episode and think, "Maybe he is like that" – I just thought why not just give it to them and they can just laugh at me.'

Order of the Phoenix premiered in the UK on 3 July 2007 and in the USA on 8 July. It was released in America on 11 July 2007 and in the UK the following day. In the midst of all this, and to celebrate the opening of the film, Daniel became the youngest actor to be immortalised as a waxwork figure at Madame Tussauds in London. The figure had Daniel dressed in a suit and tie. 'Apparently I look really mature, which some people say is about time,' joked Daniel.

Ben Lovett of Tussauds commented: 'It's been great for the studio's sculptors to recreate someone who we've all watched growing up on the big screen.'

Daniel's waxwork was situated in the Blush area of the museum alongside the likes of Tom Cruise, Brad Pitt, Samuel L. Jackson and Julia Roberts.

Meanwhile, Daniel had endeared himself to his Japanese fans even more. He attended a premiere in Tokyo in June and addressed the audience in Japanese to be greeted with loud cheers. Wearing a white suit and before a spectacular firework display was launched, Daniel said Japanese fans were the 'strongest' the Potter team had had over the years. 'You're incredible,' he told the delighted crowd. Outside, thousands of fans had gathered on the red carpet with scores of children wearing black capes and wigs. Some burst into tears when they realised they would not be allowed inside the grand cinema at Tokyo's Roppongi Hills entertainment complex.

Daniel was nominated for another Saturn Award for Best Performance by a Younger Actor and an Empire Award for Best Actor. He won the National Movie Award for Best Performance by a Male.

Daniel was certainly winning worldwide recognition for the boy wizard, who just like him was now growing up and had left that little boy behind. 'It kind of is sad. I'm not that little, innocent, lovely little thing anymore. It's very nostalgic and weird, but I'm very proud to have grown up. And also, when I look at those first films and I see that, I think, "God, we had no idea what we were doing." To a certain extent, all of us didn't. It was new ground.' But he added that maturing on screen was only natural: 'It probably seems strange to everyone but me. I don't think of it being a case of me having grown up on screen. I have just grown up.'

He was soon to prove this in a dramatic and professional way.

CHAPTER 4

NAKED AMBITION

He stood there totally naked. The sweat trickled down his back in the knowledge that, while his eyes could only make out dim images before him, he was under the scrutiny of hundreds of anonymous spectators. Daniel Radcliffe, aged just seventeen and seemingly destined to remain forever known as a boy wizard, was determined to cast his own spell – the one that would transform him from child star to acclaimed actor.

There had been many cigarettes smoked – a habit Daniel has 'behind the scenes' but feels uncomfortable doing in public – much going over and over his lines and a honed focus in his dressing room to prepare. Then the call came. Now he had to walk onstage. He even allowed himself a little smile as he thought of how proving he was not just a one-trick-pony actor could not be a more fitting phrase to come into his head right now. But as he was to say some years later: 'For a teenager with serious acting aspirations, it would have been incredibly stupid to have turned this down.'

For Daniel had chosen the complex and controversial psychological play *Equus* for his West End stage debut. Losing the technique needed to perform in films and learning new ones for the theatre was challenge enough. But for his very first experience of treading the boards he was to be in a play in which, literally, he was exposed to the public and critics alike. Much was made of Harry Potter going full frontal and simulating sex in a London theatre, which greatly irked all those involved with the project. 'We are not doing it as an excuse to show Harry Potter's willy' was how producer David Pugh summed it up. Pugh defended the publicity material of a naked Daniel (top-half only), saying, 'We want people to know they are going to come and see a show about a young man, not a young boy … This is a boy who is now making his own decisions, and, rather than just being seen as a sort of Shirley Temple, is determined that he wants to act for the rest of his life, and this is his way of putting himself out there.'

Daniel said he was not uptight about posing for the *Equus* publicity shots because it was one of his 'hyper days' and he had just done the nude scene for the first time in rehearsals. 'I was basically wanting to get my kit off as much as I possibly could to try and get used to the idea and in front of as many strangers as I could. I'd be like, "Ready now? Is this where I take them off?" And they'd be like, "Dan! Hold back! Wait! Just give us ten minutes, please!"'

But some websites were receiving comments from parents who were worried about Daniel's dramatic departure from his family character. One said: 'We as parents feel Daniel should not appear nude. Our nine-year-old son looks up to him as a role model. We are very disappointed and will avoid the future movies he makes.' Another wrote: 'I am curious as to how and why his parents said this was okay.'

One educational website even made Daniel's stage appearance part of a lesson plan: 'QUICK DEBATE: Students A believe Daniel Radcliffe should not act in the play *Equus*. Students B believe Daniel Radcliffe is making a good move. Debate this with your partners. Change partners often.'

The *Daily Mail* reported how 'utterly dismayed' Warner Bros. were said to be that 'the sixth-former will not only cavort naked for a full ten minutes during the production but will also be seen, sources say, simulating sex while riding a "horse"'. A 'source' was quoted as saying: 'Warner Bros. have been building up their publicity machine for Harry's first – chaste – screen kiss when the next Potter film comes out in the summer and now our star's out there doing full-frontal sex. We've been completely blown out of the water by this.'

Daniel was angry at the suggestion he had caused problems for Warner Bros. and denied the film company was critical of his choice of role. 'There was a lot of stuff in a couple of the less generous journals in England, who said Warner Bros. was furious with me for doing *Equus* and did not support me, which is absolute fiction. They were totally supportive from the word go. There's never been any kind of anger at anything I've done. They would never limit me.'

Daniel was also irritated by the controversy: 'Offended mothers were calling up and saying I shouldn't be doing this and that they weren't going to go and see it. They treated it like pornography and it's not. It was only seven minutes at the end of the play.'

Co-star Joanna Christie joined in the defence of Daniel and the controversial scenes, saying, 'I can't believe there are people saying he's a bad role model for children. He's an actor playing a part, and in the story he happens to have a relationship with a girl … It's an amazingly interesting, complex story. It's not about nudity or sex. It's about a lot of very complex issues. When we do [the nude scene] in the context of the play it's really beautiful and natural. I expected some publicity because of Daniel but not stories and photos everywhere.'

There was even condemnation that his character had to smoke. At first he said that the cigarettes he smoked onstage were fake and denied that he had the habit himself. He was later forced to admit this wasn't quite true after being photographed with a cigarette in his hand. A rather snide newspaper comment appeared: 'Speculation continues as to what the cigarette actually contained as the picture was snapped at a celebrity party in London. It was unlikely to consist solely of tobacco.' This claim was vehemently denied by Daniel.

Fortunately, the masses were also able to appreciate Daniel was an actor in his own right playing a challenging stage role and the genius of the powerful and disturbing concept of a troubled boy who blinds horses. Daniel's publicist Vanessa Davies commented in response to some of the criticism: 'He does not want to step away from Harry Potter but he does want to show he is a well-rounded actor capable of very different and diverse roles. He has tremendous support from Harry Potter fans.'

Despite the reported condemnation, this production of *Equus* was to make history with the highest ever number of advance bookings for a West End play.

Daniel had been approached about the role two years earlier right at the height of his Harry Potter success. He was only too aware that he was facing a possible cynical response right from the start. It was the words of his father – 'wrong foot them, Dan' – that made him determined to prove the doubters wrong. Being offered the leading role in the Peter Shaffer play was an opportunity that, as Daniel saw it, could drastically change everyone's perception of him. 'It wasn't calculated. I really wasn't a stage actor and had never done a full show. So it was nice for me to see if I could do it. It was the chance to move away from being seen as a character and being seen as an actor,' he explained.

He was very conscious that any departure from his established family-film typecasting could meet with mixed reactions. If he did another kind of fantasy film, people would say he wasn't trying hard enough. If he went off to play a hard nut like a drug dealer, he said, 'They'd say, "God, he's trying way too hard … It's also the fact that [Alan, the character he played] Strang is very different from Harry, a very violent character – he's mentally unstable, that's the long and short of it.'

So committed to the role was Daniel that, after discussion with his parents, he had left the City of London School (it's hard to remember that normal schooling ran parallel to his early Harry Potter days) after taking three AS exams in English, history, religion and philosophy (maths was never an option – 'too many little numbers on one page!' he once remarked – but he did achieve some 'reasonable' GCSEs with seven Bs, a couple of As and an A*). He was to get As in all the AS exams, disproving the predictions of all those teachers who had been so dismissive.

However, there was never any question of his going on to university as his Potter co-star Emma Watson was to do. It was 'never on the cards', he said. 'I found something that I have some aptitude for – I hesitate to say that I'm good at it because I'm so far away from being finished at school and I've still got a lot to learn, but I certainly think that I'm better at this than I would be at anything else. So I'm going to try to just focus on that and try to make as long a career for myself as possible.'

The excellent result in English was to encourage Daniel to think more about writing for himself because 'as an actor you're always ultimately going to be saying somebody else's words'. He didn't think he had enough staying power or skill to one day write a novel but he loved writing short stories and poetry, describing them as his 'two passions'.

Equus was first performed in 1973. But no other performance – even that starring Richard Burton in 1979 – would create such a stir as this one, with its star shaking off the mantle of schoolboy sorcerer overnight. Of course, there had been many revivals of the play both in London and on the local theatre circuit. There was also the 1977 film with Peter Firth in the main role (which Daniel deliberately chose not to watch in case it influenced his own character interpretation), and all required the raw exposure of actors playing the character of Alan Strang. Daniel wanted to play it his way. 'I still don't want to be a big over-the-top actor. That's never going to be the way I work. But I think I've got better at striking a balance where I'm being real but still being expressive,' said Daniel.

During the weekend preview performance of *Equus*, Daniel found himself about to expose all publicly for the first time. He was onstage facing Royal Shakespeare Company actor

Richard Griffiths at London's Gielgud Theatre. It must have been daunting for Daniel to be working with such a big name. Griffiths had also won the 2006 Tony and Olivier awards for Best Actor in a Play for his performance in *The History Boys* and past film appearances included *Gandhi*, *The French Lieutenant's Woman* and *Chariots of Fire*. Griffiths played the other lead role, psychiatrist Martin Dysart, who tries to help the tormented teenager, while coming to terms with his own demons. It was not the first time the two had met, of course, for Griffiths had appeared in the Harry Potter series as Vernon Dursley. Among the rest of the cast were Jenny Agutter as magistrate Hesther Salomon (in the 1977 production she played Jill Mason), Jonathan Cullen and Will Kemp (who with a wire-form 'head' played Nugget the horse and The Young Horseman).

The play was directed by Thea Sharrock. Daniel already had her firm support, and she had made it clear that Harry Potter and Daniel Radcliffe were indeed separable. 'We could all finally see it,' she said. 'I felt excited to find this character with him and prove to the world that this was something he could do.'

Producer David Pugh was joined by Dafydd Rogers. It wasn't the first time the three had worked together, as Pugh and Rogers had given Daniel his first ever chance to work in the West End as a celebrity guest in *The Play What I Wrote* at the Wyndham Theatre in 2002. The celebration of legendary British comedy duo Morecambe and Wise was directed by *Harry Potter and the Chamber of Secrets* co-star Kenneth Branagh and featured a surprise appearance each night. Daniel – listed as 'playing himself' – actually played the son of Count Toblerone in a sketch called 'A Tight Squeeze for the Scarlet Pimpernel' and had to wear a dress and wig. 'He brought the house down for three shows – two on Boxing Day!' said Pugh.

In fact, Pugh had first met Daniel as a tiny baby when his mother Marcia was his secretary. 'She was superb, she got pregnant, which was a bit of a bugger because it was only me and her running the office,' recalled Pugh. 'We were producing *Steel Magnolias* at the time and then she had a son called Daniel who spent the first nine months of his life in a Moses basket underneath her desk. So that's how I met Daniel Radcliffe.'

As with the part of Harry Potter, there had been another 'bring me that boy' moment involving Daniel when Shaffer, after some reluctance, finally agreed to the new production of *Equus*. 'He said, "If you find the boy, I'll think about it,"' said Pugh. Co-producer Rogers recalled Daniel as being 'phenomenal' at the first reading, saying, 'A lot of people think it was one of those cases where Daniel said he wanted to do a play, but we wanted to do *Equus* and when he did the workshop he was wonderful, so we put the production together from there.'

Originally, Branagh had been approached about playing Dysart and directing the production, but there were artistic differences, said Pugh, and so Thea Sharrock was called in. The project was to be the biggest gamble of her career and she wanted it to work for Daniel and all those involved. 'With Dan, I do feel a huge sense of responsibility,' she said at the time. 'It's a huge personal risk for him. One has an overwhelming sense of wanting to protect him, wanting to work him as hard as possible, so that when he goes out there he's going to do himself proud.'

Daniel then did a reading and Shaffer came over from New York. 'We did the reading at the Old Vic where it originally started, and Daniel was superb as was proven,' remembered Pugh. 'Everybody was dubious but I just knew he could do it.'

There was someone else who had been a major mentor for Daniel even before the first of the six-week-long rehearsals. Knowing that projecting professionally onstage was so very different from speaking on screen, Daniel enlisted the help of voice coach Barbara Houseman who once worked in the voice department of the Royal Shakespeare Company and to whom many actors are indebted. She still works with Daniel today.

For this role, Daniel said, he practised and practised to ensure that he did not face the pitfalls of other actors who have made the same move to the stage, 'either not being heard or screaming and wrecking their voices'. In short, he said, he wanted to do it all in the right way. The two worked together for a year and a half. Exercises included Daniel sometimes reading vowels from text and sometimes just the consonants. It was all new to him: 'The techniques are so different from film, even just the basics about projecting your voice without sounding as if you're yelling your head off.'

This wasn't the only way he prepared for the role that was to be a life-changer. At the start of the play, Daniel, as Strang, had to sing the Milky Bar advertising jingle. By his own admission, he was initially 'screwing up the tune', which resulted in his being sent to a singing teacher. He also undertook method sessions in which he had to imagine that different parts of the room were different emotions, and had Alexander Technique lessons to teach him to stand and move properly. All this was particularly demanding for Daniel: as already mentioned, he was later to reveal that he suffers from dyspraxia, a neurological problem that impairs the organisation of movement and affects how the brain processes information. Fortunately, he has a mild level of the disorder, which affects up to eight per cent of people in Britain, but ironically the affliction comes from the word 'praxis', meaning 'doing, acting'. Daniel has said that suffering from dyspraxia was one of the reasons he wanted to become an actor, feeling that he had underachieved at school.

He certainly wasn't underachieving in the run-up to *Equus*, even taking intense acting lessons in preparation for his stage appearance. There was nothing he wouldn't do to meet this new challenge; and *Equus* was indeed a challenge. It would also remain a memorable change of direction for Daniel, who would later say, 'You know what? That play gave me the taste for pushing the boundaries and for doing something that bit different. I have discovered that, when you are acting, the best quality you can have is fearlessness – that is what you should aim for. You should be willing to try anything. You might fail, but at least you've made the attempt. That's what I aspire to. You learn as much in failure as you do in success – or rather, you should do, if you've got any common sense.'

The play begins with the psychiatrist Dysart's monologue about how helping his young patients only makes him realise that his own life is unsatisfactory. It is revealed that there is one boy in particular, Alan Strang, whose plethora of mental problems, including the rejection of his parents' conflicting religious beliefs, leads him to violence. This culminates in his blinding of horses – animals that figured in his life via the stories his mother read to him as a child and which now hold a sexual draw for him. He gets the chance to commit his horrific acts when taken on at a stable. One horse, which Strang calls Equus, is ridden bareback and naked. As well as the nudity, Daniel also had a sex scene with Jill Mason (played by Joanna Christie), as his character tries to beat the conflict of his natural urges and his parents' condemnation of sex being unnatural and dirty. But Equus has been a witness to this – and must be blinded.

Shaffer would probably see this résumé as doing a great injustice to his work in which he has Strang seeing the horses as representative of God, confusing his adoration of God with sexual attraction. Also important is Shaffer's examination of the conflict between personal values and satisfaction and societal mores, expectations and institutions.

'In reference to the play's classical structure, themes and characterisation, Shaffer has discussed the conflict between Apollonian and Dionysian values and systems in human life.'

David Pugh was more down to earth about the sex scene, saying, '[Daniel] had to get his kit off with a very beautiful girl. Quite frankly, I'd have been scared witless too.'

The *Daily Mail* noted how Harry Potter would be seen onstage with an actress 'resting her naked body against his while caressing his bare flesh against the provocative backdrop of a haystack'.

Shaffer may have 'discussed conflict' in the play, but he didn't discuss much with his latest leading man. The first time he and Daniel met was when the cast put on what Daniel describes as a 'ramshackle production' for the writer after a couple of days of workshop rehearsals. Daniel was impressed that Shaffer, aged eighty-two, had walked up six floors to view his performance. It was another year before they met again. But Daniel is eternally grateful for Shaffer's trust in him – and that at the time he was seventeen, the exact age Shaffer insisted *Equus* character Alan

Strang had to be: 'Peter was very, very keen that was the age he was,' Daniel emphasised.

And so, Daniel Radcliffe was about to appear in his first major stage role. It was a testing departure for him with the concern that no one would want to see Harry Potter violent, sexual and screwed up. And it was all predictably accompanied by publicity focusing on what Daniel quite justifiably said was simply part of the play: everyone wanted to know how he felt about being stark naked in front of an audience every night. For a hitherto boy wizard, he gave some very mature answers: 'I love the speeches in *Equus*. The rest can work itself out. If you sign up for something, then you know full well what you have to do. If you get nervous about it, then tough. There's no time for procrastination or doubt. It's integral to the plot.

'Before anyone had seen the play, they had come to the conclusion that it was some gratuitous pornographic scene we were doing, which is so the opposite to what it was in reality. It is nerve wracking and scary but once you accept the fact that everyone knows you are not going to look your best...'

One person breathing a sigh of relief that in the end artistic merit overrode the whole Harry Potter-goes-naked frenzy was co-producer David Pugh: 'What I'm really proud of is that there hasn't been a night when we've had a giggle or a wolf-whistle,' he said afterwards. 'We've brought people into the theatre, some who've never been before, and we've held their attention. That's the achievement.'

Undoubtedly, it had been an exceptionally brave decision for a self-conscious lad of seventeen who had actually asked his father if he'd get away with wearing pants instead of being totally naked. Daniel also confessed to what he called 'Michelangelo's

David Effect': 'He [David] wasn't very well endowed, because he was fighting Goliath. There was very much of that effect. You tighten up like a hamster.' But he learned to accept the onstage 'shrinking': 'The first time it happened, I turned around and went, "You know, there's a thousand people here, and I don't think even one of them would expect you to look your best in this situation."'

Daniel had, in fact, had regular sessions at a gym to tone up for the nude scene. His efforts had certainly paid off, with Thea Sharrock admitting, 'We all said, "Wow! Oh my God!" when we saw him.' But Sharrock also knew Daniel would shape up for his first serious West End appearance too. 'If you want to be an actor, then you need to be tested and I can't think of a more testing part, apart from Hamlet, for this age. Is he ready for the challenge? The peculiar life Dan's led has prepared him for things that most people will never have to deal with. To watch the ease with which he deals with things is extraordinary and immediately gave me great faith in the fact that he had as good a chance as anybody of pulling it off, if not better.'

Daniel certainly needn't have worried about his naked physique. When snatched 'grainy and out of focus' pictures taken of him onstage with co-star Anna Camp found their way on to the Internet when *Equus* transferred to Broadway the following year, they were responded to in a highly favourable way, with women saying what they would like to do with this grown-up Harry Potter and commenting on every part of his body. Not unexpectedly, similar enthusiasm was voiced in more graphic detail by male fans. Shaffer voiced his fury about the snatched pictures in no uncertain terms: 'Whoever did this is a creep.'

Stage technician Rachel Juozapaitis raged that art had been turned into pornography. 'It's just wrong. He still has to do some Harry Potter films for the kids…' (In fact, Daniel had postponed his next Potter film to do the play.) The production team refused to set an age limit for those seeing *Equus* because, they said, 'one fourteen-year-old is not the same as the next fourteen-year-old' and left the decision up to parents. '*Equus* is on the school syllabus and I would never stipulate what age people should be able to see it,' commented David Pugh.

And all those involved in *Equus* strongly defended the contentious scenes. 'There is unquestionably a very dark side to the play – that's what makes it so visceral and exciting – but it doesn't take away from the fact that it's an exceptional piece of playwriting and it's time to see it again,' said Sharrock. 'It's too good for yet another generation not to see it. At some point, you have to hold your hands up and say you can't please all of the people all of the time. But perhaps some of those people will come and see it and be bowled over by Daniel's performance – not Harry Potter, but Daniel Radcliffe – and forgive us for doing it. He's not a fictional boy who lives in a book.'

However, the naive boy in Daniel came out in an interview with *Empire* magazine –and he talked bottoms. Bottom hair to be exact, and how he had had it removed with a sugaring process that rips it off: 'I was very self-conscious about arse hair, so I made the ill-fated decision to have it removed. It was fucking painful. I only had it done once and now I no longer care about my hairy arse. But it's not as bad as you'd think.' He gave himself six out of ten.

Daniel was not so laid back when one newspaper ran the headline 'Hairy Botter'. It wasn't even a reference to his bottom, but to his private parts. Daniel was unimpressed, not just because of the 'crap pun' but because anyone had found it necessary to comment about something so natural in a teenage boy. 'It's that thing of being shocked that I should have hair, you know, anywhere else than on my head. It's not so much they don't want me to grow up. It's that they're annoyed that I'm growing up adjusted. They'd rather I was growing up and going wild and crashing cars.'

Several years on, Daniel would still be asked 'naked questions' about *Equus*. He tried to fend off some of the salacious interest by admitting in one interview that nudity really was no big deal and that in fact he and his parents were quite used to it at home. 'I grew up always walking around naked, well not always, but it was never an issue in my house. I've seen my mum naked, seen my dad naked. I don't actively seek to find them naked, but it's never been a particularly big deal.'

But it still didn't come easily to him in public performances. 'There's this whole myth that it's easier for me to get naked onstage than it is for women, which is absolute crap in my opinion. If there's a naked woman onstage, that's fine, the guys are happy to see a pair of tits. As a man you feel like you're being more assessed, which is frankly not the way I'd choose to have my assessment done, in front of 2,000 people every night.' And if he had heard the words 'Harry Potter is waving his other wand' once, he'd heard them a thousand times. It was a lot of fuss about one, albeit slightly prolonged, nude stage appearance. He told *Time Out*: 'Some people were always going to be salacious and focus on the nudity but the people that mattered sat up and said, "Okay, that play's no joke. It's a bold move. He wants to do something serious."'

After the preview performance, more than four hundred fans mobbed Daniel as he left the Gielgud Theatre and police were called in. Daniel was escorted to his car by security staff, but Jenny Agutter and Richard Griffiths had to make their exit through a window in the melee. David Pugh commented: 'You try to get Richard Griffiths out of a back window – it was a bit touch and go.'

Daniel's first 'official' night in the West End, on 27 February 2007, culminated in a standing ovation from an audience littered with celebrities. Hollywood actor Christian Slater said, 'The work that Daniel did onstage was incredible, extraordinary. I take my hat off to him completely. He became Alan Strang. I never thought for one second I was looking at Daniel Radcliffe – I was watching Alan Strang.'

However, it was not all plain sailing for Daniel when he took the stage each night. There were those who still saw Harry Potter standing in front of them as well as those who just wanted to get to him – whatever. He received a letter from a woman who told him she was in London for the weekend and asked that he look out for her in a certain seat. She would be wearing a red scarf, she wrote. She also gave the name of her hotel and room number. It was made even more embarrassing because Daniel's father had opened the letter. 'I didn't look, believe me,' said Daniel. 'And I didn't see her … but she sort of propositioned me.'

There was also the night when enthusiastic fans took advantage of the additional audience seating for 60 people onstage. Remaining on the stage in between scenes, Daniel was constantly bombarded with urgent whispers from the group of fans. 'They kept saying, "Dan, Dan, look at us.

They were talking to me the whole time. I rarely get angry with audience members but I came off and begged to have them moved.' He continued with the second half of the play without further disruption.

Some audiences reacted in a way that dispirited the cast and production crew. 'We had a couple of very odd laughs,' Daniel said. 'After a certain point there was nothing funny about the action. I thought if you are laughing now you are not seeing where this is going. Not to tar a whole audience with the same brush, but when there are a couple of them laughing you just think, "Really?"' Another night, Daniel couldn't help noticing a youngster in the front row texting throughout the whole play. 'I wanted to shout, "Put it away and watch!" It was slightly ironic considering the play is about alienation.'

Daniel couldn't even wind down after the play because he knew there would be herds of fans and photographers waiting outside the theatre for him. He loves the genuine fans and felt bad that he was too exhausted to meet some of them. What he doesn't like are the large numbers of autograph hunters who make money out of him. Of course, it is sometimes hard to tell these from the genuine fans, but there are times, such as during the 2013 Film Independent Spirit Awards, when footage of Daniel signing away among the crowds outside clearly shows that many of them are middle-aged men shoving Potter merchandise his way. One can be heard shouting for Daniel to sign, saying, 'I'm not in your face like everyone else', and at one point Daniel shouts, 'Please don't punch over her head' when some old enough to know better are jostling a girl.

In fact, there are a lot of men of a certain age who simply look out of place in these situations and one can understand Daniel's feelings about them: 'They will instantly sell the autographs and I can't stand them because they are so aggressive and just foul-mouthed with everybody. The autograph hunters are so rude to people that I actually try not to sign for them whenever I can. I did say to this one guy, "Look, I signed for you, it has to be twenty times by now. I'm really sorry, I'm not doing it again." And they're always blank pieces of paper. They just go and sell them. And you think, "Why would I bother with you when I can sign for somebody else?" They haven't seen the show. They're just hanging around the stage door! I just don't think it's right.'

Outside the theatre after each *Equus* performance, there were also the paparazzi to face every night. It was an intrusion Daniel did not need after a long stint onstage. So he came up with what he called a 'cunning ruse', wearing the same jacket and hat each night, 'so they could take pictures for six months but it would look like the same day, so the pictures became un-publishable. It was hilarious because there's nothing better than seeing the paparazzi getting really frustrated.'

The London reviews in general were good, with the huge praise heaped upon Richard Griffiths equalling that given to Daniel.

In *The Telegraph*, Charles Spencer wrote: 'Better yet, Daniel Radcliffe brilliantly succeeds in throwing off the mantle of Harry Potter, announcing himself as a thrilling stage actor of unexpected range and depth. Those of us who have watched the Potter films with our families have always liked Radcliffe, who has a rare natural charm about him, and he has improved greatly as an actor as the series has progressed. Despite minimal previous theatrical experience Radcliffe here displays a dramatic power and an electrifying stage presence that marks a tremendous leap forward. I never thought I would find the diminutive (but perfectly formed) Radcliffe a sinister figure, but as Alan Strang, the play's teenage anti-hero who undergoes psychotherapy after viciously blinding six horses, there are moments when he seems genuinely scary in his rage and confusion. There are fleeting instants when you even detect a hint of Voldemort-like evil in his hooded eyes.'

Peter Brown said in the *London Theatre Guide*: 'The most intriguing and interesting question for me was whether Radcliffe could pull off a substantial and demanding role on the stage. After all, there's a world of difference between doing a few seconds on a film set (maybe with lots of coaching before it) and playing to a large audience onstage for over two hours. In fact Radcliffe does manage, more or less, to pull it off. He certainly seems confident in the role, and presents us with a vulnerable, edgy, and sometimes rather scary, but naively child-like Alan Strang, who's been bombarded with differing philosophies and attitudes that have somehow got strangely jumbled in his brain and emerged as horse-worship.'

'Forget all the prurient press speculation about Harry Potter's private parts. The revelation of this revival is that Daniel Radcliffe really can act, proving that his screen appearances as J. K. Rowling's boy-hero are no flash in the magic pan,' wrote Michael Billington in *The Guardian*.

There was more praise in *The Stage*: 'His energies are so focused within the character, they almost glow, Potter-like, from within – his arms locked firmly by his side, his voice almost without pitch but cracking with teenage angst and emotion. Unlike many stars of the big screen, he has the ability to expand his range and fill a stage.'

In fact, Rowling, Harry Potter's creator, was there in the audience on opening night. That meant a lot to Daniel, the boy she once described as the son she never had – 'It's going to be weird for her to see her long-lost son blind horses!' said Daniel. It was also unfortunately the night a Harry Potter fan in the audience threw a toy owl with a note attached onstage – albeit, Daniel was to say, 'a very sweet note'.

Equus finished its successful London run on 9 June 2007. Producers Pugh and Rogers claimed that at a cost of £700,000 it had been the 'most expensive production of a straight play to hit the West End'. But it recouped all that in just nine weeks. Daniel's brave decision to shake off Harry Potter had paid off. He had now made a name for himself in his own right: 'It was the first time some people started to know my real name. They started calling me Daniel. And I had now actually become aware of the process of acting. With Potter I was really just saying the lines like I myself would say them. I didn't have the process of turning Harry into this or that. *Equus* was so very different. It required a different mental attitude. It was the first time I was saying lines I would never say myself. I had to create a character.'

As Dominic Cavendish remarked in *The Telegraph* shortly before the show ended: 'Just a week on Saturday, Daniel Radcliffe will take his final curtain-call in *Equus*, hop back on his broomstick and fly off to shoot the next Harry Potter film, his reputation as an actor transformed.'

This was not the only acting departure Daniel had undertaken that year. He had also fitted in eight weeks of filming the ITV drama *My Boy Jack*, based on the Rudyard Kipling poem.

Wearing a fake moustache and with his hair slicked back, he took the part of Kipling's son John Jack, a First World War veteran who went missing in action. Daniel said of the role, 'That was quite hard for me because I still haven't grown up to the extent that Jack has in the film. I had to act older than I am, which is much harder than acting younger I think. But when you like a character, no matter how hard it is to get under his skin, it becomes a lot more enjoyable because it's a pleasure getting to know him better. As long as I keep doing work like this and having a good time doing interesting things, I think you've got to give everything a go and just see how you fare. Sometimes it will come off and it will be great, and sometimes it won't and it'll be horrible but at least I'll have tried.'

David Haig (who wrote the screenplay) played Rudyard Kipling and other cast members were Kim Cattrall as Carrie Kipling and Carey Mulligan as Elsie Kipling. 'I think what David [Haig] has done is just amazing – it's a labour of love and he has been labouring at it for such a long time,' said Daniel. 'He knows every character, particularly Rudyard, inside out, and I have to say he was an absolute pleasure to work with. Especially when we'd suddenly look at each other and realise we could actually pass for father and son.'

Haig said he found Daniel 'extraordinarily interested and interesting and a bright guy', adding, 'Not for one second was he anything but an actor who had been employed to pay and investigate that part.' The film, shot in Ireland, had Daniel's old friend Rebecca Eaton from his *David Copperfield* days as an executive producer with Brian Kirk as director, and was shown on Remembrance Day. The filming, which took place around Dublin and ended at Kipling's family home in East Sussex, was hard, with Daniel and the rest of the cast exposed to mud, rats and being soaked by rain machines. 'It was Glastonbury all over again but with guns,' he said. 'But when you're actually in the trenches and it's freezing cold and there are rats everywhere, that does make it slightly easier to imagine yourself into that situation. But equally you can't ever hope to fully comprehend what it was like to be there.'

The crucial scene where Jack is sent over the top from the trenches into No Man's Land – and the soldiers' nightmare – was particularly hard for Daniel. There was an explosion scene and he had been warned that he would lose 70 per cent of his visibility because of the smoke. 'When the explosions did go off, the air was just filled with dirt and for about five seconds you could see nothing and you were sort of running blind. I think those five seconds were the closest you ever really came to experiencing what it was really like.'

My Boy Jack received mostly positive reviews. Critic Brian Lowry wrote on Variety.com: 'It's not exactly *Equus* but Daniel Radcliffe's maturation into this young-adult role is merely one reason to watch a poignant, splendid "Masterpiece" production … If there were any doubts, it also demonstrates that for Radcliffe, there is clearly life after Harry Potter.'

James Walton in *The Telegraph* wrote: 'Happily, Radcliffe's presence never felt like merely a ploy to increase the ratings – although presumably it won't have done them any harm. For a start, casting a real teenager served as a constantly jolting reminder of just how young First World War soldiers were. (When he sailed for France, Jack still wasn't 18 – and so needed a letter of permission from his dad.) One minute, we saw a boy having a sneaky fag with his sister and moaning about his parents. The next, he was commanding a platoon of 20 Dubliners, most of them older and far more worldly than he was. And through all of this, Radcliffe created an entirely convincing sense of a young man trying unconvincingly not to be scared – and doing his unconvincing best to impersonate a grown-up. At the same time, Radcliffe was wise enough to leave the real actorly fireworks to Haig, who mapped Kipling's changing feelings about the war with great clarity – from the early, almost excited patriotism to the terrible grief and guilt when Jack was killed on his first day of action.'

Daniel said of the role: 'For many people my age, the First World War is just a topic in a history book. But I've always been fascinated by the subject and think it's as relevant today as it ever was.'

In July 2007, Daniel, together with his Potter co-stars, left imprints of his hands, feet and wand on the hallowed ground outside the famous Chinese Theatre in Hollywood, thus joining a legion of legendary acting names before him. 'When you see all those other names, I think we were all just a little bit in shock that we had been asked. But it was amazing, absolutely just fantastic.'

Equus opened on Broadway on 25 September 2008. This remarkable debut was blighted by family tragedy for Daniel. A couple of weeks into the play, his paternal grandmother Elsie Radcliffe died, aged 79, after a long illness. Daniel's initial reaction was of course to return to Britain for the funeral that October but his parents decided Elsie would have wanted her grandson to carry on. A spokesman for Daniel said: 'It's been a very difficult time but Dan chose to remain in New York after discussions with his family. They decided it was what his grandmother would have wanted. She was a strong supporter of Dan and his career and she wouldn't have wanted him to miss a performance.' It was indeed a hard time for Daniel, keeping on top of the eight performances a week and dealing with the loss. He still managed to stop to talk to fans outside the theatre but one night, still in an emotional state, he found the pushing and shoving so bad that he threatened to leave unless the crowd calmed down.

It was the play's first Broadway revival since its debut when it had won the Tony Award for Best Play in 1975 and run for more than a thousand performances from 1974 to 1977. So it was particularly rewarding for Richard Griffiths and Daniel to be asked to repeat their roles for the New York stage. The rest of the cast was an all-American line-up, with Anna Camp taking the role of Jill Mason – 'Dan said he and I are in it together and that the more you do it, the more comfortable you get. Hopefully by the 100th performance I'll be less nauseous,' she said of the sex scene. The cast also included Kate Mulgrew, Carolyn McCormick and T. Ryder Smith, with Thea Sharrock back as director.

It was another new challenge and Daniel was determined that he would continue to give the part his all. His concerns about stage appearances are that, if people pay 'extortionate' amounts of money to see a play, then it is down to him to reward them with his best performance – every night – 'you have to make it fresh every time you do it'.

One unexpected change to the script was the name of the horse Strang 'talks' to. It was originally called Trojan but was switched to Hero for the US audiences, as Trojan is the name of an American condom brand. There was also some criticism about the 'semi-nude' pictures of Daniel in the role being used in promotional material – 'This is not the sort of thing that's taught at Hogwarts' – and that mighty film giant Warner Bros. were concerned about how it would all affect Harry Potter's future – 'Unlike the boyish Harry, Radcliffe's character smoked, dealt with harrowing sexual themes and appeared nude for one scene of the play.' Any Internet search at the time would have revealed site after site exploding with comments and pictures about Daniel's nudity – and complete photograph galleries devoted to it.

The Daily Intelligencer website was even more cynical: 'In honour of the opening of ticket sales for Peter Shaffer's *Equus* on Monday, publicists for the show have started doing what they do best – disseminating sexy/angry shots of 19-year-old Daniel Radcliffe's exposed torso. We've always thought this marketing campaign – while a little hot in a pervy, exploitive way – is off the mark. Poor little Daniel is trying to shake off his Harry Potter image, not become a stripper. He wants people to see *Equus* for his acting, not his wang … unlike the images from the London performances, these pics don't even have a woman in them. Or a horse! It's like "Oi! Come and see this lil' chap take his knickers off …"'

Reviews such as 'he was more than just an actor who played a junior wizard' were later to save the day.

Daniel may have made a conscious decision not to watch other Alan Strang characterisations in a bid to make his interpretation his very own, but for Broadway he found another way to tweak and freshen up the role. At Richard Griffiths's suggestion, Daniel watched the 1971 film *A Clockwork Orange* for a new take on the violent mind. The film, adapted from Anthony Burgess's book and which put director Stanley Kubrick in the annals of cult cinema, starred Malcolm McDowell as sociopathic Alex. It was pretty horrific – but it was also useful for Daniel. 'I didn't want to just rehash the performance. I wanted it to be a lot stronger and have a lot more anger. Also, the ideas they play with in *A Clockwork Orange* are so similar. It's about taking away what makes someone an individual so they fit into society as a whole.'

Griffiths had become a close friend to the young Daniel. They were already acquainted from the Potter films, but now Daniel needed someone to guide him in this departure from the norm. And Griffiths, with a lifetime of stage acclaim and accolades behind him, proved a kind, encouraging and loyal mentor. Daniel was to speak often of how Griffiths showed him such warmth during their stage time together, saying, 'It was my first time doing a play, but, terrified as I was, his encouragement, tutelage and humour made it a joy.' Griffiths would joke that he didn't like kids, but his fatherly concern was obvious. The age gap of more than forty years did not prevent mutual respect but rather demanded it.

Daniel was never to forget learning at the feet of such a master and Griffiths admired the teenager's fast learning. 'He's got a lightning-fast mind and picks up things very rapidly. Once he gets it, he's got it.' Above all, Griffiths was surprised that Daniel had been successful in the transition, for he had initially had his doubts that even Harry Potter's magic would work: 'When you get someone who's been a very famous, high-powered star who has to make the transition to being a working actor, they very often have nothing to bring to the table except being told what to do. When they're offered an adult character, they woodenly spit out the dialogue – out come all these tricks they've relied on in the past. And they have terrible status problems. The minute you become a junior member of an acting company, you're just a dogsbody like anyone else.'

Daniel had proved him wrong, but their time of working together was to become tragically poignant when Griffiths died in 2013.

Just as in London, *Equus* at the Broadhurst Theatre on Broadway had sell-out performances and met with rave reviews (not that Daniel would have seen them as he refuses to read any reviews, negative or positive, for fear they will affect his performance), some being more heavyweight than others. In the *New York Times*, Ben Brantley wrote that Daniel had stepped 'into a mothball-preserved, off-the-rack part and wears it like a tailor's delight'. 'Alan Strang is, in a sense, a tidy inversion of Harry Potter. Both come of age in a menacing, magical world where the prospect of being devoured by darkness is always imminent. The difference is that for Harry that world is outside of him; Alan's is of his own creation … Like many beloved film actors Mr Radcliffe has an air of heightened ordinariness, of the everyday lad who snags your attention with an extra, possibly dangerous gleam of intensity. That extra dimension has always been concentrated in Mr Radcliffe's Alsatian-blue gaze, very handy for glaring down otherworldly ghouls if you're Harry Potter. Or if you're Alan Strang, for blocking and enticing frightened grown-ups who both do and do not want to understand why you act as you do.'

In general, the consensus was that Daniel had 'cast a sorcerer's spell over hard-to-please New York critics'.

Variety's David Rooney said, '[It was] an astute career move for the "Harry Potter" frontman as he confidently navigates the transition from child stardom to adult roles ... Radcliffe provides *Equus* with a raw emotional nerve centre that renders secondary any concerns about its wonky and over-explanatory psychology.'

Clive Barnes of the *New York Post* described Daniel's performance as 'beautifully understated and withdrawn'. Linda Winer of Newsday.com said he had 'bravely established himself as a smart, intense, wildly serious stage talent'. (Though she did add that *Equus* 'always was pretty much of a crock – pseudo-serious humanity-on-trial hokum dressed up in mythic profundity'.)

Critics Charles Gross and Jeff Goodman discussed the 'highly anticipated' play on the TV show *Two On The Aisle*. Said Goodman: 'I never read a *Harry Potter* book or saw a Harry Potter film so I don't care about that ... Daniel Radcliffe did this to get away from that role. I thought it was a great Broadway debut. I think he did it brilliantly.' He also slapped Gross down for continually calling the young *Equus* star 'Harry Potter'.

Many of Daniel's acting friends had attended the opening night. But perhaps one of the biggest accolades was that Daniel's Harry Potter co-star Alan Rickman cut short a holiday to see the young actor perform. This touched Daniel who credited Rickman with giving him a lot of guidance. 'This was much appreciated. He's an actor who I admire and who is always trying something new and daring.'

There were some critics, of course, who simply didn't like what they saw. Under the rather cruel headline 'Ready for the Glue Factory', reviewer Dan Kois had to admit that *Equus* was 'a sensation once again' but added: 'The crowds are there not for Peter Shaffer's drama but for Daniel Radcliffe and his magic wand. Obsessive fans of Harry Potter – writers of erotic fan fiction, for example, hoping for an unobstructed view – are urged to sit house right. For the rest of us, the question isn't whether Radcliffe can act; as we know from his increasingly adequate performances in the Potter movies, he can, a little bit. But can he hold a stage? … That he's not terribly convincing isn't really Radcliffe's fault. His Strang is shouty and uncomplicated, and he overplays the weirdness – he's so skittish in his biggest scene that it's a wonder that Anna Camp, playing the girl, even bothers to get to first base with him, much less naked. But he's always compelling to watch, especially in his tender interactions with the production's primary horse, played by Lorenzo Pisoni…'

The *Daily News* gave Daniel just one mention in its review: 'Let's get right to it – Daniel Radcliffe, the marquee man-boy and the reason *Equus* has trotted back to Broadway. Yes, he's terrific and gives a passionate performance as Alan Strang, the 17-year-old stable hand who worships – and blinds – six horses. Yes, he's nude in a scene, but not gratuitously. And yes, he's (at least partially) in good company in the revival of Peter Shaffer's play, which intrigues but shows its age…'

By the time *Equus* ended its New York run on 8 February 2009, Daniel had endeared himself to Broadway. During the whole of the run, he had never missed a single one of the 156 performances. There was a near miss one night when he was sick before going on, but he refused to let the audience down. It would take having a leg amputated before he missed a show, he has said. 'I would have to be seriously ill to do that. It's my job, my work ethic, and ethic that my parents always had and which they instilled in me.' And it was an ethic he had learned right from the start on Harry Potter. He hated the idea of bringing a halt to filming and thus affecting everyone else around him on set. If ever he was feeling ill and it was suggested a doctor should be called, Daniel would insist he was fine because he didn't want to be an inconvenience. 'That feeling makes me not want to worry people.'

Rather eerily, a student was later to present a thesis on the whole *Equus* event – 'The Male Nude, Celebrity Body: Daniel Radcliffe in Peter Shaffer's Equus' – submitted to the Graduate College of Bowling Green State University. The thesis, eighty pages long, made numerous references to Daniel's nude scenes and cited more than thirty reference sources. In some places it was pretty heavy going:

'In this thesis I argue that the casting of Daniel Radcliffe is actually a reinforcement of the themes of the script, rather than simply a cynical commercial strategy that takes away from the message of the play ... For example this role is a transformative one for Daniel Radcliffe and the trajectory of his career. He shows his manhood and becomes something new – an adult actor of serious fare...'

Master's degree analysing aside, it had been a challenging time for Daniel, finding his feet on the New York stage. And it had sometimes been a somewhat lonely existence. No actor can come offstage and relax. The adrenalin is still running and it was no different for Daniel. He would leave the theatre and still be unwinding at 2am or 3am, watching cricket scores on his computer or tuning in to the History and Discovery channels on TV.

During his time in New York, Daniel also took part in the

20th annual fund-raising Gypsy of the Year competition. The event raises money for the Broadway Cares/Equity Fights Aids charity. He and the rest of the *Equus* cast performed a song, 'The Love That Dares Not Speak Its Neigh'. It was enough that Daniel was suffering from a bad cold and sore throat when he had to sing it (he continued with singing lessons while in America) and dance that evening, but he had also written the song himself, having worked on it in his spare time. 'It was a fun, silly song. It was cool that we beat the musicals at their own game!' he joked afterwards in one of the many, many interviews he gave.

That same night, Daniel auctioned off a pair of his jeans, which went for $4,000. But that wasn't all: the *Equus* cast raised a record $203,747 with all their combined efforts and won the 2008 Fund Raiser Award. A pictorial hardback book, *One Day in the Life of Daniel Radcliffe*, was also to contribute to the Broadway Cares cause, with photographer Tim Hailand donating a percentage of sales to the charity. Hailand had spent the whole of 13 January 2009 with Daniel, photographing him behind the scenes and around New York. There were pictures of Daniel asleep in bed, eating his breakfast, at rehearsals and, no doubt to the joy of many fans, stepping out of a shower. Hailand said: 'There are a lot of young girls that want to get close to Dan and this is a way to get close to him. You mostly see pictures of Dan as Harry Potter or in paparazzi photos.'

Daniel provided footnotes to some of the fifty images.

In July 2009, Daniel scooped two *Equus* awards at the Broadway.com Audience Awards at a ceremony held in New York's Waldorf Astoria hotel – for Favourite Leading Actor and Favourite Breakthrough Performance. He was also nominated for the Drama Desk Award for Best Leading Actor in a Play, which was quite an accolade from the American circle of professional theatre critics, writers and editors.

Daniel felt honoured that America had accepted him. He has spoken about returning to the Broadway stage in the future, saying, 'It's an amazing town and an amazing community.' So comfortable was he with the place he had called home for several months that Daniel looked upon it as his sanctuary for three weeks after an exhaustive run in the London production of *The Cripple of Inishmaan* in 2013. It was obviously a much-needed break, for when asked at the time about future stage work he said it was like asking a woman who had just given birth if she wanted more children.

New York has become a real second home and he now spends a lot of his time there at his apartment in the West Village area. He loves the city's 'incredible energy' and defends America against any critics, saying, 'I think in England we sometimes make fun of Americans for being so positive but I am actually all about that. I love enthusiasm.'

His feelings are certainly reciprocated with reports on Twitter after sightings of him ranging from the interested: 'Just saw Daniel Radcliffe having a cheeky Chinese dinner in NYC' to the more hysterical: 'Just seen Daniel Radcliffe. OMG!'

But the best aspect of walking the streets of downtown New York for Daniel is that he is largely left alone. 'The West Village is a very easy place for me to just walk around and not really get noticed. I've only had one experience with the paparazzi since I've been here. I've been very lucky.'

Just as he said on his very first visit to America when he was only eleven, Daniel finds it more chilled than Britain. 'The other thing I love about New York is that people are kind of much cooler. I remember I got lost at one point in Central Park. I went in one entrance and then came out like three miles somewhere else and just had no idea where I was. And I was looking around for someone to ask directions to, and I saw a guy in an ambulance. Not somebody being stretchered on; they were parked up. And I knocked on the window, because I figured if anyone is going to know the city … And I said, "Excuse me, do you know how to get back to West 69th or something?" And this guy just said, "Oh, you're doing *Equus* here, aren't you?" And I said, "Yeah! That's really cool that you know that." Everyone's so aware of the actors and stuff in New York that everyone's just really, really kind of cool about it and laid back. So I think everywhere else in the world you get reactions. But New York people are pretty kind of chilled about the whole thing.'

Daniel once said that Halloween in the city was his favourite day as he could walk around the streets in a mask and not be recognised. 'It's the most surreal feeling, to be able to walk with my head up and look in people's eyes. It's very bizarre. The fun thing to watch is me walking through a crowded street, particularly if I'm with my girlfriend, because it looks as though she's my carer. I basically keep my head to the ground and follow her feet.'

In Britain, Daniel won the Dewynters London Newcomer of the Year Award at the Theatregoers' Choice ceremony in February 2008, and *Equus* won an award for the Best Play Revival. The announcement the same night that his *Equus* publicity shots took the prize for Theatre Event of the Year may or may not have pleased him. And what should have been a fairly serious event hit the headlines when the host, actor James Corden, planted a kiss on his lips when he went to collect his award. Together with Daniel's now infamous full-frontal images, the moment was to go down in YouTube history.

Surprise kisses apart, Daniel had achieved his aim to shed Harry Potter. He was now nineteen years old, and had matured greatly. As he was later to confess, 'Being nude in the theatre every night in *Equus* was hard but I would never have given up the chance to appear in such a great play. It was the most exciting thing I've ever done. I love Harry but I want people to realise that I have chosen to be an actor.'

Later, when he looked back at the experience, Daniel said that *Equus* was more important than he realised at the time and that '[He] felt it had been a good choice'. The half-blood wizard had become a full-blooded actor in his own right.

CHAPTER 5

A PARALLEL POTTER UNIVERSE

Daniel fumbled under the girl's skirt, stroked her stomach and moved in for the kiss. Then it got more steamy. It was all enough to provoke Internet comment. 'She's a slut!' and 'No she's not. Harry Potter has moved on – get over it.' But many did not feel comfortable with Harry lying on a bed with a girl – he would never do that with Hermione.

Daniel had somehow fitted in six weeks of filming *The December Boys* in Australia between his commitments to Warner Bros. and took on the project after completing the fourth Potter film, *Goblet of Fire*, and starting the fifth, *Order of the Phoenix*. The only similarity to his legendary role was that he was again playing an orphan – cigarette-smoking Maps – and was to experience his first screen kiss and sex scene. This time he was an orphan without the magic and special effects and with a lot more realism: 'If you said that if you can play one orphan you can play another one, that would mean that both orphans would have to be the same character and that's not the case. It wasn't about using what I know of Harry to portray Maps at all. And in terms of Maps's background I have always assumed that his parents were alive and had not wanted him, or at least that that is what he'd been told.'

Daniel also got to 'moon', once more baring the Radcliffe bottom, or as he said 'the genuine Radcliffe ass'. The independent drama directed by Rob Hardy was based on a novel of the same name by Michael Noonan and told of the lives of a close group of friends growing up together in a Catholic orphanage in Australia in the 1960s. Nicknamed the December Boys because their birthdays all fall in that month, the four boys discover life when allowed to go on a seaside holiday. Daniel said that he hadn't really planned to take on an independent film role but just loved the script. 'It was another challenge. Unlike Harry Potter, for this character I had to say more but speak less.' In an interview with Australia's *Herald Sun*, Daniel said he wanted people to accept him in this new role. 'Hopefully, people will accept me doing something different. I think a lot of people are more open-minded than they're given credit for. But obviously there will also be people who just want to see me as Harry. You're never gonna convert those guys, so what's the point worrying about it?'

Daniel was given good advice from a director, not one he had worked with but one he had encountered in his acting circle, which was to help him move away from his stereotyping. 'One of the things he said to me, which I really took to heart, was that, whatever I did next and for the foreseeable future, I had to try to make sure the film was an ensemble piece, rather than the film hanging on my performance,' he said. '*December Boys* is such a piece and, while initially attention in the press might be focusing on me, once people get there they'll watch the film as a whole rather than analysing my performance.'

To help him 'connect' with Maps, Daniel created a special playlist on his iPod: 'I recall there was a lot of Elliott Smith on there. It was troubled guitar-wielding men, mainly. And a lot of Nirvana, Radiohead, [Nine] Black Alps and stuff like that. It was a fairly dark CD, but it helped. Music for me is one of the most helpful things that can get you into a scene. If I'm starting from scratch, then music is the main thing I will go to first.'

Ever diligent in his research, he even talked to friends who had lost parents when they were young to find empathy in the role, and to the Catholic woman who had been his film-set tutor for several years. 'It was really good to talk to her actually about Catholicism and how it can, if your faith is shaken or you do something that feels natural, contradict what your faith says you do. She was just telling me about how Maps would feel about what he's doing based on his background. It was very helpful.'

There was also another accent to perfect with the help of coaching over six months. 'The Irish and Australian accents are easy to caricature and I knew Australians would be the hardest to please … I was half doing an impression of the squeaky-voiced teen from *The Simpsons*. I was going for what his voice would sound like if it were a little bit deeper but equally atonal.'

There was also the pleasing discovery that, for once, Daniel, having just turned eighteen, would be one of the more senior members of the cast. As Harry Potter, of course, he was always one of the youngest on set. 'Suddenly I was on this set with these three kids that were a lot younger than me and had done a lot less,' he explained, 'so I was suddenly one of the senior members of the cast and I did feel really protective of all the other kids for some reason. But I actually quite enjoyed that aspect of it, of being treated like an adult rather than one of the young ones and, because my experience of being on a film set at that age had been totally joyous, I wanted to make sure it was the same for them.' It was a total role reversal for him, he said, and he felt very paternal – even to the extent that he now understood what some of his directors in the very early Potter days had had to contend with. 'There were times when it was towards the end of the day and I was really tired and they [the other child actors] had almost as much energy as they had at one o'clock in the afternoon. And I found myself saying things like, "PLEASE stop shouting so loudly in my ear!"'

It was quite a leap from being the child star to the grown-up, something Daniel was still finding hard to come to terms with. 'When I turned eighteen I expected to wake up and find I had a full beard and that there was a voting form lying by my bed. But it doesn't all happen at once. I looked at myself and thought how now I had to act like a man and not a boy and I wasn't quite sure how to do that.'

It was to be no surprise that Daniel was questioned more about his intimate scene with Australian actress Teresa Palmer who played Lucy, the girl in the bed scene, than anything else. He said that, unlike *Equus*, when the time onstage meant he got lost in the character, filming presented more time to get nervous. 'We filmed the sex scene that night, so I wasn't too tired yet luckily! But I was nervous, definitely. It was the first love scene I had ever done and, although it wasn't exactly imposing, I was certainly aware and wondering, "God what do I do? What don't I do?"' It was very fumbling and sweet. Daniel did get to touch Teresa's breast. 'I was sort of worried, you know, certain things, but it was OK. No matter how beautiful someone is, when you're surrounded by crew who are taking measurements on the focus and making sure you're in the right light, it becomes totally clinical. And clinical is not a word I would associate with any good sexual experience … Luckily Teresa was very, very good at helping me to chill.'

It was not Teresa's first time at screen kissing and she put Daniel at ease, but it was the very last scene to be shot and both actors were exhausted. 'By that stage you are just on auto-pilot,' she said. 'We didn't even have time to think about what we were doing. It was a case of "Let's do it".'

And, although most people watching the film might still have seen Harry Potter lying there, for Teresa it was different. She was to confess that she hadn't known who Daniel was and had never seen a Harry Potter film. 'It wasn't until someone told me and everyone made such a huge deal about it that when I first met him I was shaking.' But by the end of filming, nerves had been replaced with compliments for her co-star. 'He is so brilliant and talented. At the same time he has all this amazing success and fame and all these things, which you think he would be affected by. But he's unaffected and unassuming. Just a regular eighteen-year-old guy.'

The scenes were shot between 23 December and 24 December and it was certainly an unusual away to spend Christmas. But happily Daniel was not alone. His father had accompanied him throughout the whole shoot and his mother had made a couple of visits. The family were all together for a Christmas 'down under'.

Unfortunately, Daniel's choice of project in his bid to depart from the Potter mould was not well received this time. *Empire* magazine commented: 'The first question, of course, is how Radcliffe does, shorn of the lightning scar and wand – and the answer is not bad. He manages the Australian accent with barely a quaver, and gives a good impression of a much less secure character than we're used to seeing from him. But his face is still curiously blank, rather detracting from the effect of spot-on voice work and body language. Perhaps it's the role, but he'll need to do more to prove that he has that movie magic outside Rowling's world.'

In his own personal Internet insight of 'More Movies That Suck', Roger Ebert said: 'The sight of Harry Potter smoking is a little like Mickey Mouse lighting up … Radcliffe is convincing as the young man; he proves he can move beyond the Harry role, which I guess is the objective of this movie, but I am not sure it proves he has star power – not yet, anyway, unless his co-star, so to speak, is Harry Potter.'

More harshly, another suggested that Daniel's next move should be to talk to his agent: 'Radcliffe looks faintly uncomfortable throughout, as well he might.'

However, Daniel did not regret taking the role. He would always be his own man when it came to making career decisions. 'Maybe I'm rebelling against what people think I should be doing, but it is not a conscious thing. I'm making my own choices and, if some people feel that is slightly unorthodox, that's their issue more than mine, really. It doesn't bother me.'

The December Boys was released on 14 September 2007, the day Daniel completed his punishing whirlwind of publicity tours in Australia and throughout Europe. Three days later, he was back on the Harry Potter set. On reflection, it is incredible to understand how he coped with the pressures. 'Sometimes I can feel a bit sorry for myself if I've been lying down in the mud for the night shoot and then I have to get up at 4.30 the next morning,' he once said. 'But my mum and dad have always said, if anyone's complaining, "Well, you're not down a mine". Actors give themselves a bad reputation, and I think it's a shame. It's why some people resent them for being famous and think they do no work comparatively. But it's a great job. And no, it's not down a mine.'

Filming for *Harry Potter and the Half-Blood Prince* began on 24 September 2007 and yet again there was a demanding schedule, with locations ranging from Fort William, Scotland, to Gloucester Cathedral and Lacock Abbey in Wiltshire (when residents were reportedly told to black out their windows with dark blinds for the night-time shooting).

One star new to the cast was Jim Broadbent, as Horace Slughorn, and the man at the helm was again director David Yates. He was still working on *Order of the Phoenix* when he was asked to direct *Half-Blood Prince*. Yates described the latest Potter as 'a cross between the chills of *Prisoner of Azkaban* and the fantastical adventure of *Goblet of Fire*'. Daniel has said that, compared to *Order of the Phoenix*, he found *Half-Blood Prince* a bit light. Yates recalled, 'I remember very early on, before we started shooting, he came into my office and said, "David, I just think, you know, some of this is a bit light, isn't it?" He loves the intensity and the darkness. I said, "Dan, no, no, no. It's really great. This is our opportunity to shift gear for a movie. You know, we've got plenty of dark stuff coming up and let's just enjoy the playfulness."'

In fact, Daniel, curious as to what Harry's final fate would be, had discussed it with Jo Rowling one night at dinner. He wanted to know if he would be facing an on-screen demise. 'I think my exact words were probably as tactless and unsubtle as: "Do I die?" and she said, "You have a death scene." So it was very obvious to me that it didn't mean I died,' recalled Daniel. It was a conversation he was to keep secret for a long time despite being frequently quizzed about how the whole Potter saga would end. 'It was great fun. I'd say, "I know something", and everyone would go, "What, what?" and I'd say I wasn't going to tell them! I quite enjoyed that to be honest. For months and months in interviews and to endless journalists I was just lying and said I knew nothing.'

This latest sequel saw Harry starting his sixth year at Hogwarts and discovering an old book marked 'the property of the Half-Blood Prince'. It also featured the first death of a major character – Professor Dumbledore, now played by Michael Gambon. Daniel admitted he found the scene particularly difficult to film as he had never had to deal with bereavement in real life (although sadly he was later to lose his grandmother). 'Before that, I'd never experienced any kind of sadness. So it was very tricky. It's also a tremendous pressure, because you know that a lot of people watching will have felt that. I tried to play it quite quiet because that's just how Harry is.' If Daniel was hoping for some moral support from Gambon for this difficult scene, he would be disappointed. Although describing Gambon as both 'the least professional' and 'most respected actor' he has ever worked with, Daniel said that, while Harry was lamenting over Dumbledore's body and 'really pulled out all the stops to convey the emotion', after the fourth take he looked down to see Gambon had dozed off! 'I had to prod him awake,' he said. So much for impressing someone with your skills!

Sometime later, Daniel was to admit that he 'hated' his performance in this sixth Potter film: 'I wasn't entirely thrilled with my performance in *Half-Blood* – I found it quite samey, and didn't think there was enough variation in it – so I worked hard to make sure that, if the seventh film came out and I was still unhappy with it, I'd know it won't be from lack of trying.' He added about his Harry Potter appearances, 'I am a harsh critic of myself and I have to say I have not been proud of all of them.'

One acting challenge for Daniel came when Harry takes a potion that alters his state of mind. Despite his self-critical view of his performance in this particular Potter instalment, Daniel said he liked these scenes. 'To be honest I just let the more manic side of myself that I suppress for twenty-three hours of every day loose for a while on set and just became a kind of uncontrollable, vaguely irritating but sort of vaguely amusing person that I sort of keep hidden. I just let him out and run mad for a few days and it was great fun to be able to. It is a side to the character that hasn't really been seen before. We always sit next to each other, so David Heyman [producer] leaned over to me and said, "That's my favourite piece of acting that you do in this film", so maybe I should have really been playing him slightly more manic all along.'

Daniel's mother Marcia commented that she was seeing

more and more of her son in the Harry character, saying to him, 'Harry has started to argue like you argue.'

The film also featured Harry's second kiss, this time with Ginny Weasley (played by Bonnie Wright), sister of Ron. It followed Ginny telling Harry, 'Close your eyes and then you can't be tempted.' Bonnie had already had discussions with David Yates about how the relationship between Ginny and Harry was to develop but she still found it strange kissing her co-star. 'We've known each other so long and it was weird having to look at someone in a different way. Surprisingly on the actual day it all seemed to be okay. You just kind of treat it like any other scene. That sounds silly and probably boring to others! But I think in order to make it realistic you have to just go for it!'

This kiss – which was actually just a very brief nibble on Harry's bottom lip – and the general scene took two days and around thirty takes to complete. Daniel was a bit taken aback when he saw it all later, saying, 'My God, my lips are like the lips of a horse, kind of distending away, independently away from my face, trying to encompass the lower half of hers. So I apologise, Bonnie.' It was all as strange for Daniel as it was for his female co-star. 'It was quite weird for me because I've known Bonnie since she was nine and I was eleven. Very strange. But we got through it. It was good. And it'll get a bit of a cheer from the Potter fans.'

There was also another underwater scene, but fortunately for Daniel it was not quite as demanding as before and filming took two days. A stuntwoman wrapped herself around him 'as a kind of lady inferi' (one of the dark wizard corpses of Harry Potter), and Daniel said it was one of the 'coolest' moments of his career when he burst through the water surrounded by a circle of fire. 'What they did was they had a pipeline underneath the surface of the water that shoots up bubbles of kerosene or propane, and they kind of ignited just after the surface. So the surface kind of goes black with soot, which is horrible, but it's also great fun. And then I get to climb up on the central island and I see Michael Gambon there, just looking like God or Moses and swirling fire around his head. It was one of those moments where I went, "It doesn't matter how many more films I do, I will never have this scene or anything like it ever again."'

The last scenes for the *Half-Blood Prince* were filmed on 17 May 2008. Shortly after, tragedy was to strike one of the cast. Eighteen-year-old Robert Knox, who played Marcus Belby, died from stab wounds he had received while protecting his young brother Jamie from a knife attack outside a London bar. A spokesman for Warner Bros. said: 'We are deeply shocked by the news and our thoughts and sympathy are with the family.'

Daniel had not known Knox well but said he was 'a great ball of sunshine' and that everyone who knew him liked him. He said the attack was cowardly and that Knox's death 'cast a long shadow. What a waste, a stupid, tragic waste.'

Another red carpet, another premiere. Daniel attended the world premiere of *Harry Potter and the Half-Blood Prince* in London on 7 July 2009 – another premiere taking place in a heavy downpour. The American premiere was on 9 July, at which Daniel said that, although he could be very hyper, on this particular night he was keeping 'quite calm' and 'very level headed', adding, 'I'm quite pleased with myself for that.' It was noted by one watching commentator that Daniel was on 'an impressive charm offensive' that made it clear 'which of the three stars is still going to be making bank when he is fifty'. Special praise for Daniel was earned when he put a group of TV reporters on hold and made a beeline for an eleven-year-old girl, Danielle, from a magazine called *Scholastic News*. Daniel answered Danielle's questions, thanked her for being 'very, very kind' and left the little girl nearly dropping her microphone in excitement. 'It was an adorable interaction that won us over for good,' said one critic.

Daniel's 'charm offensive' also helped ease the backlash following remarks about religion he had made in an interview with *Esquire* magazine, which appeared that week. He had, some critics said, 'risked the wrath' of fans and 'box-office prospects' by declaring himself to be an atheist, furthering the belief that 'the Christian right has long been suspicious about Potter's "anti-Christian" message. Radcliffe's admission will do nothing to ease the concerns of those religious zealots who fear the Harry Potter phenomenon,' commented Examiner.com.

Daniel's admission he was an atheist was accompanied by his remark that he was 'very relaxed' about it. 'I don't preach my atheism but I have a huge amount of respect for people like Richard Dawkins [a leader of the New Atheism movement] who do. Anything he does on television I watch.' It was a brave revelation by Daniel, coming as it did at the release of the *Half-Blood Prince*, and he was aware it might not go down well in some quarters. 'That's half of America that's not going to see the next Harry Potter film on the back of that comment,' he said.

Examiner.com reported that the *Potter* books 'continue to threaten and anger some Christians. Tales of the schoolboy wizard are taken very seriously by some Evangelical Christians. One of the largest Christian groups in the country, Focus on Family, denounced the books as "witchcraft".' It added that the Church of England, had, however, 'published a guide advising youth leaders to use Harry Potter to spread the Christian message, as the characters face "struggles and dilemmas that are familiar to us all"'.

There was to be some more controversy over this particular Potter instalment. The film went on general release on 15 July 2009 – a timing that, despite claims there had been a writers' strike, was reportedly linked to Warner Bros. wanting another Harry Potter summer success and delaying the original release date of 21 November 2008 'to guarantee the studio a major summer blockbuster'. In a statement, Warner studio chief Alan Horn said: 'We know the summer season is an ideal window for a family tent pole release, as proven by the success of our last Harry Potter film, which is the second-highest-grossing film in the franchise, behind only the first instalment. Additionally, like every other studio, we are still feeling the repercussions of the writers' strike, which impacted the readiness of scripts for other films, changing the competitive landscape for 2009 and offering new windows of opportunity that we wanted to take advantage of. We agreed the best strategy was to move *Half-Blood Prince* to July, where it perfectly fills the gap for a major tent pole release for mid-summer.'

This decision did not win favour with many, especially those publications whose lead-in times meant they were publicising the film months ahead of it actually appearing on screen. And Horn had earlier told the Associated Press: 'The picture is completely, absolutely, 100 per cent on schedule, on time.

There were no delays. I've seen the movie. It is fabulous. We would have been perfectly able to have it out in November.'

Shortly before *Half-Blood Prince* went on general release, Daniel did a cover shoot with *Time Out* whose staff were under instruction, 'no wands, no glasses and no scars', just Daniel as himself. It was seen as something of a breakthrough for the now nineteen-year-old star. According to *Time Out*, Daniel was 'like a pig in shit' about the shoot, said his publicist Vanessa Davies. 'It's the nearest he'll ever get to shooting an album cover,' she said, as Daniel lay on a bare mattress looking moody. He also obliged with some photographs on a roof, jumping up and down and giving everyone a few tense moments: Harry Potter might be able to fly but Daniel Radcliffe can't.

By this time, Daniel had already started filming the last two Potter films and the end was finally in sight. 'I've got a year left of shooting so I'm not thinking about the end yet,' Daniel said. 'Probably on the last day I'll get emotional but not for the reasons anyone would expect. Not because I'm leaving behind a character. I will be sad about that, but that'll happen six months after. That's normally when I think, "God, I could have one more go at that."'

One project Daniel talked about at the time was playing photo-journalist Dan Eldon who was just twenty-two when he was killed by a mob in Somalia. Although it was a possibility he said he was really interested in, it appears that the necessary funding did not materialise.

In December 2008, Daniel appeared on the Bravo channel in an hour-long *Inside the Actors Studio* interview with James Lipton at New York's Michael Schimmel Center. He was the youngest guest ever to be interviewed on the show. In line with all other guests, Daniel was asked ten set questions, such as 'What is your favourite word?' ('Verdurous. I don't even know how it is spelled to be perfectly honest with you, but it's a great word meaning lush and green and wonderful and Keats uses it to great effect "through verdurous gloom and winding mossy".') 'What is your favourite curse word?' ('Bollocks') and 'If heaven exists, what would you like to hear God say when you arrive at the Pearly Gates?' ('Well, I am not religious. We'd just be standing there and he'd be smoking a pipe and, um, he'd look up from the fireplace and say, "Isn't it amazing we're the same."') His least favourite word would be 'mediocre' if applied to himself and his favourite sound is a cricket ball hitting a cricket bat – 'at 90 miles an hour and speeding off to the boundary. Wonderful.' In answer to what turned him on, Daniel said, 'Bathtubs,' but refused to say 'explicitly what turns me on sexually'. His biggest turn-off was unprofessionalism in people 'in whatever their job is'. Similarities between him and Harry Potter were, he told Lipton, 'an innate curiosity about the world … a stubbornness not to involve people and to solve our own problems. And I pick people up on stuff. I'm very irritating to argue with, like Harry would be, I'd imagine.'

Answering yet another question from another interviewer about character similarities, Daniel said it was always a case of Harry finding himself in a certain situation and asking if he would have the guts to do something. He certainly had the guts for that kiss with Ginny and it no doubt contributed to the *Half-Blood Prince* being the top-grossing film in the UK in 2009, taking £50.7m, and to Daniel being nominated again for the MTV Movie Award for Best Male Performance and the People's Choice Award for Favourite On-Screen Team with Rupert and Emma. It was all just adding to the incredible success that was Harry Potter.

CHAPTER 6

BEATING THE DEMONS

Coping with so much fame at such a young age was always going to cause problems for Daniel. Although he never falls down on commitment to any work project, and has handled hundreds of interviews over the year with maturity beyond his years, there were demons. And his hopes that he would disappoint those 'waiting for me to cock up' were being sadly dashed.

He was only seventeen when he moved out of his parents' London home in a bid to be independent. This had more to do with the rebellion any teenager might go through than fame. He said he wanted to be able to smoke freely without having to hide it from his mother and father. He felt, he said, that he was under too close a scrutiny from them: 'Because of the life I've had, I'd grown up quicker than most people. I felt like I was entitled to move out.'

For a while, Daniel was able to lead a fairly normal life, watching his beloved cricket on television and 'bad TV on a Friday night' and, like most teenage boys when they first leave home, relying on his mum to do his washing. He wasn't very good at ironing either. But it was not long after Daniel started to live on his own that he started drinking. Initially, he has said, it was to make himself 'more interesting'. And it wasn't just drinking at parties or to be sociable: this was heavyweight drinking. He had become the drunk everyone wanted to avoid. 'I became a nuisance,' Daniel admitted. 'I became the person in the group who has to be looked after.' He would hit local bars, but, when it reached the stage when he was too embarrassed to return to them because he had no recollection of his previous behaviour, he drank alone.

The *Daily Mail* reported on Daniel's eighteenth birthday saying that now he was 'officially getting his hands on £20m of earnings' it was a good excuse to go 'a little wild'. In fact, Daniel watched the Test Match cricket with old school friends at Lord's on his birthday (he appeared on BBC Radio's *Test Match Special* on the final day of the England versus India match) before heading out for the night to a private members' club in Soho. The *Mail* reported: 'There, under the watchful eye of his mother Marcia and father Alan, his chums sang "Happy Birthday", drank their way through scores of bottles of beer and wine, sank cocktails and dined on a selection of hors d'oeuvres including crispy duck pancake, foie gras, rare roast beef and crayfish.'

It would be six hours before Daniel was led out on to the fire escape at the rear of the building and down a back street to his limousine. His mother had the stern fixed gaze of someone who has just spent far longer than she liked in the company of boisterous youth. And by the time they arrived at the family home, her son, still in his England cap, was looking decidedly worse for wear. He looked pale and was said to be so unsteady on his feet that he had to be led across the pavement by a minder. Daniel's publicist Vanessa Davies denied he had been drinking while watching the cricket but added, 'The question as to whether Daniel was or wasn't drinking alcohol at his birthday party last night I am not willing to discuss. Daniel is now eighteen and the question of whether he chooses to consume alcohol at a private function or not is completely up to him.'

All of this was contrary to the privacy Daniel had hoped he would have at his special birthday bash. He was also aware, he said, that, now he was officially an adult, he was going 'to be more sort of fair game'.

At the height of his drinking, Daniel said later, he managed to be 'fun for the first four drinks' but after that 'it was a rapid, rapid decline where I had to be helped home. I was living in constant fear of who I'd meet, what I might have said to them, so I'd stay in my apartment and drink alone. I was a recluse at twenty.' He was, he said, a 'really annoying, loud, inappropriate, messy drunk'. There were the nights he did what many drunks did – dialled up ex-girlfriends just to talk. It was the only time Daniel was also to admit to having one-night stands with no meaning.

Looking back, he now realises he was too young to have struck out on his own. It was hard enough for any normal teenager but Daniel was far from that. He was confused and miserable and being on his own just wasn't healthy. 'When I was unhappy in any way, it made it too easy for me to hide it. I'd done *Equus*, which had gone so well, but I still couldn't get rid of that committee of voices in my head saying that you're going to fail. I think there was a part in the back of my head that was going, "This is all going to end. And you're going to be left in this nice apartment. Just living here. And being reminded of what you did in your teenage years for the rest of your life."'

David Thewlis, who played Professor Lupin in the Potter films, once said that even when Radcliffe was young, 'He would joke that he'd be in rehab by the time he was eighteen, and by twenty-seven he'd be hosting a game show called *It's Wizards!*'

In one of a series of interviews with Daniel for *GQ* magazine, Craig Mclean recalled what happened when the two had met in June 2009. 'Now unchaperoned after moving out from his parents' house and embracing long-awaited, boozy adulthood, the actor was on fire. Having polished off a fistful of fags and a run of whisky sours and double bourbons, Radcliffe – only a month before his teenage years were finally over – ordered us tequilas. "I love tequila. It's a dangerous thing. It's one of those things like Jägermeister, where you get a certain type of drunk off it," he said with knowledgeable relish. Shortly after, he was proving it.'

The relationship between Daniel and his parents at that time was being stretched to the limit. The danger of his being found out by the press or of being photographed looking the worse for wear came closer and closer. 'People are always looking to say, "Kid star goes off the rails". But I try very hard not to go that way because it would be too easy for them,' Daniel said. In short, his role as Harry Potter, the family favourite wizard,

Child stars: A young Daniel, with co-stars Emma Watson (*left*) and Rupert Grint (*right*), poses in London after being announced as Harry Potter after thousands auditioned. ©*Getty Images*

Above: A wide-eyed Daniel, 12, enjoys the glitz of his first film premiere. ©*WireImage*

Below: Daniel with the woman who started it all, author JK Rowling. ©*Getty Images*

Above left: Daniel and Emma have fun on the set of hit MTV show *TRL*.   ©WireImage

Above right: Arch-nemesis?: Daniel and Ralph Fiennes joke about on the red carpet at the New York premiere of *Harry Potter and the Goblet of Fire*.   ©WireImage

Below: Walk of Fame: Harry Potter's amazing success is confirmed as Daniel, Emma and Rupert have their hands, feet – and wands – commemorated outside the legendary Grauman's Chinese Theatre.   ©FilmMagic

Bittersweet: Daniel, Emma and Rupert celebrate the end of an era at the London premiere of the final Harry Potter film.

©REX/David Fisher

Theatre magic: Daniel has made a name for himself on Broadway, both in the much-talked-about *Equus* (*above*) and as the all-singing, all-dancing ambitious J. Pierrepont Finch in *How To Succeed in Business Without Really Trying* (below). ©*AFP/Getty Images* ©*Getty Images*

Above left: Ghostly: Daniel shooting for *The Woman in Black* as disturbed widower Arthur Kipps.

©*REX/Moviestore Collection*

Above right: Daniel proves he always has time for his many devoted fans at the horror film's premiere.

©*REX*

Below: Daniel with the rest of *The Woman in Black* cast.

©*Getty Images*

Above: Daniel is an actor at the top of his game, recently appearing as poet Allen Ginsberg in *Kill Your Darlings* (*above left*) and in the Broadway critical success *The Cripple of Inishmaan* (*above right*).

Below left: Posing with his 2014 Broadway.com Audience Choice Award for 'Favourite Actor in a Play'.

Below right: As well as acting, Daniel has used his fame to promote awareness of gay teen suicide prevention with The Trevor Project. In 2011, he received the Hero Award for his continual efforts.

his contract with Warner Bros. and his whole life were under threat, for there were times he would arrive on the Harry Potter set drunk from the night before: 'I can honestly say I never drank at work, but yes, I went in still drunk. I can point to scenes where I'm just gone. Dead behind the eyes,' he later revealed. He had developed a taste for the liqueur Baileys. 'I thought, "Gosh, that's nice. I could drink a huge amount of this."' It would have made things more pleasant, he said, for the people doing his make-up because 'they'd have smelt Baileys on my breath in the morning instead of vodka'.

The downside of filming the iconic series was that an impressionable Daniel had got to meet a couple of older hell-raisers. 'It put me around people like Richard Harris and I heard all their amazing stories about their drunken nights. That was what I was desperately trying to pursue.'

Director David Yates was quick to defend Daniel, saying that 'most teenagers in the UK drink heavily. It's a national pastime.' He said Daniel had never betrayed any hint of being drunk on set.

This was backed up by producer David Heyman: 'It didn't affect his performance and it most certainly didn't affect the making of the film.'

Emma Watson was unnecessarily put on the spot when she appeared on the David Letterman show in the USA in 2011 and was asked what she knew about Daniel's drinking. She loyally answered, 'To be honest, it's really not something that I genuinely know much about – he is the one to talk to about it.' Rupert Grint was just as protective of Daniel when he was quizzed about the same thing, and said he was unaware of any problems.

Cruelly, *Vanity Fair* ran an Internet piece entitled 'Let's Guess Which Harry Potter Scenes Daniel Radcliffe Filmed While Inebriated' and included a handful of scenes in which they said Daniel appeared 'dead-eyed'.

It was a case of having too much too soon. Daniel once said that if he could understand exactly what happens when fame is found so young he would be 'an extremely successful child psychologist'. An insight into what being a child star could lead to was given by Jack Wild, who had shot to fame in the lead role in *Oliver!* in 1986. Wild wrote advice to Daniel soon after he was chosen to play Harry Potter. 'By the time the Harry Potter film is released, he will be a world-class star, hyped to high heaven, just as I was … Like other child stars I paid a high price for my instant success. I hope and believe that Daniel can avoid my mistakes … Daniel is going to have to cope with the wonderful opportunities as well as the tremendous strains and temptations of stardom.' Fortunately for Daniel, he would handle it all, eventually, unlike Wild who became an alcoholic and was to tragically die of cancer in March 2006.

Daniel said that, despite the bad times, he felt he had managed fame quite well because he had remained level headed. 'As soon as you start to believe you're a star, that's the moment you start to screw up. But also the other thing about the word "star" or "celebrity" is that it's fleeting. There's a phrase in football, "Form is temporary and class is permanent", and that's what I aspire to. I want longevity rather than a quick-burning career.'

The dark years for Daniel were between eighteen and twenty-one, the age he finally realised he needed to get his life in order. 'Yes, I had become very reliant on alcohol and then there came a moment when I realised something destructive had crept into a routine.' Daniel was glad when his teenager years were over because 'anything that's bad just goes away and stops being a problem after a while'.

Daniel was pushing himself too much; bouncing from one project to another was exhausting and he never really had time to take stock of what he wanted. 'I wanted to close the gap between the real me, what was going on in me, and the person that people perceived,' he said. But he did not blame the pressure of being Harry Potter for his reliance on alcohol. 'I can't say that, because it could have been something I stumbled upon in my life anyway. It wasn't the pressure of Harry Potter. It was the pressure I put on myself.'

Meanwhile, pressure from the press was not helping his fragile state. In November 2009, the *Daily Mirror* ran a front-page story headlined 'Harry Pothead' alleging that Daniel had announced 'I love weed' while at a London party held by a friend of his then girlfriend Laura O'Toole. A guest, twenty-six-year-old Wadia Tazi, was quoted as saying that Daniel had pulled out a joint, lit it and that he 'looked spaced out and didn't look like he knew what was going on'. He said Daniel had allowed a female guest to drag him into a toilet and draw a moustache and beard on him in felt-tip pen. And that he had been 'surprised' by his behaviour. The report said Daniel's actions caused concern for a minder he had with him and with Laura.

Daniel has always refuted claims he has taken drugs of any kind – 'I've been around some amazing people and still managed to keep a real childlike view of the world. I'm not into drugs' – and, in a serious rebuttal to this story, one of his team stated: 'We categorically deny the allegations …

Daniel does smoke the occasional roll-up cigarette but he was not doing anything more than that.' Legal action being taken over the accusation was also spoken about. Daniel did win some sympathy from certain press quarters, with a specially favourable piece in online newspaper the *Huffington Post* appearing shortly before the release of the final Potter film: 'The stories of troubled adulthoods following childhood flame are legion, with a certain extra mettle required to avoid the fate. Perhaps appropriately, given his character's legendary magical powers and storyline of simmering bravery and valour, it seemed that Daniel Radcliffe, the big screen's Harry Potter, would defy those pitfalls and reach that star status, so calm and collected and level-headed, he. And as his final Hogwarts adventure rushes toward worldwide release, it does indeed look as if he will be the exception to the rule, a star in his adult years akin to a Ron Howard or Michael J. Fox.'

One time when Daniel needed to offload on someone, he chose Harry Potter co-star Gary Oldman to whom he had become close. Daniel was not able to fully admit his drinking problems but he hinted he was in trouble. Oldman told him he had too much to lose and at one point took him aside to bolster him after negative press reports. 'Don't listen to what they say in the papers,' he said, and slipped Daniel a piece of paper with the words, 'Keep your eye on the work, OK.'

But Daniel was not ready to pack up the drinking just yet. That he was never pictured obviously drunk during this time was a combination of good luck and good friends – some of whom were offered money to dish the dirt on him.

In July 2010, the month before he decided to give up drinking for good, the *Daily Mirror* cruelly got the closest to exposing what he was later to admit – his becoming reliant on alcohol. Daniel, the paper said, had been celebrating his twenty-first birthday 'quite a lot, despite the fact it was over a week ago'. He was also pictured in the *Daily Mail* having another celebratory day out watching the cricket at the Oval. The *Mail* commented on how Daniel had just got back from celebrating his landmark birthday with a couple of friends in St Petersburg, adding, 'But the Harry Potter star showed he is no ordinary Muggle as he flew back to London for another party with friends.' It said Daniel appeared to be 'sporting a slight hangover judging by the red rings around his eyes'. On another occasion, the newspaper pictured Daniel leaving a theatre accompanied by video footage of him 'playing the bongos during a wild night out'.

Daniel was not happy: 'I was walking from the theatre to my car and it was, "Daniel looks exhausted and frustrated" and it's like, yeah, cos I had your ugly pap in my face. There's stuff like that that gets annoying but it's more than worth it because I have a great job and dealing with the tabloids actually comprises a very small part of my life.'

Even as late as 2012, a long time after Daniel announced he had stopped drinking, there were reports he could have fallen off the wagon. American journalist Randy Jernigan suggested Daniel had dropped back into his old habits because of the pressures of performing in the London production of *The Cripple of Inishmaan*. One newspaper said he had been 'Jäger-bombed' (Jägermeister spirit mixed with an energy drink) at Beauty Bar, a bar on New York's 14th Street. It was said he requested a Dusty Springfield song, 'got into a twist' with the DJ and was then encouraged by his entourage to get a cab home. It is no wonder that Daniel often feels there is someone lurking around every corner who is out to exploit him and that he needs to have people around him who won't betray him. 'You get chancers out there who just want to make a quick buck, but as long as you tune into them and who they are … The best thing I've learned is, if you're going out, never go out alone – you leave yourself vulnerable. If you've got someone else there you trust, they can say, "Be wary of that person." I probably used to be too trusting of people.'

But back in 2010 Daniel had already realised what the booze was doing to his body and to his life in general. It was a 'pathetic' stage, he said. 'For a long time people were saying to me, "We think you have a problem", but in the end I had to come to the realisation myself … I am a fun, polite person and drinking turned me into a bore.'

The turning point came after filming finished on the last Harry Potter film when Daniel realised he was both at a loss as to what to do with his days and going further and further into a dark place: 'I had so much more time and I was going out more and celebrating and I woke up – in my bed, thankfully, but I don't know how I got there – and I thought, "You can't do this anymore."' He needed to get back on course without the eyes of the world upon him and without journalists trying to catch him out. 'I was a teenager making my mistakes as I went along. And the fact some of those things were pounced on, or could've been, by the press, is frightening. I wouldn't wish that on my worst enemy.'

Even harder for Daniel was the fact that not only were his parents being followed by reporters but his relationship with them had also become very strained because of his drinking.

All the reports about his problems were never exaggerated, he has admitted, but only he knew the full truth.

This was one of the reasons why he was to launch a blistering attack on CNN anchorwoman Isha Sesay after she decried his drinking admission as a publicity stunt. 'It was the angriest I've ever been,' said Daniel. 'I will never forget her name and I can't wait to meet her. She made some comment about my drinking and said how it was weird timing, like she was inferring I was helping publicise Harry Potter. Like Harry Potter needed publicity ... I think any intelligent person would have some compassion and not say something like that just because it's an easy thing to say, but she did.'

Daniel feels the whole drinking problem should now be laid to rest. 'The time I talked about all that initially was a huge mistake. I thought the narrower the gap between people's perception of me and the reality of my life, the better, but actually the more information you put out there, the more people have to speculate on. And I don't like being talked about. I don't put myself out there to be judged. I made the mistake of doing that the first time.' He has also said, 'Being self-critical is good; being self-hating is destructive. There's a very fine line there somewhere and I walk it carefully.'

His late teens were the hardest times for Daniel. He was trying to be normal, all the while being famous. In February 2012, he told the *Daily Mirror*: I have a crazy life ... somebody will tell me we're going to an airport and I know vaguely what we're doing, but I have no idea so I take it a day at a time.'

He wanted to be like any other young man going out and having fun. He wanted to be left alone to enjoy life. But because of who he was and because of the great public persona he presented, Daniel felt this sometimes proved impossible. It was no wonder he often felt he wanted to escape into drink and felt so insecure. In an interview in November 2013 with Simon Hattenstone, Daniel said he was frustrated when all his friends were going to clubs and under-18 nights. 'I couldn't because there's a level of anxiety I get when I go out. Even if the people aren't remotely interested in you, it's in your head, and if you start dancing, you think everyone's going to say, "Look at Harry Potter, dancing like a twat"'.

At its height, the Potter image had taken over his life to the extent that even in some interviews he was mistakenly called Harry instead of Daniel – or Dan, the shortened form he prefers. It was as if fiction had blurred reality. 'I am thrilled to have this in my life, but it is separate from my life, you know? It's nice to be called Dan. And actually I started correcting people. You do feel a bit of an idiot for doing that, but at the same time in the long run it is better for us. I know it's better for me.'

So, going into his late teens, fame got on top of Daniel. He still had the hyperactive personality he had inherited from his childhood and still had excessive energy to burn. It was something he had to learn to control 'so I just don't go nuts for four hours and crash and burn'. He became frustrated at what he felt was a loss of freedom and he found it hard to cope with the mobs that surrounded him if he did go out. 'People would start taking photos and then they go on the Internet and then everyone knows about it. Then more people arrive because they've seen it on the Internet.' At this time too, he said there was 'definitely a level of frustration around … I did have to think where I went more than a lot of my friends and you do get a little frustrated at that age, but ultimately it's childish, petulant – "I want that too".'

Then there was the problem of knowing who he could trust and who he couldn't. 'When you're in the position I'm in you have two options: you can both shut yourself off from everybody, from the world, and not live a full life. Or you can welcome everybody into your life and occasionally somebody will try to take advantage.' Genuine friends are as important to Daniel as his family is. 'Good friends are completely honest with you. They stop you becoming arrogant and keep you grounded.'

Becoming public property was never going to be easy. 'I think in terms of all the media attention that you get and all that stuff, I think the one thing you have to be careful of is that fame does not become a part of your identity. You have to find out who you are aside from what the media say you are. If you've become reliant on them for kind of a sense of self, then you're really screwed.' He told *GQ* magazine that press attention was all part of the job but that the 'integral moments' of his growing up were mercifully spared. 'There's a difference between having a record of what I looked like when I was growing up and of me actually discovering masturbation in front of people! All those private teenage moments happened behind closed doors. Thank Christ!'

Generally, Daniel has an excellent relationship with the press and certainly no one could ever fault how he has always allowed them to probe and pry without too much complaint. He was even open enough to once admit stealing a Mars bar from a shop when he was little – but the tale lost its edge when he added that his conscience got the better of him and he put it back: 'That was really rubbish but the tabloids have led on less.'

Although obviously he would rather not have the label 'celebrity' or the intrusion that accompanies it, he knows it goes with the territory. 'Don't get me wrong, I have a very good relationship on the whole with journalists, but there were times, particularly in the later years of my teenage years, when I definitely would've liked to start a fight between journalists if I could have done. So it's a huge amount of fun to play around with all that stuff – stuff that you know sort of plays into people's perception of you – and slightly subvert that. It's a joke within a joke, another layer for people who are sort of in the know.'

Daniel regrets being so candid as to once say he had lost his virginity to an older woman. He has also admitted there is one comment he regrets making to journalists more than any other in his entire career. 'I said sarcastically, "I'm going to try to be single when I'm on Broadway because I'm going to be in a show with loads of dancers", basically implying that I'd like to sleep with all the chorus. Oh, Jesus! … What a douchebag thing to say! What kind of arrogant twat do I think I am?'

In fact, the interview was with *Dazed & Confused* magazine and referred to his appearance in *How to Succeed in Business Without Really Trying*, and what Daniel actually said was: 'I said to a friend the other day, "Dude, I'm doing a show with dancers. I've got to be single." He was like, "Don't sleep with anyone in your own show. That's a mistake." It's good advice but I'm not sure I'll stick to it.'

The comments naturally provoked some response, with one girl fan writing on the celebitchy site: 'Be on the lookout,

Broadway dancers! DanRad is single and ready to mingle. He's so fucking cute. I know he sounds like a poon-hound in this interview, but I get the feeling he treats his girlfriends like gold and is probably pretty romantic and sweet. That being said, I would LOVE to have a one-night stand with him. My guess? He's probably such a little flirt, and I bet he totally surprises you in bed.'

There have also been the unfounded rumours about various film roles and more bizarre stories. In 2005, there was speculation that Daniel, together with fellow actor Jamie Bell, was in the running to play a young James Bond in a film adaptation of the book *Silverfin*. Some years later, it was reported Daniel would be taking the part of Freddie Mercury in a film about rock band Queen ('I'm completely wrong for the part!' insisted Daniel) and that he was to appear in a remake of the classic war movie *All Quiet on The Western Front*.

Later came speculation that he had 'missed out' on the lead role of Christian Grey in the film adaptation of E L James's erotic *Fifty Shades of Grey*. But Daniel had not wanted the role! Refuting the story, he said, 'I think there was approximately no people waiting for me to play the part, including myself. I have to say, no offence to anybody as I'm sure they're going to do a great job on the movie, but it's not something that I think would have been a good next step for me.'

Daniel has his 'top five' of totally untrue stories: How he had shot up two feet in height in five weeks, being the victim of a stalker, requesting two former SAS men to walk his dogs, drinking a special beer brewed in a Belgian monastery, and having a sculpture made of himself in *Equus*, which had pride of place at home.

There are ways, Daniel once said, of making his celebrity life easier, such as not going to film premieres of someone else's film or other events he is not involved in. The desire to have some private life is the reason why he doesn't go on Twitter or Facebook: 'If you tell everybody what you're doing moment to moment and then claim you want a private life, then no one is going to take that request seriously.' He also does not understand why anyone would value his opinion 'that highly'. But as *The Guardian* pointed out, 'that doesn't mean Radcliffe is absent from Twitter or Facebook – a brief search reveals dozen of unofficial fan club accounts offering news about the star, from the Netherlands to Thailand to Brazil, with tens of thousands of followers.'

At one time, Daniel did not even have an email address because he didn't have time to check his inbox regularly: I don't have an email because, I did have one for a while, but I checked it so irregularly that people would be getting pissed off at me that I wouldn't reply to their emails.' Daniel has, however, confessed to being 'a big texter', and becoming an avid fan of Skype while staying in New York.

Luckily for Daniel, those difficult teenage years are behind him. But life, he has said, is still not without its problems. 'Your 20s are weird. You feel like you should be grown-up but actually you're not. You're constantly torn between that thing of "I'm young!" and then "I'm not!" There are certain expectations you have about your 20s when you're a teenager and none of them really happen. You think everything is going to be simpler but life gets more bloody complicated. I hope to be more settled.' It had been a difficult transition from his teens, he said. 'At twenty years old I was trying to be like "cool guy". It's nothing to do with Potter; it was just being twenty and being a dick,' he admitted. 'I think that's bullshit. I'm fucking not that guy. I'm nerdy: I like books and I like quiz shows and that's just fine.'

Today Daniel is back on track. 'I'm not somebody who likes worrying people. So, if I know I'm a worrying drinker, would I ever drink in front of people that I would worry?' His whole attitude to going out and having a good time has changed, too. 'As much as I would love to be a person that goes to parties and has a couple of drinks and has a nice time, that doesn't work for me. I'd just rather sit at home and read, or go out to dinner with someone, or talk to someone I love, or talk to somebody that makes me laugh.' Now, he has said, he likes it when he is an observer of drunks rather than being one. 'I quite enjoy it until everyone starts slurring, and you're like, "You've told me this fucking story three times already!"'

After a Christmas party on Broadway, Daniel said, 'I had fun going into the rooms of people I knew had got really fucked up the night before, and shouting at them. Just to be an arsehole. If you're going to be sober, you might as well be smug about it.'

Reflecting back on those dark days, Daniel realises there were other ways he could have found an outlet for what he called 'youthful excesses'. He does not miss the drinking – or the blackouts – and can now have fun in other ways other than looking at the bottom of an empty glass. 'I don't want to give the impression I'm a boring bastard that never goes out. I still have a really good time. It's about going "If I continue like this, I will jeopardise my career, and the thing I love."' If he was to give advice to his younger self, he says, it would be simply, 'Don't try too hard to be something you're not.'

Cutting the umbilical cord with Harry Potter did have its

perks as far as press attention was concerned. 'I think word must have got round that I'm boring. They're not going to get anything interesting. They're even bored of the "me smoking a fag" story.'

It is no wonder that, when once asked what magical power he would like to bring to his own life, Daniel has said 'to be invisible'.

CHAPTER 7

TRIALS AND TRIBULATIONS AT THE END OF THE POTTER ROAD

Daniel walked out of the hospital and immediately lit a cigarette. He was not only exhausted, having just finished his Broadway run in *Equus* a few days before, but he was also emotionally wrecked. It was 11 February 2009 and Daniel, accompanied by co-star Tom Felton, had just paid a traumatic visit to one of his oldest Potter friends.

David Holmes was in the spinal unit of London's Royal National Orthopaedic Hospital following a stunt that had gone horrifically wrong on the set of *Deathly Hallows*. The twenty-five-year-old stuntman, who had doubled for Daniel right from the start of the Potter films, had suffered serious spinal injuries while rehearsing a flying scene involving an explosion on 28 January 2009. Though he was wearing a harness, the blast had flung him to the ground. The accident happened at the Leavesden Studios. It was devastating for former competitive gymnast Holmes who was heard to declare after he fell, 'I can't feel my legs.' Holmes had been rehearsing the 'jerk back', one of the most dangerous stunts in the business. The scene involved him, as a Harry Potter lookalike, flying through the air in a harness and then appearing to be hurled back by an explosion. One source commented: 'David had done the stunt earlier that day but he said that it was harder to perform than usual and that it hurt when it was pulling him back. It's a dangerous stunt and David knew that. Most stuntmen get double their daily pay to carry it out. It went terribly wrong and David was thrown so far that he missed all of the safety mats. He hit the ground very hard.'

It was to be another two weeks before the set was reopened. There was talk in some quarters that there was a Harry Potter curse, the most dramatic rumours being that Daniel had been the target of a death threat and was placed under 'extraordinary security' when travelling to and from the set. *The Sun* newspaper reported that Daniel had been given a 'chase car' to follow his own in case of an emergency and that he now had four ex-SAS protection men. An 'insider' was quoted as saying, 'There is real concern for Daniel's welfare. The bigwigs haven't said what has been going on. It's all hush-hush but security has been massively ramped up.'

Belief in a Potter 'curse' was further strengthened in 2009 when Jamie Waylett, who played Vincent Crabbe, was found in possession of cannabis. In October 2011, he was charged with possessing a homemade bomb following his involvement with the London riots (in March 2012, he was jailed for two years after being found guilty of violent disorder).

In March 2010, in yet another example of how dangerous the stunts could be, the Hogwarts set for the final Potter saga was destroyed in a blaze at Leavesden Studios when filming the last battle scene went disastrously wrong and explosives set light to scenery. Six fire engines raced to the scene and it took forty minutes or so to get the fire under control. A fire service spokesman said: 'There was a big battle scene involving a lot of pyrotechnics and explosions. The mocked-up castle of timber, steel and plastic somehow caught alight.' Around £100,000 of damage was caused; Daniel, Emma and Rupert were not among the 100 crew and cast on set at the time.

Back in October 2005, Harry Potter's flying car, which appeared in *Chamber of Secrets*, had been stolen from a Cornish film studio. The 1962 Ford Anglia was said to have initially been found abandoned by a group of travellers in a lock-up garage with its number plates missing. But it ended up dumped outside a castle near Falmouth after it was believed the gang had trouble selling it. Police Constable Tim Roberts was reported as saying: 'It seems we have now located the Harry Potter car. I'd love to think Harry had driven it there to take part in some adventure at the castle but the reality is probably a little less interesting. It seems to be in good order. I would guess whoever left it there did so with their tongue firmly in their cheek.'

Another more tragic indication of the cruel jinx apparently hanging over the Warner Bros. franchise took place in June 2010 when crew member and electrician Danny Espey, who had worked on four of the Harry Potter films, was found by his twelve-year-old daughter hanged in his garage.

The main shooting for *Deathly Hallows* began on 19 February

2009 and was completed on 12 June 2010. Bill Nighy as Minister Rufus Scrimgeour and Frances de la Tour as Madame Maxime joined the cast. Film agency Film London described the plot: 'In *The Deathly Hallows*, the now post-pubescent Harry (Daniel Radcliffe), Ron (Rupert Grint) and Hermione (Emma Watson) are on a mission against the clock to find and destroy the source of Lord Voldemort's immortality and end his reign of darkness forever. Ralph Fiennes reprises the role of Potter's nemesis Voldemort and key cast, including Michael Gambon, Helena Bonham Carter, Alan Rickman and Jim Broadbent, accompany the core characters to the bitter end.'

The film was also to feature a topless, silver-painted Harry and Hermione in an intimate dream-like sequence. The short scene showed Hermione kissing and embracing him with her hand cupped under his chin and came as Ron attempted to destroy one of Voldemort's horcruxes (pieces of his soul). In a bid to distract Ron, Voldemort torments him by showing him the couple together. Emma Watson was to say the scene was 'like some weird social experiment' as it was like kissing her brother. Daniel said they had chewed lots of gum beforehand to freshen their breath and that, although he had been expecting it to be a 'slow, soft kiss, it was passionate and rigorous'. He added, '[Emma] is a bit of an animal, she is, she was great. But then I'm not complaining, there are tens of thousands of men that would cut off limbs to be in that position.'

Co-star Rupert Grint had to leave the set because he was laughing so much. The kiss scene took five takes to perfect. There was plenty of publicity for the film, of course, with one promotional short showing Daniel wearing a bra and saying the words, 'Look away, I'm hideous.' The scene was part of a complicated Harry Potter plot, which diehard fans understood right away, and as Daniel was later to say, 'It was better than wearing stockings and suspenders, which was the other option they toyed with at one point.'

The scene involving seven Harry Potters took much, much longer – an incredible ninety-five takes – which wasn't, Daniel wanted to stress, because he wasn't doing it right. 'It was a very complex technical shot using a motion-control camera, which is a camera operated by a computer rather than a human being. It can recreate the exact same move every time. And basically, I would stand in one place, and the camera would do the shot. And I would stand in a second place and the camera would do the shot. But if I was standing an inch too far to my left or too far to my right, then I would be standing in a theoretical me that would be put in there later. So yes, it took a long, long time, but it's one of those sequences that's wonderful to see when it does then come out on to the screen, because it looks so good. All that work paid off, for sure.'

In June 2009, some very special visitors stopped by on the *Deathly Hallows* set. American First Lady Michelle Obama and daughters Malia, ten, and Sasha, who was getting an extra special treat for her eighth birthday, toured the studios and met the stars. A birthday party for Sasha was held on the set's Hogwarts Grand Hall. The VIP party was in response to a personal invitation that Daniel had extended in January that year when he'd been in America for Barack Obama's inauguration as President – whom he described as 'both Martin Luther King and JFK' and 'a symbol of progress' – and discovered the women were visiting London later that year. Daniel had announced, 'I'd like to take this opportunity to issue a public invitation to the

Obamas that, if their daughters would like a private tour of the Harry Potter set, I would be honoured to be their personal tour guide.' Michelle Obama had already said that Harry Potter 'is huge in our house' and that the US President himself often read the books to their daughters.

VIP visitors apart, *GQ* magazine's Craig McLean gave an insight into the real Daniel on the Potter set. 'Out the back of the studio canteen we find Daniel Radcliffe. He's skulking next to a Portakabin storing boxes of crisps, hiding from the children who are visiting during half term (each member of the cast and crew are allowed one bunch of visitors to the HP set). He's smoking a roll-up but can't be seen puffing away by the kids. That would spoil the magic. He's bloodied, dirty. They've just finished filming a scene in which Harry fights arch-enemy Lord Voldemort (Ralph Fiennes). The actors had rolled heavily over a precipice. Fiennes had landed a few punches "off the padding" and had caught Radcliffe's face. "And I kneed Ralph in the bollocks – by accident," he adds hastily, grinning.'

Daniel went on to tell McLean the fight had been an 'intense experience' but that he had learned a few tricks of the trade from Fiennes. 'I learned from watching him, the way he used his body and his hands, especially when Voldemort first regains his human form. It's fantastic.'

Fiennes paid equal tribute to his young co-star: 'Daniel had to put up with a lot from me. Here's a boy who's tied up with a man pushing his finger into the wound on his head, laughing and delighting in the pain he's causing. He had to act as though he was in agony and terror without having many words to say. I was full of admiration for him.'

Daniel was to win varied accolades in 2009 including being voted number eighteen in *Portrait Magazine*'s 'Top 30 under 30' list. Incredibly, though, he was well below his Harry Potter co-stars, with Bonnie Wright taking second place, Evanna Lynch third place and Rupert Grint fifth place. Emma Watson was voted in at number eight.

Despite the tight filming schedule, Daniel had taken time out for something particularly dear to him: raising funds for David Holmes. He had held a gala in April 2010 for the stuntman who was now confined to a wheelchair and no longer able to work. At the event, guests paid £100 a ticket and an auction featured a pair of signed boxing gloves donated by Angelina Jolie and Brad Pitt, which alone raised £4,000.

There were some obligatory events too. In June, Daniel joined Bonnie Wright and Tom Felton at the opening of The Wizarding World of Harry Potter theme park in Orlando, Florida. 'It's brilliant going round your own theme park,' he said. 'You don't have to queue; you don't have to pay! I went on the Dragon Challenge roller coaster five times.'

J. K. Rowling was also present at the event, which was attended by thousands of fans.

That same month, he was the cover star of magazine *L'Uomo Vogue* in a shoot that had him in a bowling alley – 'Mr Harry Potter's new look Daniel Radcliffe' was the tag line. In August, Warner Bros. threw a belated afternoon wrap party in a field near Leavesden Studios, which Daniel attended along with Rupert Grint, Tom Felton, Jim Broadbent and David Thewlis. The funfair theme meant cast and crew had the chance to enjoy traditional rides, including dodgems and a ghost train, and a fleet of ice-cream vans was on hand.

In October 2010, Daniel was diversifying again, with his voice being featured on an episode of *The Simpsons*. He and fellow British actor Hugh Laurie provided the voices in the 21st annual 'Treehouse of Horror' Halloween special.

There was also the most dramatic photo shoot Daniel had ever done. The November issue of fashion and culture magazine *Dazed & Confused* featured Daniel in a series of pictures taken by Serge Leblon, in which his face was painted gold, his hair slicked back and his eyes smothered in black make-up. He wore clothes by, among other designers, Duckie Brown, Prada, Dolce & Gabbana and Alexander McQueen. The session, the magazine said, was an attempt to 'bring a certain edge to the young star'. Daniel had not been the obvious choice for such a shoot said the magazine's editor Rod Stanley, 'which of course was one of the reasons we were interested in working with him. He was open and enthusiastic about our visual direction even though he was slathered in paint and feathers at the time.' Daniel was the magazine's cover star that month, with his hair and face covered in white and gold paint and the words 'Daniel Radcliffe – Shape Shift'.

The magazine's stylist Robbie Spencer said: 'Daniel was a dream to work with, a true professional and incredibly down to earth and mature for his age. He totally understood what we were trying to achieve, and was really into being transformed into this alter-ego character. He gave a lot of himself to each shot.'

One fashionista went deeper: 'For Daniel Radcliffe I believe this shoot was a way for him to well and truly stamp on his wizard's cloak and tell the world that he's not a boy but a man, a man who can be as daring and striking as any other male in the performance industry.'

Daniel simply said, when you are covered head to toe in make-up, 'the only thing to do is go for it…'

Harry Potter and the Deathly Hallows: Part 1 premiered in London on 11 November 2010. Although he found premieres intimidating, Daniel announced: 'There's nowhere I would rather be. Over the last ten years it's been some of the most surreal, bizarre moments of my life but in a lovely way. There's certainly nothing I would have swapped it for.' One time when asked about the manic reaction he received on such nights, he made it clear that it could have been any young boy on the red carpet and the response would have been the same. 'It isn't me they are screaming at. Whoever got the part would have had the same mania for a few weeks every year.'

Some fans felt they were being ripped off with the splitting of the final instalments into Parts 1 and 2. David Heyman defended the move: 'When Steve Kloves began working on the screenplay, it became clear we would have to omit too much to do justice to J. K. Rowling's book in one film.' But the two films were filmed back to back and treated as one as far as production was concerned.

'I find it hard to believe we made Part Two at the same time as Part One but I couldn't be more pleased with it,' Daniel commented. He also defended the two-film split: 'There were a lot of cynical people when it was announced and they thought it was all about making more money. I felt like saying to them, "Well, you adapt it into one if you feel you can." It took the time in the first one to set up the story and by the second we could tie up all the loose ends.'

The young cast had lots of fun in the year and a half it took to film, said Daniel. 'It was fantastic. It was a really, really good shoot, lots of running around, lots of getting fiercely competitive with Emma about who was the faster across the ground. I'd definitely say me, but she would give you a different answer, definitely. I think she's probably better over long distance, but short distance? I'll have her every time.'

This particular Potter instalment seemed to really test the young cast with its frenetic pace and demanding action. 'It was an exhilarating shoot,' said Daniel, 'but exhilaration is only a state that you can keep up for so long. We were shooting both films back to back for eighteen months. At the end of it we were on our knees, really struggling. It was a huge challenge. But I feel like, in a way that they have so much energy and momentum, because we did them all at once. It was all mad. We were shooting one movie and then going to Part Two. And it was all just kind of crazy, but somehow it all came out pretty well. So we were obviously doing something right. If we spent the whole time being exhilarated, I think I might have collapsed of exhaustion at some point – which I didn't.'

There were more murmurings of how dark this Harry Potter epic was – the cinematography was by Oscar-nominated Eduardo Serra who had worked on *Girl with a Pearl Earring*. And it was the first time Hogwarts School was not seen in a Potter film. 'We were away from the magical environment of Hogwarts, which felt very safe even when the characters were in utter jeopardy,' said director David Yates. 'Suddenly Harry, Ron and Hermione are trying to survive out in the big, bad world, and it's a dangerous place. They feel isolated and alone and very vulnerable. It makes the adventure much edgier and more grown-up, which really appealed to me and to Dan, Rupert and Emma as well.'

The film was released on 19 November 2010, smashing box-office records and taking around £17.5m that opening weekend. Josh Berger from Warner Bros. commented: 'The opening of the film has become an extraordinary worldwide event.'

Reviewers were now more than aware that Potter fever was mounting with the completion of the back-to-back filming. And they made note of the fact that one of the scenes in *Deathly Hallows: Part 1* had been specially created for the film and was not in the original book. This was a scene in which Harry and Hermione dance together in a tent to a radio playing the Nick Cave track 'O Children'. One critic commented: 'It manages to be sweet, funny and tear-jerking all at the same time.'

Chris Tookey in the *Daily Mail* wrote: 'The most praiseworthy aspect of all is that this episode – unlike the one before it – once again gets Harry (Daniel Radcliffe), Ron (Rupert Grint) and Hermione (Emma Watson) working as a team. The most memorable sequences in the film are not, for once, the action scenes but the acting ones. There's a delightful one where director David Yates allows Harry and Hermione simply to dance together, in a desperate attempt to rediscover some fun and human contact in a world that seemingly has room for neither.'

Yates recalled how screenwriter Steve Kloves had suddenly come up with the idea for the dancing scene. 'I said, "My God, you're right, that would be great" [...] I find it very tender, very funny, very moving. For me it's about them becoming grown-ups, growing up in a very painful way ... I like the notion that they find comfort in each other when everything seems to be falling apart. It's a very natural thing to do, trying to provide warmth for each other as friends. For me it's a very special moment in the film but I know it drives some people nuts.'

Daniel said that Emma was a much better dancer than him and he had just 'muddled through', but he added, 'When I saw the film and that scene came on, I thought that was the coolest Harry Potter would ever be.'

There had been speculation that Jo Rowling was to write another *Harry Potter* book – which naturally caused some consternation among those involved in the film franchise. Could yet another movie be on the cards? What would be the effect on the long-term cast? Daniel had to admit he was more than a little relieved when the rumours turned out to be false. 'I think I always knew there were only going to be seven books. Because in the books you get seven terms of Hogwarts. I did have a mild moment of cardiac arrest one day when I picked up my phone and looked at the browser and it said, "Rowling promises eighth *Harry Potter* book", and I was like, "Arghhh! What?!" I saw her the other day and I said, "Jo, you're not going to do any more, are you?" She said, "No, don't worry. No more Potters." Which I think slightly worried her because it looked like I'd had a horrible time doing the films.'

In August 2011, Harry Potter's last two films won seven Teen Choice Awards. *Deathly Hallows: Part 1* scooped Best Sci-Fi Fantasy, with Emma Watson winning a Best Actress Award and sharing another with Daniel, who won the Summer Movie Male Star Award for *Deathly Hallows: Part 2*. Daniel, who was appearing onstage in *How to Succeed in Business Without Really Trying*, could not be present but gave an acceptance speech via satellite: 'Thank you very much for this amazing award ... Thank you for an incredible ten years. It has been an absolute dream.'

In December that year, he won the MTV award for Entertainer of the Year and the rather unusual award of being the actor MTV News was 'most thankful for in 2011'. He was nominated for the MTV Movie Award for Best Male Performance for *Deathly Hallows: Part 1*, for the Best Kiss (shared with Emma Watson) and for the Best Fight, shared with Rod Hunt, Rupert Grint, Emma and Arben Bajraktaraj.

The awards, of course, meant a lot to Daniel, but they came at the end of a year that had seen him gravitate away from Harry Potter. He said: 'I've done some work I'm really proud of in that time ... I've got so much better ... I think the next year will be the big one for me. In fact the next two or three years are going to be pretty important. This year is not a breakout year, it is a breakaway year.'

CHAPTER 8

HORROR
STAR

On 19 July 2010, just a few days before Daniel's twenty second birthday, it was announced that he was to play the character Arthur Kipps in horror film *The Woman in Black*. When questioned about why he wasn't taking a break, Daniel replied, 'Somebody said to me after Potter, are you not going to take a break? And I said no, I cannot afford to take a break: This is the time when the film world will be watching to see what we do next and we can't afford to be seen to be inactive. That fear of failure is something that will panic me a lot.'

The film, based on the novel by Susan Hill, enjoyed a long run in the West End from 1989. Central Television had also broadcast a version in December that year in which Kipps was played by Adrian Rawlins, the actor who was to later find fame as Harry Potter's father. This new production had a script written by Jane Goldman, goth and horror lover and the wife of TV chat-show host Jonathan Ross. Daniel had been given it to read literally hours after filming his last shot for the final Harry Potter film. He was immediately excited about the opportunity to take on a horror movie role, and not just any horror movie but one from the renowned Hammer production company: 'It's great because we can push the horror a little more because Hammer's there. We can go back to old standards of creepy toys and a haunted house and all those kind of things that recur. And because it's Hammer nobody questions it.'

There was also some satisfaction, he confessed, in Harry Potter appearing in a Hammer horror and 'freaking people out' – even though Daniel has said he is too much of a coward to watch horror films himself: 'Being on the other side of the screen is OK though, it's fun.' It was the first Hammer production for many years and Daniel was thrilled to be part of such a legendary film institution. 'The Hammer banner is wonderful, it's a fantastic thing for me, particularly because, having been in the British film industry all my life, it means that if you're not working with people who actually worked on the Hammer films, you're working with their kids.'

The role called for Daniel to look older than his years and it would be the first time, he proudly announced, that he would be playing a father. 'I was struggling in vain to not come close to making a face that would make people think of Harry.' And how would he characterise a Harry face? 'I have to accept the fact that my face is going to remind people of Harry because I played that character. If I try to avoid being expressive in that same way, all I'll do is stop being expressive, and I won't be any farther away from that character.'

Ever the workaholic, Daniel also said he wanted a project to work on after finishing Harry Potter and before embarking on the play *How to Succeed in Business Without Really Trying*. He never had any particular plans about what he would do after completing one play or film, but said he simply wanted to carry on with what he felt he did best, all the while still learning: 'There's no blueprint for where I should be. I see myself as a young, good actor who still has a lot to learn. There's nobody at any point in their career who is the finished article. The next couple of years for me are about finding people who are really going to push me. I've never trained, so the only way I'm going to get better is with taking risks and working with people who I think are going to improve me.

'Obviously, I've been very lucky in general in my career, but I feel that I've been very lucky in terms of having directors come along at the right times who have taken me to the next level of where I needed to be. Over the next couple of years I'm going to hopefully come on in leaps and bounds. To me it's what this process is about. I just want to work with people who are going to stretch me.'

Joining Daniel in his new film was fellow Potter co-star Ciarán Hinds as Samuel Daily, Liz White as the ghostly woman Jennet Humfrye, Alisa Khazanova as Mrs Drablow and Janet McTeer as Mrs Daily. Little Joseph Kipps was played by Misha Handley, Daniel's real-life godson, whom he had suggested for the role. 'The way I sold it to him was I said, "Misha, I am playing this part and I haven't done this before, can you help me?" So it was kind of like we were playing a game. He was like, "There are a lot of people playing this game", and I said, "Yeah, they're all in on it."' The film was directed by James

Watkins and the producers were Brian Oliver, Simon Oakes and Richard Jackson.

Of course, Daniel studiously read the novel in preparation. He also organised a visit to a psychologist to gain greater insight into his character's personal torment and how his chilling experiences would affect him. For it was not just the scary aspect of the film that had attracted him or that it was simply something so different for him: he was also drawn to the relationship between the characters, he told interviewers. 'It's very hard to pin down what you're looking for in a role but I like to be challenged by something I've not done before. What appeals to me is a really good script, a good story that unfolds through exchanges of the character rather than reading pages and pages of exposition. I don't like bad writing riddled with clichés … a script with sentimentality is something I can't stand in films. If I feel it is trying to emotionally manipulate the reader in a way I am not naturally feeling, I find it off-putting.'

When asked if there had ever been a role offered he would definitely not take, Daniel said there was the time he, Emma and Rupert were offered the chance to appear in a remake of *The Wizard of Oz*. Daniel would be cast as the cowardly lion. 'That was definitely one part I wouldn't want to consider,' he said. 'Occasionally you'll get some script in for some crappy fantasy thing and you just go, "Well, no, guys."'

One challenge for him was creating the staid fatherly character; he admitted that he had to rein in his normal enthusiasm in order to do this. 'I am quite hyper and energetic but this time I had to get into the part of someone who was coping with the circumstances he found himself in,' he said. 'I have this very excitable energy about me, and Arthur should not, and it would be completely wrong for the character. One of the things James Watkins was keen on was trying, as he put it, to "take the fizz out of the bottle, to let it go flat", stripping away my natural zeal, the attack I have with everything, and actually showing somebody who has been devastated by their loss to the point where they're in a state of emotional paralysis.'

Physically, Daniel would look very different, with darkened hair and sideburns (specially grown for the part). Watkins declared: 'He's sexy! We played up his fantastic blue eyes and this is a totally different Dan who bought into this as a way to reinvent and reintroduce himself.'

Daniel loved wearing his fitted grey suit and waistcoat and getting to wear a fob watch. 'It's how I would dress all the time if that wouldn't get me beaten up in London,' he joked.

This project was to be the first time Daniel was not accompanied by one of his parents. But his father wrote to him with words of wisdom, which he was never to forget: 'On a film set there's always going to be somebody who's going to cause a delay. Try and make sure it's never you.' Despite the bad times he would later face, Daniel always heeded this.

The story is set in the nineteenth century and tells of young London solicitor Arthur Kipps having to travel to the remote Yorkshire village of Crythin Gifford to advise on the affairs of Mrs Drablow who has just died. Her home, Eel Marsh House, is, of course, spooky and Kipps soon discovers the presence of the ghostly Woman in Black – and that local children are mysteriously dying. The ghost is seeking revenge for the death of her own child. Does Kipps run? No. Despite suffering from the trauma of his wife's death while giving birth to their child, the fearless Kipps stays around to find out what it is she wants. At one point, Daniel's character wanders around the house in silence for nearly twenty minutes, a particularly tense interlude.

The complexity of Kipps's personality appealed to Daniel: 'It's about loss and what happens to us if we don't move on from loss and I absolutely knew it was what I wanted to do next.'

Filming started on 26 September 2010. There was to be a gruelling schedule with no less than eight different locations including 'home of horror' Pinewood Studios. Most of the shooting was done in Essex and Sussex with Cotterstock Hall in Northamptonshire providing the eerie setting of Eel Marsh House. The original idea to shoot *The Woman in Black* in 3D had been scrapped.

Filming ended on 4 December that year. Daniel, who has admitted to being afraid of the dark when younger, at times found the whole creepy experience somewhat unsettling. Even one of the American posters for the film spooked him. 'I am a slightly jumpy person anyway … it was just a sepia photo of two kids with their eyes scratched out. In the middle of the night I got up to get a drink of water and jumped two foot in the air because I suddenly thought there were two eyeless children staring at me.'

One scene in *The Woman in Black* called for Daniel to be submerged under marsh mud – a particularly challenging ordeal for him because he has said his biggest fear is being buried alive. He also, incidentally, suffers from coulrophobia, a fear of clowns, has a fear of being murdered and of there being a nuclear war. He doesn't much like cockroaches and has said that Yellowstone volcano 'gives me nightmares'! On a lesser scale, Daniel's list of hates include chewing gum, people who eat and talk at the same time, cake, rudeness and being patronised.

That December, Daniel managed to fit in filming for one of his favourite shows, the BBC's *QI* with host Stephen Fry. Shown on Christmas Eve, it proved that Daniel knew quite a bit about some of the most obscure subjects. He impressed his rival team, which comprised comedians Lee Mack andAlan Davies, by accurately answering the question 'What is the oldest trick in the book?' and giving some pretty informative answers to other questions, too. The programme ended with his team member Graham Norton beheading Daniel with a guillotine.

The Woman in Black had its London premiere on 24 January 2012 and was released in America on 3 February. It was the biggest-grossing movie that opening weekend. In fact, it was the biggest US opening for a Hammer film in the production company's history, raking in $20m, well over the predicted takings.

Released in Britain a week later, it was also the highest-grossing British horror film in twenty years, taking £3.15m at the weekend box office. Daniel, however, didn't just sit back and wait for a reaction to the film. He had embarked on a five-week press tour to promote the film. This had taken him on a return trip to Moscow, where, on 16 February, he had attended a premiere of the film and a photo call. With director James Watkins at his side, and through an interpreter, he answered a series of questions in Russian at a press conference. The film had cost around £10m to make, said Watkins. Daniel patiently responded to his interrogation by the Russian press, answering questions such as what difference did he find between screen and stage acting – 'acting is holding off self-consciousness to be natural and it's easier onstage' – and confessing how nice it was to be able to talk about a project other than Harry Potter – 'I think by the end of it the journalists had run out of questions and were probably bored hearing all the same answers'. After a hectic tour, which had included Madrid and Paris, Daniel was no doubt looking forward to his planned three-week holiday before heading to New York to start filming *Kill Your Darlings*.

By June 2012, *The Woman in Black* had made $127,730,736 (around £77m) worldwide. It was a pleasing result for Daniel who was forever being asked the reasons why he took on such different roles. 'People ask those questions a lot,' he explained. '"Why are you searching to be so different?" or "Is it intentional that you want to be so diverse?" And the answer is, "Yes, it is." But I don't think that's something specific for someone coming out of a franchise. I think any actor worth their salt wants to show as much versatility as they possibly can. Over the next couple of years, it's going to be about doing as much work as possible and making it as varied as possible.'

But there was a black cloud hanging over *The Woman in Black*. Many felt the 12A certificate given by the British Board of Film Classification (BBFC) was not appropriate for a film that included so many gory scenes and it was to become the most complained-about film of the year, even though the BBFC website gave a warning about 'a number of scenes of supernatural horror and threat'. This did not save the BBFC from receiving no less than 120 complaints. All this bemused Daniel who was relishing being in a film in which the spookiness was a world away from the family sorcery fun of Harry Potter. 'I do take a small tincture of pride about it being the most complained-about film. I would have thought from the trailer that you could see what kind of a movie it was going to be. I said at the time, if your kid is under twelve I would advise them not to see this film. Apparently there was a girl at the British premiere who fainted and, when I heard that, I was like, "We did something right."'

Despite being such a massive box-office success, the reviews for *The Woman in Black* were mixed. The *Daily Mirror* remarked: 'As for boy wonder Radcliffe, this isn't a performance likely to fend off the usual comparisons between him and a piece of cardboard. Not that this should put you off a film this frightening and this moody. Prepare to have nightmares.'

Time Out's Tom Huddleston wrote: 'Hanging on to your movie career is a trial for any child actor, but for Daniel Radcliffe, who is associated not just with youthfulness but with one very specific, well-loved role, it's going to be an uphill battle. He's made a good first step with this smart, spooky adaptation of Susan Hill's bestselling novel – famous also as a long-running West End show – but the sight of Harry Potter with mutton chops and a two-year-old son can still take a spot of getting used to. Radcliffe is solid rather than spectacular, but that serves the film.'

The *Hollywood Reporter's* review stated: 'Curiosity about the actor's first adult screen role and first part since leaving Hogwarts behind should ensure healthy returns for the CBS Films release. And the good news is that the former Harry Potter carries the film quite capably.'

And *Empire* magazine commented: 'Radcliffe plays a challenging role well, frequently with nothing to react against as he tiptoes around Eel Marsh House waiting for something horrible to happen. He's got good eyes for looking terrified: huge and always a little bit aghast, even in repose.'

The Woman in Black was to win a handful of awards and nominations including Best Horror Film of the Year in the *Empire* Awards. Daniel was a Best Actor runner-up in the 2013 Fangoria Chainsaw Awards (for horror and thriller films) and Marco Beltrami won an ASCAP Award for his musical score.

Daniel had succeeded once again in his brave decision for diversity and he was happy at the reaction to it. 'Somebody said to me, "Do you think your Harry Potter fans will stick with you in this film?" and I was like, "If they stuck with me through *Equus* they'll stick with me through this!" This is nothing in comparison to that. I think this is a very good first step. I was under no illusion that people would see this film and go, "Christ! He's not Harry Potter anymore. He's completely transformed." I didn't ever think that was going to happen. But I think it's a good first step in that I look very different. I'm playing a man rather than a boy. It's a different type of film to be in, and all that stuff is very useful at this point for an audience to see that I'm going to try and do different stuff.'

The Potter team were to miss out on the big ones at the BAFTA Awards that year, which Daniel presented, admitting he was 'terrified' because at one ceremony he had forgotten the nominees' names. Among the awards he handed over was Supporting Actress to Minny Jackson in *The Help*. *Deathly Hallows: Part 2* did win a BAFTA, for special visual effects. It wasn't a bad way to end the Potter series.

CHAPTER 9

A WIZARD'S FORTUNE

Of course, Harry Potter did not only bring Daniel fame but a massive fortune too – though reports vary considerably when it comes to totalling his wealth. But he *has* topped the Rich Lists a few times and there is no doubt that with each Harry Potter film Daniel's worth both as an actor and a commodity for Warner Bros. grew and grew – in quite a mind-boggling way. If the figures added up, at the end of 2013 and the beginning of 2014, he was 'worth' around £60m and is certainly the wealthiest of the Potter child star trio.

Daniel has said that he was nineteen before he became fully aware of his earning potential, telling an interviewer at the time, 'I only found out what I was worth two months ago. Seriously, I'd never wanted to know, but eventually I got so sick of hearing all these ridiculous figures that I asked my agent. She told me and my jaw hit my toenails. I won't tell you what it was, but it was very surreal. You just go, "Oh. Well, that's nice. I'll buy you several drinks then, shall I?"'

But there aren't many lads who are given personal advice on wealth management by the Queen's bank Coutts, which is what happened shortly after his eighteenth birthday when his parents also allowed Daniel some financial freedom. It *was* rumoured that he treated himself to a green Fiat Grande Punto or a Golf GTi for this landmark birthday – but he hadn't taken any driving lessons. (One of the reasons he turned down a potentially lucrative car advert deal.) He said of turning eighteen, 'I don't plan to be one of those people who suddenly buy themselves a massive sports car collection or something similar. I don't think I'll be particularly extravagant. The things I like buying cost about £10…'

Daniel has, however, invested in some works of art. He bought *Mona D, Mary And Me*, a work by New York-based artist Jim Hodges whose work has been described as 'exploring themes of fragility, temporality, love and death utilising a highly original and poetic vocabulary'. The media he uses range from graphite and ink to gold leaf. Daniel said the Hodges work bears the words 'Oh for crying out loud', which he liked because it is something his mum always used to say, and that it is 'basically a drawing of blue ink on white paper'. He saw the work at one of the world's largest art fairs, the Frieze Art Fair, and fell in love with it, but the dealer said they wanted to sell it to a more prestigious collector. 'Jim got word of this. Turns out he's a massive Harry Potter fan and insisted they sell it to me. Ever since then I've been really good friends with Jim and his best mate Tim, a photographer.' It was through the two gay men that Daniel was introduced to New York's transvestite community, which apparently offered more than just a colourful social scene: 'If you want to go out on the street without being recognised, without even being looked at, go out with a 6ft 8in beautiful transsexual. No one gives you a second glance.'

Other collected works include one by Damien Hirst (a butterfly painting, the cost of which Daniel has always refused to disclose), a Craigie Aitchison hanging in his London flat, an Andy Warhol, and portraits by American artist Elizabeth Peyton (he especially likes one of bad-boy musician Pete Doherty). Daniel admits these are something of an extravagance 'because you don't really need a painting'. He has even considered investing in stamps – 'I was told it's the new thing!'

The money trail has to be traced back to the first Potter film in 2001 to get an idea of how Daniel's standing in the franchise increased; before *Harry Potter and the Philosopher's Stone*, he had barely made a ripple in the acting pool. What he was paid for this is reported to be between £150,000 and £250,000; not an inconsequential amount for a boy of ten but meagre compared to his earnings by the time the last Harry Potter film hit the cinemas. The second in the series, *The Chamber of Secrets*, earned him £1.7m, the third, *The Prisoner of Azkaban*, £3.4m, the fourth, *Goblet of Fire*, £5m. Quizzed about his wealth at this time, Daniel shrugged and said he had no idea about it. 'It is in a bank. I am fourteen. I don't really use it. I don't care and I don't need it,' he told one interviewer. The fifth film, *Order of the Phoenix*, reportedly earned him £8m and the sixth, *The Half-Blood Prince*, £9m. The last two, *Deathly Hallows: Parts 1 and 2*, each reportedly earned him £13m. It was, one observer noted, 'a display of how dependent Warner

Bros. have become on his image … to the world at large he is Harry Potter and can't be replaced'.

Various Rich Lists chart Daniel's accumulation of wealth: he appeared on *The Sunday Times* Rich List in 2006, which estimated his personal fortune to be £14m, making him one of the richest young people in the UK at the time. In 2007, this had risen to £17m (though incredibly it only gave him the position of 33 on the British Young People's Rich List). It was no wonder that Daniel, naturally cautious and responsible with money, felt he should spend some of his fortune – in America. In 2007, he bought a £3.2m fifth-floor apartment on 40 Mercer Street, Manhattan. It was very much an investment (his portfolio is overseen by his mother) and Daniel never actually moved in. Instead, he rented it out for £3,000 a week.

In February 2008, Daniel paid just over £3m for a three-bed apartment in the same area. What made the apartment special, apart from its 2,450sq ft floor area, which included a unique 'eat-in' kitchen with marble and granite surfaces, butler's pantry and 500-bottle wine cellar, was the stunning view of the Hudson River through the semi-circular glass walls.

By 2009, aged just nineteen, he had become Britain's richest teenager, worth around £30m – with the prediction that at the end of the Harry Potter series this could rise to £70m. Daniel, it was pointed out, was now wealthier than Princes William and Harry (£28m each) and only the then F1 Championship leader Jenson Button and Newcastle United striker Michael Owen (£40m each), both twenty-nine, were young higher earners. That same year, Daniel topped the Forbes 'Most Valuable Young Stars' list. In 2010, Daniel ranked fifth on the *Sunday Times* Young Millionaires list, worth a reported £42m.

In February that year, he was hailed as the sixth highest-paid Hollywood male. By October 2010, still only twenty-one, Daniel had now amassed around £45.7m according to a wealth list drawn up by *Heat* magazine. This made him the wealthiest star under the age of thirty.

Daniel was now the owner of a third New York property. It was his most costly one to date, a £3.6m five-bedroom house with a 36ft garden in Greenwich Village. The location was described by Sotheby's as 'one of New York's most picturesque tree-lined cobblestone blocks'. The main house, built in 1847 by a sea captain for his daughters, covered 3,000sq ft, boasted six fireplaces and a huge balcony and had a one-bedroom apartment on the ground floor. It was said to be 'soaked in sunlight throughout the day' and the 'sizable open garden and backyard is cooled by beautiful old trees and landscaping'. The previous owner, Ann Emonts, said the deal, as usual done via Daniel's mother Marcia, was 'super fast' and that not being able to tell anyone who was buying her home was 'sort of a fun secret'. It was rumoured that Daniel spent around £100,000 refurbishing the place, with a friend quoted as saying, 'He's created a cool, stylish bachelor pad to bring home beautiful girls, when he wishes. He called in a fancy interior designer to create special lighting, soft furnishings and a hanging music system, to get the party started. He's really excited to be twenty-one and living in his own pad in New York. He's tarted it up to the nines. He's young, free and single in New York, with a fantastic apartment, and a stack of cash in his pocket.'

There was also the Australian apartment in the Toorak suburb of Melbourne, which Daniel's parents had purchased after holidaying in the country some years before. 'We just joke about me being the high-earner, to be honest. That's the way to deal with it. They don't think of me as the bread-earner of the family.'

Financial records published in 2010 by Gilmore Jacobs – the firm set up in 2000 by his parents to manage his assets – revealed that Daniel had fixed investments worth over £18m, with the three properties in New York worth a total of £10m. There was also the London house, valued at around £730,000, close to his parents' home in Fulham.

Daniel was back on the *Heat* magazine lists the following year as the richest young British entertainer. And he still could not understand why everyone was interested in the money he had earned. 'It's very strange. Because they wouldn't ask anyone else. I think it's because I'm young. There's a fascination of, "Wow, what would I have done if I had the money at that age?" And, the truth is, I don't really do anything with it! … I'm very grateful for the money, I feel amazingly lucky to have it. It's something that I can't quite comprehend. But it's not the motivating factor in my life and it's not the thing that drives me – probably because I have it, I realise – but I'm in a fortunate position where I don't now have to work for the money and I can pick things I'm interested in. Gary Oldman says it's called "Fuck it money!"'

In 2012, it was reported that Daniel was dropping his support of Labour for the Liberal Democratic Party because of its stance on taxes. He said he felt it was only right that the wealthy should pay higher taxes. 'I think if you make a lot more money than most people – like I do – you should pay more tax and subsidise people who work just as hard as you, but don't earn as much.'

Following this, there were several attempts to get Daniel embroiled in a discussion about politics generally but he would not be drawn. 'They're all quite uninspiring, the politicians at the head of all the parties,' he said. 'My parents are left wing, and I would describe myself as that. But also you know what? I wouldn't describe myself as that. Because I don't have to. Because I'm not a political party. Most people are a little bit of each and we change our mind on various issues.' A few years earlier Daniel had defiantly said that the reason young people are reluctant to vote is because they believe all politicians are the same, regardless of what party they belong to. The next time he would get interested in the political scene, he said, was when his old friend comedian Eddie Izzard (who once gave Daniel support when he was being bullied) stood for London mayor in 2020, adding that current mayor Boris Johnson only got in because 'he hosted *Have I Got News For You* a few times. It was a vote for celebrity.' In that particular election, Daniel said he was the only person of his age he knew who had actually voted – 'Not one of my friends even registered.' He hoped that could change if Izzard entered the political arena. 'He's really interesting, super-smart and brings a huge amount of integrity – something that we definitely don't have today.' Apart from that, Daniel said he found politics 'disillusioning; it's just bickering, it's exhausting'.

On 23 October 2013, Daniel was pipped to the post as Britain's richest celebrity aged thirty or under. He had held the number-one place since the *Heat* magazine poll started three years earlier. Daniel was now 'worth' around £56.19m but came second to *X Factor*'s hugely successful boy band One

Direction and their £59.3m (although, of course, Daniel does not have to split his wealth five ways!).

Daniel once joked that he might use some of his vast wealth to buy twenty Porsches and just crash them for the hell of it. But it was only a joke for he is incredibly responsible – and charitable – with his fortune. 'I don't know what to do with it. I'm very fortunate to have it and it gives you room to manoeuvre … But the main thing about having money is it means you don't have to worry about it. And that for me is a lovely thing. It's not for fast cars and hookers.'

True, he has homes in America, Australia and London and several other indulgences, but he also spends a lot of money on the ordinary things of life, such as books, music and hosting his friends on a night out. 'The only time I will spend a wad of cash in one go – and this is going to sound so nerdy – is in bookshops. I've gone out of bookshops with a pile of fifteen to twenty books before. It's excessive. I have this thing in bookshops where if I see this thing that there's a good chance I may never ever see again or sounds interesting then I have to get it.' Daniel has said it was the *Harry Potter* books that originally got him back into reading. Now he is passionate about it. He once listed his five favourite books: Hemingway's *The Old Man and the Sea* – 'probably the first book by a really classic author that I ever read, and it was then that I realised that things were classics for a reason, and they weren't all just really, really, really hard work'; *Germinal* by Emile Zola – 'the first sort of longer and more European novel that I ever read, and I remember reading it in like five days. It's a long book, and I'm a slow reader, but I just did nothing else'; *Fear and Loathing in Las Vegas* – 'this was given to me on my fifteenth birthday by a friend, and I just thought it was the funniest thing I ever read and kind of amazing and captured the period of time brilliantly'; *The Master and Margarita* – 'my favourite, favourite book in the world ever by Mikhail. To me it's the greatest exploration of the human imagination, and it's about forgiveness and life and history, and it's just the most incredible book that I've ever read; I read it once and then I read it almost immediately again'; *Harry Potter and the Philosopher's Stone* – 'I think it's fair to say that, if we're talking about the five books that have most influenced my life, I think it would be pretty churlish of me not to say *Harry Potter and the Philosopher's Stone*, for giving me everything that I have and everything that I will have.' Daniel said that a song by the band The Divine Comedy called 'The Booklovers', which lists many literary icons, was also an influence. 'I took it upon myself to try to read at least one book by every author on that list. I have done about twenty of them.'

Collecting books aside, Daniel is happy to admit he is not the world's biggest spender on a day-to-day basis. In an interview with *The Guardian*, he said, 'Anyone who is my friend knows that I don't spend money. So they can hang around with me as much as they like and they still ain't going to get anything. Ha ha! They barely even get a birthday gift – if they're lucky.' He gets as big a kick out of spending £7 on a purchase as spending more phenomenal amounts. He rarely goes on holiday and his trips abroad are normally accompanied by a gruelling time on a film set or a tortuous round of publicity interviews. 'I don't particularly like taking breaks,' he admitted. 'I've never taken a break.'

Daniel once said he would never know just how much he is

worth and neither would he ever defend the wealth acting had brought him. 'I have no idea how much money I've got. Do I deserve it? Fuck no! No actor does. But at the same time, you wouldn't turn it down, would you? Stinking rich, yes, that's the one. It doesn't matter what you do, no matter what line of work you're in, you can never really deserve that amount of money. It just so happens I'm in an industry where those sums of money are dealt with. And I'm very lucky to be in a position where I don't have to do a job just for the money.' Financial security gave him a lot of freedom as an actor, he said, and he could afford to be selective in what he did, especially as he got older. 'I'm in an unusual position for a twenty-three-year-old to be able to have a say in what I do – that's the sort of luxury money can't buy. Well, actually money does buy it. That's not really true…'

But the money certainly affords him a lifestyle alien to others his age. He is able to buy clothes from prestigious American company Brooks Brothers whose average suit costs around £2,000, Grenson shoes (around £200 a pair) by the established Northamptonshire firm of William Green (he gave them good publicity when he sported a pair of their Bert Cap Toe Oxford shoes (around £350) at the premiere of *Woman in Black* in 2012) and the top end of the top range of Ray-Ban sunglasses (the £150 classic 3016 design is one of his favourites).

Behind the scenes, Daniel devotes time and money to charity and there are many organisations and causes he supports including Book Aid International, which provides books for schools in Africa. In February 2006, Daniel paid £30,000 for a 'family tree' of Sirius Black at an auction for the charity. It had been donated by Jo Rowling. At the same event, Daniel also successfully bid £3,700 for a handwritten play, *Murder*, by Tom Stoppard and £980 for a humorous piece of writing by Iain Banks. In all, the event raised more than £63,000. Unable to attend the auction himself because of filming commitments, Daniel made the bids via his mother Marcia, who commented, 'This should put paid to anyone who says that Daniel doesn't like reading. He hasn't stopped since he read the first *Harry Potter* books and he loves Iain Banks and Tom Stoppard.'

Daniel also supports the Lupus Foundation of America (a 'Green Room Book' he autographed raised £18,000 at auction), Save the Children and the UN. His favourite charity is Demelza House, a children's hospice in Sittingbourne, Kent, for whom he once designed a 'Magic Chair' that could be transformed into different items. It was sold through Habitat with proceeds going to Demelza House. Daniel was proud of his design, saying, 'Why have one toy when you can have many? That's what I figured anyway. And it was that thought process which led to the birth of my cu-bed; a very important product which can magically be twisted and reshaped into many different forms … A den one day, a bed or a barricade the next.'

There is also the Get Connected helpline for young people under twenty-five in the UK who have problems but do not know where to get help. Daniel confirmed his support for the group in 2009 and also made a generous donation. 'I am delighted to pledge my support for Get Connected, and mark their tenth anniversary by becoming their first Best Friend,' he said. 'The free confidential helpline finding young people help for any problem is a vital and unique service. We live in a world that is so full of choice and information; it is often impossible to know where to turn or what to do.'

Fiona Clark, interim chief executive of Get Connected, praised Daniel for his 'big-hearted commitment' and added: 'We feel extremely privileged that Daniel Radcliffe has chosen to support Get Connected and help us launch our new Friends scheme in such an exciting way. His generous contribution will assist us immensely as we work towards raising greater awareness among young people and expanding our services to be available for young people whenever they need help.'

Since 2009, he has supported The Trevor Project in America, which works in a similar way to the UK's Samaritans, providing a helpline for sexual minorities with suicidal tendencies. 'My work with The Trevor Project has taught me that the best thing I can do as a straight ally is show my support of lesbian, gay, bisexual and transgender people. When we let someone know that we accept them for who they are and that we are safe to talk to, we can help save lives. It's as simple as that,' he said. Daniel's patronage of the charity was recognised when he was honoured with a Trevor Hero award. Receiving it, he said, 'I have always hated anybody who is not tolerant of gay men or lesbians or bisexuals. Now I am in the very fortunate position where I can actually help or do something about it.'

On another occasion, Daniel made a more heartfelt statement following the suicides of five gay teenagers in America. It was 'heart-breaking' he said. 'These young people were bullied and tormented by people who should have been their friends. We have a responsibility to be better to each other, and accept each other's differences regardless of sexual orientation, gender identity, race, ability or religion and stand up for someone when they're bullied. When a friend is feeling depressed or says they're thinking of killing themselves, we must take it seriously and get them help. My deepest sympathies go out to the families and friends of these excellent young people. And to all the young people who are being bullied right now, you are not alone.'

He also gives support to the Luke Neuhedel Foundation, which works to improve the quality of life for children suffering from cancer and their families. The American charity was set up by the parents of Luke Neuhedel who died from cancer in 2002. Daniel signed a copy of the charity's book, *Loving Luke*, and it raised nearly £1,000.

Together with celebrities such as Lady Gaga, Daniel has made generous contributions to charities which give help to children and families going through difficult times. He also participated in a video called 'Mind Reading: the Interactive Guide to Emotion' in 2002 to help autistic children develop facial and vocal expressions dealing with emotions.

In February 2005, Daniel took part in raising funds for tsunami victims. He donated a Hogwarts T-shirt that was unique to cast and crew involved with *Harry Potter and the Philosopher's Stone* at a Tsunami Celebrity Clothes Auction to raise cash for the Rebuilding Sri Lanka organisation. The shirt was sold for £520. Along with other cast members he signed an American edition of *Harry Potter and The Goblet of Fire* for an auction in August 2005 in support of the establishment of Kamp Kiwanis, a facility for the disabled and underprivileged children. In March 2006, Daniel and other cast members signed a copy of *Harry Potter and the Goblet of Fire*, which was auctioned on eBay and raised £2,100 for the UK children's literature initiative the National Literacy Trust. For Daniel, using his wealth to help various charitable causes is what he finds most rewarding. 'It is the most valuable thing I do with my money. The only thing of real importance.'

It was some indication of Daniel's 'pulling power' when a staggering £24,000 was pledged in just five minutes when he appeared on BBC's *The One Show* on 14 November 2013. (Ten years earlier, a lock of his hair had been auctioned for Comic Relief 2003, at the height of his Harry Potter fame, and raised £751 on Red Nose Day.) The show was broadcast just two days before that year's Comic Relief event and hosts Matt Baker and Tess Daly asked viewers to pledge Comic Relief money for Daniel to make a confession he had never made before to fellow guest Oprah Winfrey. The confession was probably not half as dramatic as everyone would have wished. It was nothing to do with his sex life or anything controversial at all. Daniel 'confessed' to once deliberately overturning a canoe he was in with three friends, pretending at the time is was an accident. 'I've never admitted to that before,' he said. 'I then had to wait about half an hour to be rescued because I am a terrible swimmer. I've kept that secret for years.'

On 12 December 2013, Daniel was one of many celebrities to donate items for a Screen Actors Guild (SAG) auction in America, the proceeds going to the SAG Foundation's BookPALS, a programme that puts actors into classrooms so they can read to children, and Storyline Online, which attracts over two million global viewers each month. Daniel donated signed copies of *The Sorcerer's Stone* and *Deathly Hallows*, and a *Kill Your Darlings* poster also signed by Dane DeHaan.

Daniel supports many other charitable causes including Debate Mate, an international charity dedicated to 'improving social mobility', Great Ormond Street Hospital, Kids Wish

Network, Northampton Welfare Rights Advice Service, Only Make Believe, Save the Children, The Make A Difference Trust and UNICEF. Closer to home is the Holme Village Pre-School to which Daniel donated a Quidditch World Cup programme from *Harry Potter and the Goblet of Fire*, which raised £2,000, and a wand box used in the first Potter film, which raised £470 at a Fun Day on 16 July 2006 hosted by Potter co-star Warwick Davis. Another Quidditch programme signed by Daniel raised nearly £5,000 for the City of Joy charity.

Daniel shrugs off questions about money because, having worked since he was ten, his wealth is simply an accumulation of his continued career – an incredibly starry one, however – from then until the present day. He doesn't understand why people feel he is in such a comfortable financial position that he need never work again and has summed it all up by saying, 'I don't know how to do anything else.' He is also fully aware that it could all end any time and that fame – and fortune – can be fickle friends. 'You have to keep a sense of reality about what's important and never let fame be part of your identity. Fame won't be around at this level for ever, so the moment it goes you'll suddenly realise that you don't know who you are. I'm proud that I think I know who I am and what I come down to as a human being because I don't see myself as a famous person.'

He has said of his large bank account: 'Money is a wonderful thing because it gives you room to manoeuvre and breathing space to choose whatever you like professionally, but, yeah … I'm very lucky … yeah. It's embarrassing to talk about. It's embarrassing that it would have some impact on the way people see me. That is not something I enjoy.'

Scottish director and actor Peter Mullan who worked with Daniel on *Deathly Hallows* described him as 'the sweetest, nicest multimillionaire I've ever met. He's a total sweetheart and lovely in every sense of the word. Utterly genuine. Nothing is put on. I was impressed.'

Does he ever wish he had less money? 'Only because it would come up less. Most people in life would agree money is a topic that is not appropriate to bring up. You'd never ask anybody else how much they make, but because I am in a position where you are "filthy rich" from a young age, it becomes a curiosity. I'd hate for someone to make assumptions on me based on what my bank balance is. I'm sure some people do.'

In December 2013, it was reported that Daniel could look forward to an extra celebratory Christmas – his company had made a £6m profit, with Gilmore Jacobs boasting assets, including his Harry Potter earnings, of £54,079,238. Ready cash in the bank was rumoured to be over £9m – an increase of more than £5m on the previous year. It got better. In the 2014 *Sunday Times* Rich List published in May 2014, Daniel was said to be worth £66m, around £6m up on the previous year. His latter stage appearances were mainly behind the increase.

Rich List editor Ian Coxon said: 'It's a small amount in comparison with films but he will get paid quite well because he's big box office and he's been wowing the critics.' It is a wowing that currently makes Daniel, number ten in the list, the wealthiest young actor – with his friendly 'rival' *Twilight* star Robert Pattinson netting £60m from *his* mega film franchise. Fellow Potter stars Emma Watson and Rupert Grint were said to have fortunes of £30m and £25m, respectively. Coxon's forecast for Daniel was certainly hugely optimistic: 'I would personally put money on him being the outstanding talent of the next ten years in terms of British entertainment in stage and film. I just think he's got it. He seems to me to be a consummate actor, able to turn his hand to a lot of different roles and he's quickly established himself as a big name above and beyond Harry Potter. He's obviously an exceptional actor because he's equally at home onstage and on the big screen. He can go from strength to strength.'

But, as has been noted, Daniel's best response to being asked why he isn't a 'fucked-up egomaniac', despite becoming famous at eleven, a multimillionaire by the time he was nineteen and worth such a staggering amount before reaching twenty-five, is: 'I had really good parents. And I got lucky and I loved it.'

CHAPTER 10
DANIEL DIVERSIFIES

High-kicking, singing and dancing, despite being dwarfed by his 6ft 4in co-star, Daniel was thoroughly enjoying his first-ever musical. He was back on Broadway and loving it. But this time it would not all end on a high note.

Daniel had undertaken many dance sessions for the energetic role in the stage revival of *How to Succeed in Business Without Really Trying*. He had worked in one-to-one sessions with former dancer Spencer Soloman in London for many months before his arrival in America. (Soloman was later to become Daniel's personal assistant and with the approval of Daniel's parents shared his New York apartment to keep an eye on him. He also planned Daniel's schedule, dealt with agents and publicists, and even informed Daniel when it was time for a shave.) It was no wonder he impressed observers during rehearsals, with one saying, 'In each run-through he threw himself into every kick, pivot and strut, and with some assistance, flipped from a boardroom table into the arms of waiting cast mates.'

A source close to the production was quoted on how Daniel had worked hard on getting in shape. 'Daniel wants to completely resculpt his body and has taken Cristiano Ronaldo as his inspiration. He envies his muscle definition and is hoping to get a similar six-pack for himself. Daniel is taking his fitness regime really seriously. He's stopped drinking, knocked the fags on the head and is watching every mouthful. He put on a little timber last year and is keen to get down to a more svelte shape. He's already lost nearly a stone in the past month.'

The work-outs no doubt helped counter the effects of Daniel's love of an 'unbelievable' macaroni cheese with bacon dish from a New York oyster bar and fish shack called Ditch Plains.

Daniel also had to perfect his American accent. It was to be another courageous choice and a vastly different project from previous ones. He knew he had a hard act to follow in a show described as having an 'impeccable pedigree' after its successful Broadway runs in the sixties and in 1995. *How to Succeed in Business Without Really Trying* had also come out on the big screen in 1967. It was, critics emphasised this time around, a musical that rested on the shoulders of its young male lead. And that was to be Daniel.

He had been approached in September 2008 during preview performances of *Equus*. Producers Neil Meron and Craig Zadan went backstage to meet him. Daniel recalled: 'They were very complimentary and they said to me, "So you can sing?" For a moment I paused and wondered what they were talking about, then I realised that in *Equus* I have to sing the Milky

Bar theme. But I wasn't aware that this was a qualification to do a Broadway musical …' Daniel was left a bit bemused but a couple of days later he was receiving emails from Meron and Zadan saying they really wanted him to be in a show – although it was only after meetings with Daniel and his agent that they actually came up with which show that would be.

It would be the first time Daniel would sing professionally. Before that he'd been a self-confessed karaoke addict. 'I'm one of those people who say, "No, No, No, I can't, I possibly couldn't", and then I'm elbowing people out of the way to get onstage.'

Ever the glutton for punishment, Daniel had barely had time to breathe between projects. He had finished the last Potter film in July 2010 and it was two months before he started filming *The Woman in Black*. At one point, both projects ran parallel. 'It was kind of weird,' he explained, 'because I was rehearsing nine hours a week dance rehearsal, six hours a week singing rehearsal for this fun, joyous musical and at the same time I was preparing for the demoralised, devastated, introspective, detached character, so it was kind of a weird balance. But it was one of those moments as an actor you just kind of have to celebrate the situation you are in because having two such different exciting jobs to juggle at the same time is a blessing.'

Daniel would be following in the footsteps of Robert Morse in the original productions, and Matthew Broderick in the latter production, as J Pierrepont Finch, a young window cleaner with big ambitions to become an advertising mogul who ends up as chairman of the board at the World Wide Wicket Company. Daniel's co-star was the lanky 6ft 4in John Larroquette as his boss J B Biggley. He was delighted to be working with Daniel, he said. 'I couldn't ask for a better partner and a leader … he's a workaholic like I am and he sets the bar for discipline and we try to follow that lead.'

On Daniel's part, as ever, he just wanted to keep each performance fresh. 'It's all very well doing it for a couple of months, but then the middle of the year comes and everyone who was really excited about the show has already seen it. But there is always someone out there for whom this is their first Broadway show … and I may never get the chance to dance like that again.'

The point was made that twenty-one-year-old Daniel was taking on a role that had previously been played by actors in their thirties, but director and choreographer Rob Ashford said his youthfulness gave a different slant to the character: this time, instead of fully understanding ambition, he would be naive about it: 'Dan brings his own youthful energy to Finch. Like Dan himself, his Finch doesn't sit back and contemplate. He dives into a problem and solves it. Dan is at once innocent and fiercely intelligent. He could not be a better fit for Finch. He's the type of guy who would leap off a cliff and figure out how he's going to land halfway down.' Dan also threw himself into rigorous training for the role with 'determination and fearlessness'.

The musical had Daniel tap-dancing in a whole new round of interviews too. One of the most bizarre was on Susan Blackwell's *Side by Side* show in which she got Daniel washing windows, sorting laundry and cleaning the toilet at her apartment in between firing questions at him. The show ended with the two of them sitting next to each other on the floor of Blackwell's shower and her licking his cheek. Daniel looked relaxed through it all, but generally it was a stressful time. He was onstage every night in what would be a nine-month run and there were days when long stints of singing combined with equally long stints of answering endless questions affected his voice. But he was determined not to miss a single performance. He sweated so much during each performance that he warned the first two front rows of the audience they would get wet as he did handstands, knee-slides and danced until his hair was plastered on his head. At one point he did a Jackie Chan-style kick-up, springing from a lying position. 'It's about training yourself to be able to learn choreography, step by step,' Daniel said. 'Once you put the hours in, it's just about learning and learning and repetition and repetition until you pick it up.'

Just as in *Equus*, there were eight shows a week – but, while the part of Alan Strang had been emotionally draining, this one called for high degrees of stamina – and often a breakfast comprising lots of maple syrup. Daniel was full of aches and pains and had lost around half a stone in weight. 'When I started it was a shock to the system. But I have so far had a perfect stage record and I want to keep that. Stuff like that is very important to me.'

To help relax from the high that always accompanies an actor ending a performance, Daniel would tune into American football when he came offstage. It made him something of an expert on the sport. 'I probably know every starting player's name in the league. Actually, I don't know why I'm being modest, I definitely know every starting player.' He also recorded episodes of the quiz show *Jeopardy!* that he watched before finally retiring for the night. On one rare evening out with the rest of the cast, Daniel got to have a go at his beloved karaoke singing Elvis Presley's 'Hound Dog' and 'Feeling Good' by Muse. 'That was my proudest moment because I actually did that rather well.'

How to Succeed in Business opened its preview performances at New York's Al Hirschfeld Theatre on 26 February 2011 with the official opening on 27 March. Daniel, who had to sport slicked-back hair, a check jacket and blue bow tie in his role, was again determined to keep the show 'fresh every single night' to prove himself. 'I know a lot of people thought it was a slightly confusing choice for me to make but I like that,' he said. 'If you're enthusiastic enough about stuff – even if you're not good at it – your enthusiasm will get you to the point where people allow you to do it enough so that you become good at it.'

Crowds outside the theatre that first night greeted him and the *New York Post* described how, despite obviously being exhausted, he handled it all with his usual friendliness. 'He cheerfully poses for pictures, signs posters and indulges questions. "Are you going to get a Tony?" – "I don't think so, but thank you for your optimism." "Why are you so cool and not an arsehole like so many actors?" – "Uh, a lot of actors are pretty cool. But there are some arseholes." "Will you sign my tie?" – "Of course." He signs his last autograph, then hops into a giant black Denali and speeds off. A grown woman who just missed getting his signature nearly breaks into tears.'

Some were not so effusive, with *The Guardian*'s Leo Benedictine saying that 'no matter how expertly he flaps around and gasps for breath, Radcliffe on Broadway remains a fish out of water'. This was a great disappointment to Ashford, who before the opening had gushed: 'I'm excited. I'm excited for the audience, for everyone.'

In the *LA Times*, Charles McNulty said: 'He [Daniel] gets an A for effort but he doesn't have the theatrical stature to pull together this choppy production.'

Ben Brantley of the *New York Times* only rated Daniel a six out of ten, adding: 'He conscientiously hits his choreographic marks, speaks his lines quickly and distinctly (with a convincing American accent) and often sings on key … You truly want him to succeed, just as you hope a favourite athlete or hip-hop artist will avoid elimination on *Dancing With the Stars*. But you don't particularly want his character in the show to succeed, and that really is a problem.'

The mixed reviews continued, with Scott Brown of *New York Magazine* making a cynical reference to the role for which Daniel had become most famous: 'Radcliffe has often struck the ungenerous mind – mine, I mean – as a nice, lucky kid who was in the right place at the right time. He was the boy who looked like Harry Potter, therefore Hollywood made him Harry Potter … Radcliffe, *Equus* aside, has always given off a just-happy-to-be-here vibe. He still does, and it might be his greatest asset here.'

The *Chicago Tribune*'s Chris Jones added: 'He doesn't have to play the role like a Broadway wise guy. He can play him as a risk-taking, flying-by-the-seat-of-his-pants kid. That feels like a pretty apt description of Radcliffe himself in his first Broadway musical.'

Other critics said Daniel was 'out of his league', was 'not animated enough to make Finch soar' and that his singing was not up to scratch.

The criticism, had it reached Daniel's ears, would have hurt him greatly after all he had put into *How To Succeed in Business*. He said, 'The wonderful thing about my job is that it makes me do things I would never do otherwise. One time I said, "You will never get me to dance; that won't happen. But then I had dance lessons for three hours each weekend when I wasn't doing Harry Potter and then upped it to nine hours. Then there were three hours a week of singing lessons. It would be nice to think that if you put enough work in something happens. I don't brag about stuff but me being such an uncoordinated mess and so scared I felt it was one of my proudest achievements.' He always had a fear of failure, he said, together with 'a fear of mediocrity and not meeting the goals that I have set myself. There is the fear of falling in my mission.' He added, 'The thing is, in a few years' time I'll be twenty-one, twenty-two and that's when all the guys who've been at drama school will come out. They've been learning dance or singing and all that stuff, and I'm going to need to compete with them because I won't have Harry Potter as my safety net anymore.'

Worse was to come. Daniel caused a furore among the executives of Warner Bros. when he said he would take to the stage in *How To Succeed in Business* rather than attend the London premiere of his final Potter film, *Harry Potter and the Deathly Hallows: Part 2*, on 7 July. He was not allowed to be released from his New York contract and it ended with a furious Warners having to pay the show's production company more than £300,000 to cancel performances of the musical – literally buying out the entire theatre for five nights – so that their star would be where they wanted him to be. His priority, they said, was to promote Harry Potter and not be on the Broadway stage.

The negotiations were said to be 'bitter'. One source said: 'This is the final film so it's a big deal. A grand world premiere is being planned as well as a US premiere and a press tour. They absolutely couldn't do it without their big star.'

Warner played down the drama, with a spokesman saying: 'Everything is fine. Dan is promoting the film and is happy to do so. With all productions there are scheduling issues, but everything has all been worked out. Warner Bros. is very supportive of Dan, and there is no issue.'

The premiere of the last ever Harry Potter film was indeed a big deal. Some fans travelled more than five thousand miles to catch a glimpse of Daniel, even sleeping out nights before. Above all, Daniel was there on the red carpet. It had cost him dearly in more ways than one. He made a speech to the waiting crowd: 'I don't think the end of the story happens tonight because – don't get too excited; it's not what you think – because each and every person, not only in the Square but also watching around the world, who will see this film and have followed these films for the last ten years will carry this story with them for the rest of their lives, and it will affect what they do. So, I would just like to say a huge thank you to all of you for giving me a job; and Jo, for letting him [David Heyman] give me a job. It's been the most amazing, inspirational, surreal, bizarre, wonderful ten years that I will probably ever have in all my life. Every opportunity I get from now on all comes back to the fact that I got very, very lucky when I was aged eleven.'

Daniel returned to Broadway shortly after to complete the run of *How To Succeed in Business*.

There were two major publicity appearances at the end of that year. In November, via a large screen, he appeared in front of around a thousand delighted aspiring journalists at the 2011 Fall Journalism Education Association to talk about his life and to answer questions. The second long interview was when he appeared in *An Evening With Daniel Radcliffe* on 5 December 2011 organised by the New York branch of the British Academy of Film and Television Arts (BAFTA) to commemorate what it described as 'the end of his Potter era'. The interviewer was acclaimed Hollywood reporter Scott Feinberg. The evening started with a roundup of Daniel's films before he once again retold his life story. Slightly under the weather with a cold, Daniel nevertheless kept his audience enthralled. He told how important it was to have Jo Rowling's endorsement of the Potter role – 'I have always felt a duty to her' – and how the boy wizard had simply become part of his day-to-day life – 'You don't sit back and see what an expansive global phenomenon it was. It was always very exciting. People expect I would have a special take on it but my experience is a very personal one.'

These were just two of the many public appearances he made. Earlier in the year, on 8 May, Daniel had given a talk at the Jewish YMCA. Among the audience of hundreds of teenage girls were his mother and grandmother, who was celebrating her eighty-ninth birthday. One public appearance Daniel had decided against was popping along to a Harry Potter exhibition in Times Square. Even though it was just a few blocks away from where he was starring in *How to Succeed in Business*, Daniel didn't think it was a good idea, saying, 'My friends made a bet with me to see how long I could go in and stay in there without people noticing me. I think it would be crazy for me to go.'

But Daniel's time in New York *did* give him the opportunity to catch up on some of his favourite musicals including *Gypsy*, *A Chorus Line*, *South Pacific* and Robert Ashford's *Promises, Promises* (which he attended with his parents and described as 'joyous').

In December 2011, Daniel was voted Entertainer of the Year by *Entertainment Weekly* magazine, beating the likes of Lady Gaga and British singer Adele. Editor Jess Cagle said: 'Ultimately, there was one person who made the most sense. Daniel is the nicest guy with one of the brightest futures in Hollywood. There's nothing he can't do. He's really interested in doing the work. Despite all his wealth and fame as a teenager he never derailed. He was never busted. Never went outside without his panties on.'

That same month, he made another appearance at the Gypsy of the Year competition, which raised another record-breaking amount. At one point, Daniel became an auctioneer, selling off the bow tie he had worn the night before onstage and raising £2,500.

Daniel made his last appearance in *How to Succeed in Business* on 2 January 2012, and his role was taken over by *Glee* star Darren Criss. The role won Daniel several awards including the Broadway.com Star of the Year. The show also won Audience Choice Award for Favourite Musical Revival and earned a handful of nominations. Daniel was nominated for a Tony Award for Outstanding Actor in a Musical, but it was his co-star John Larroquette who took the prizes, winning a Tony and a Drama Desk Award for Best Performance by a

Featured Actor in a Musical, as well as a Theatre World Award. There was comment that Daniel was a 'surprise snub' for the award but he was sanguine about it all. 'Everyone kept asking if I was OK. It was like I'd lost a fucking relative. In America, people are more openly in pursuit of awards. As lovely as awards are, I won't get caught up in it.' There was talk of the musical being turned into a film, but, said Daniel, 'The producers of the show would not be doing their jobs properly if they were not talking about the possibility of a movie.' And Daniel had other projects to focus on.

On 14 January 2012, Daniel faced one of his toughest challenges when he hosted the cult comedy American show *Saturday Night Live* and took part in several sketches. It was all a bit hit and miss, despite Daniel giving it his all, with rather lightweight, at times lacklustre, scripts. Wearing a grey suit, checked shirt and mauve tie, he opened the show with a monologue containing references to Harry Potter (who had been impersonated on the show several times, including by Hugh Jackman). At first, Daniel seemed to be making a serious statement about the film series – 'the incredible thing about the Harry Potter franchise is how it touched fans of all ages across the world. To the children I want to say that your enthusiasm is the magic.' Then he added: 'For the adults who have devoured the *Harry Potter* books I want to say they are for children…'

Critic Erik Voss commented: 'Radcliffe didn't waste any time addressing his reputation as the boy wizard and *SNL*'s history parodying the character. He then tossed a few friendly disses at the writers for their tendency to do obligatory topical pieces, worried about possible sketches of Dumbledore working in a Harry Pottery Barn or Jersey Shore: Hogwarts (complete with a lightning bolt tattoo on the Situation's abs). But for me, the monologue is all host – and I found Radcliffe to be a little stiff and very soft-spoken most of the night, undercutting several jokes.'

Daniel appeared in a number of sketches that, through no fault of his own, were just not that funny. He played an assistant with a long ponytail in a Target supermarket who was trying to 'bulk up' to impress the lady cashier. He ripped open his shirt at one point and was also the object of attention from the male manager. There was the 'Spin the Bottle' sketch, in which he had to kiss hobos, and a bizarre 'You Can Do Anything', in which Daniel played a character called Brad who was into Irish dancing and Chinese calligraphy. There was of course the obligatory Harry Potter skit, which saw him still at Hogwarts in the year 2020 – 'Did someone mention legend?' This did not win a favourable response either. In his round-up critique of the whole *SNL* show on about.com – Comedians, Patrick Bromley wrote: 'I don't know how much of my disappointment in this sketch came from the fact that the monologue had already taken the air out of it and how much was the sketch itself. While the sight of Daniel Radcliffe in his flannel shirt made me chuckle, the rest of the sketch was mostly just name-checking characters and references from the Harry Potter universe. Like in every sketch of the night, Radcliffe was enjoyable to watch even if he wasn't terribly funny, but much of what was surrounding him felt like it was going through the motions.' He added: 'I don't think that anyone could have imagined back when Daniel Radcliffe was plucked from obscurity to play boy wizard Harry Potter that he would one day be a grown, hairy man hosting *Saturday Night Live*. And, yet, here he was: grown, hairy, British, incredibly nice and sincere and happy to be there … Radcliffe managed to be the thing that came off the best. He was rarely funny, but he committed one hundred per cent to everything he was in.'

A promotional video for *Saturday Night Live* had comedian Jason Sudeikis pretending he didn't remember what films the perplexed Daniel had been in – 'I forget what they are called' – while guest singer Lana Del Rey was lambasted for poor performances of two songs. It was all a bit of a damp squib for Daniel's first go at a live comedy programme, and the reviews reflected this. In *The Houston Chronicle*, Therese Odell wrote: 'Poor Daniel Radcliffe. He did everything right: great comic timing; cheerful, almost giddy participation; and unlike Sir Charles [*SNL*'s Charles Barkley] he can actually read a cue card. And yet, the episode was dreadful – one of the worst so far this season. Radcliffe was obviously the victim of some terrible writing.'

Mike Ryan in the *Huffington Post* said he'd had high hopes for Daniel but had been disappointed. 'Oh, Daniel Radcliffe has so much stage experience, plus he's just so charming – this week will be great! It was not meant to be. I mean, there were a lot of "OK" sketches last night, but not a lot of moments that stand out. Which is a shame.'

Another critic commented on how Daniel was stranded with unfunny material and costumes 'that smacked of desperation'.

Daniel himself had had a great time. 'I'm somebody who just thrives on fear and panic and chaos,' he said, 'so for me that's just the perfect environment. I liked the fact that somebody said, "OK, there's been a slight change. Just look at the cards." Love that. Those are situations I kind of live for. It was interesting that people didn't think it was the strongest episode, but I had a blast. It's interesting. I tried and therefore people shouldn't criticise.' He said he had also loved the quick-fire costume changes and the general pace of the hour-and-a-half music and comedy show. Daniel also defended Lana Del Rey against the critics. 'It was unfortunate that people seemed to turn on her so quickly.'

It was also unfortunate that Daniel was not given a proper vehicle for the brilliant, self-effacing and cynical sense of humour he has. For, as well as an oddball video he did about American film producer and comedian Judd Apatow, Daniel made another in which he is in his dressing room with an assistant, Jake, who is there just to keep him grounded: 'I am Daniel Radcliffe and, at the age of eleven, I was part of the most phenomenally successful franchise of all time,' declares Daniel, who, while admitting he can't dance like Jake, juggle balls or do handstands, says he does 'have some of the greatest actors on speed dial'. In another scene Daniel says he needs to thank all his fans, goes to a closed window and says 'thank you' several times.

There were to be other spoof films too. In one made for T4, Daniel gives tips on how to create certain expressions as part of publicity for his horror film *The Woman in Black* – 'a film so pant-wettingly terrifying that the price of your ticket should cover the cost of new underwear'. To look 'possessed', he screws up his face to show 'you have become deranged and lost all your basic motor skills'. Looking 'scared' involves 'screwing up your facial features in the middle', and looking 'crazed' means 'doing a bad impression of Jack Nicholson in *The Shining*'. Daniel is also put up to wearing a gas mask and jumping out and terrifying presenter Matt Edmondson as he speaks to camera. The two end up wrestling to the ground with an obviously rattled Edmondson declaring, 'I nearly killed Daniel Radcliffe!' and Daniel apologising.

The obsession with continuing to work, combined with the obligatory rounds of publicity and interviews, sometimes takes its toll. In mid-2012, Daniel had to cancel some press interviews – a rarity for him. He was suffering from cluster headaches – 'which make migraine look quite tame' – and was taking twelve strong painkillers every day just to make it through. They had little effect and he was eventually forced to see a doctor and be treated with a series of injections. Ever stalwart, Daniel said it all made him feel a bit of a 'wuss', but as ever he fought back.

* * *

Daniel sank to his knees and took a bite out of the actor's outstretched hand. It was a spontaneous action and proved that he could improvise when the moment called for it! Daniel was appearing in *A Young Doctor's Notebook* for the Playhouse Presents strand of Sky Arts in 2012. The TV series was based on a collection of short stories by Mikhail Bulgakov with whom Daniel was already acquainted. Reading another of the author's books, *The Master and Margarita*, had inspired Daniel to visit the author's apartment in Russia.

A Young Doctor's Notebook is set at the time of the Russian Revolution and Daniel, now aged twenty-four, plays the part of a young doctor who leaves Moscow for a remote town where his abilities are challenged. He is also addicted to morphine. Daniel's older self – who often appeared in the same scenes – was played by *Mad Men* actor Jon Hamm. It was Hamm who, having been given a copy of the book to read through, decided Daniel would be perfect for the part. 'I love Dan,' said Hamm. 'I think he is a phenomenally talented actor … He is a wonderful comic actor. He can do that thing of talking when there is nobody there, and it is just hilarious.'

For his part, Daniel was looking forward to playing someone 'completely beyond redemption'. He also felt the series was one of the huge leaps he had made in his career and that he could now judge better what he was good and not good at. 'I owe everything to Potter but playing a character for so long gives you this pent-up energy and desire to try as many different things as possible.' Daniel's previous dancing experience was to come in handy as he had several dancing scenes with Hamm. Daniel said, 'I think the writers were like, "OK, what else can we throw at him?" It did become like a game to them to see what else they could chuck at me in the last minute, but it was fun.'

In an interview with *The Independent*, Daniel said that, in a role like this, one of his biggest drives was fear: 'It's very motivating. I don't want anyone ever to say, "You know, maybe somebody could do Dan's job better than him." In the past, they could legitimately say that at certain points. I haven't always been thrilled with my work. But the fear of not proving the people wrong who think you can't emerge from a franchise and do well, that's a very strong driving force.'

The Notebook stories are based on Bulgakov's own experiences as a young doctor, and on film produced some pretty graphic scenes including one in which Daniel as the doctor saws away at a young woman's leg and blood spurts out. As one reviewer commented: 'The horror of it, the horrible diseases, the weird growths, the bloody amputations, is described in such deadpan tones that at times it seems surreal.'

Daniel, who admitted to always having had 'a slightly overactive imagination' and despite the often surreal and gory content, agreed to the role pretty much straight away. 'The amputation was rough, you see me hacking away … That had to stay. It is pretty graphic in the book, and you can't do justice to it without that. By episode four, we were running out of blood.'

But there were some reservations from the writers, who wondered if he would be comfortable with the references to his character's height. But Daniel revelled in it, happily banging his head on low-hanging lights and letting Hamm pick him up or body-slam him. The hand-biting incident came in a scene when the young doctor was fighting with a pharmacist over a forged prescription for morphine. It just kind of happened, explained Daniel: 'It was like, what if I was in a situation like that and I really needed it. I'd bite the sucker.'

The quirky series was something of a surprise hit for Sky Arts, with the channel enjoying its best-ever viewing figures in its seven-year history. It attracted an average audience of 252,000 – beating the previous record held for another Playhouse Presents production featuring *Dr Who* star David Tennant earlier in the year – and won a cult following. The critics liked the somewhat surreal series too. In *The Observer*, Andrew Anthony wrote: 'to put it in popular … terms, Harry Potter grew up to become Don Draper. Yet strangely the combination worked, in no small part owing to the pair sharing the same scenes.' While

David Stubbs in *The Guardian* said both Hamm and Daniel were 'superb'.

A Young Doctor's Notebook ran on Sky Arts in December 2012 and a second series, forwarding to 1935, ran in November the following year, prompting one reviewer to comment: 'So strong was the appeal of seeing Daniel Radcliffe and Jon Hamm – Harry Potter and Don Draper – together that Sky Arts just had to bring back the Playhouse Presents special for another outing … Dark, but also delightful, *A Young Doctor's Notebook* is a unique telly treat that shines even brighter with its added star power. There's just four episodes, so don't miss them!'

Daniel's growing confidence allowed him to talk down the idea of another nude scene when the second series came around – one specially written in for this production. But he had just finished a year of three films in which, in his own words, he had 'got naked' and he wanted to divorce himself from what seemed to be becoming a habit. 'I'd already done nude scenes in the first season, in the bath and a couple of other moments, but there was this one scene in the second season where somebody breaks into my bedroom at night and starts intimidating me. At one point, they were trying to make the young doctor more vulnerable, and they said, "Would you do it naked?"'

Initially, Daniel agreed but then had second thoughts. 'I said, "Guys, if it's not key to the scene, I don't think I should." It was one of those moments where I felt I could say that. "Is it absolutely key for the young doctor in this scene?" I don't have a problem with it! I'm just not seeking it out. You don't want to be the guy who's known as an exhibitionist. I also thought people were going to start saying it's something Dan Radcliffe has written into his contract!'

In an article in *The Guardian* headlined 'Daniel Radcliffe: Nude no More', Ryan Gilbey took his own stance on Daniel taking his clothes off. 'The trouble is that Radcliffe's nudity has not yet had the desired effect on his wholesome image. A persona, after all, can be an awfully hard thing to kill off. When Julie Andrews exposed her breasts in the 1981 showbiz satire *SOB*, it amounted to a virtual assassination attempt on her *Sound of Music* image. But any hoped-for outrage simply refused to materialise.

'In withdrawing our peeping privileges, Radcliffe seems to have recognised that he risks being caught in a cleft stick: having gone too far in revealing himself without making the much-needed gains in credibility, he now has to relent before his nakedness becomes a running joke. It echoes the gag that Paul Kaye's spoof celebrity pest Dennis Pennis once threw at Demi Moore: if it wasn't gratuitous and it was tastefully done, might Radcliffe consider keeping his clothes on?'

Incidentally, Daniel admitted that, although he was probably 'the envy of every woman in the world' in the scene where he shared a bath with Hamm, 'the water soon turns cold'.

Daniel said it had been great working with Jon Hamm again, calling him a 'real gentleman' and adding, 'He is completely different to what people expect him to be. He may be a big strapping guy, but he's actually just a really funny nerd. He knows more about British comedy than any American I've met. I think he studied it when he was younger!'

The series was nominated in the 2014 Satellite Awards for Best Television Series, Comedy or Musical. Director Alex Hardcastle was nominated at the 2013 Shanghai International TV Festival for Best TV Film.

Daniel was just content that the series had worked. In fact, he was to declare that he was 'probably the happiest I've been in my life at the moment'. He was, he said, tired but happy. 'But then, if I wasn't tired what would the *Daily Mail* have to write about?'

CHAPTER 11

ANOTHER STAGE, ANOTHER SUCCESS

Leg dragging pitifully behind him, arm hanging uselessly by his side, Daniel was suffering the torment of being mocked by the girl he had fallen in love with. He was an object of ridicule and violence, an outcast living his life in isolation and tedium but having to put on a comical front. He was also playing another stage role that would win him great acclaim. But privately, Daniel was coming to terms with the loss of one of his closest and most revered friends.

During rehearsals for his latest project, *The Cripple of Inishmaan*, Daniel had attended the emotionally charged funeral of Richard Griffiths, the man who had taken him under his wing during Daniel's first stage performance and who had been so much a part of his life as Uncle Vernon Dursley in the Potter series. Daniel was among the three hundred mourners at Holy Trinity Church in Stratford-upon-Avon, Shakespeare's burial place and so fitting for sixty-five-year-old acclaimed Shakespearean actor Griffiths.

Daniel led the tributes, praising Griffiths for the 'encouragement, tutelage and humour' that made work 'a joy'. He recalled his very first scene as Harry Potter when Griffiths had made him feel so at ease and said: 'In fact, any room he walked into was made twice as funny and twice as clever just by his presence. I am proud to say I knew him. Richard was by my side for the two most important moments of my career.' Daniel was sometime later to tell how Griffiths also once advised him to never let the camera catch him when he wasn't thinking because the 'void would be read in his eyes'. The veteran actor told Daniel it was advice he had been given by gnarled actor Lee Marvin – who had been given it by Spencer Tracy. Daniel remarked: 'How many young people get access to *that* sort of advice and *that* sort of history?'

The Cripple of Inishmaan opened at the Noel Coward Theatre on 8 June 2013. Daniel's acting skills were again pushed to the limits with his having to present a character with not only a physical disability but an emotional one too. And there was the Irish accent to perfect – 'You don't want to go onstage sounding shit and I certainly did not want to go onstage and sound shit.'

There was to be a lot more nervous chain-smoking as Daniel rehearsed for this new and testing challenge. But by the very first rehearsal session he had learned every single one of his lines – a goal set by *Equus* director Thea Sharrock and one he reaches before any performance. Being that prepared made it less stressful, said Daniel. Even before he went onstage each night, he repeated his first line 'over and over' in his head, fearing that the rush of adrenalin he always felt would momentarily wash it away. The pressure was really on at the opening performance and his confidence and comfort in the role did not come easily initially. 'The first fifteen minutes of the first day I was just mumbling but at some point I just thought, "To hell with it, just go for it. I've got to commit to this", and it's been good ever since,' he remarked later.

The black comedy written by Martin McDonagh was first performed at the Royal National Theatre in 1996 and moved to New York two years later. This time, in conjunction with the Druid Theatre of Galway, it was another West End appearance for Daniel and was the third of five plays in the Michael Grandage Company's season 'aimed at reaching a new generation'. Director Grandage had sent Daniel four plays from the season for him to read through. *The Cripple of Inishmaan* was the one he chose. 'It was the one that stood out. It was so funny and smart. I don't think it's an overstatement to call it a modern masterpiece. As soon as I read it, I just knew I wanted to do it.' Daniel also admitted he looked forward to being 'stretched professionally'.

The Cripple of Inishmaan story is set in 1934 on the remote island of Inishmaan off the west coast of Ireland. Billy's life is empty until the arrival of a Hollywood film crew on the neighbouring island of Inishmore – something he desperately wants to be part of. They had come to film The Man of Aran – an event that had actually happened in the island's history. Though the theme appears bleak and there are scenes of violence, McDonagh's work is described as a 'comic masterpiece' and Daniel felt privileged to be asked to take part in a play penned by a writer hailed as one of today's most original Irish voices. He also had some identity with the role – the Hollywood dream, and being different from other kids, that his childhood fame as Harry Potter had catapulted him into. 'I definitely saw something that was very appealing to me,' he said. 'Because I'm short and slim, I can identify with somebody who's an unlikely fit for something and desperately wants to be part of it.'

The role of orphan Billy meant, yet again, a punishing schedule of preparation. A personal trainer was called in to ensure that the nightly onstage contortions demanded to portray a crippled young man would not have any lasting physical effects on 5ft 5in Daniel. He also consulted a voice coach suffering from cerebral palsy to fully understand how physical disability can affect someone's voice. It was Daniel's personal decision to choose the neurological condition as the reason for Billy's disability. He thought long and hard about it, coming to the conclusion that his character's useless arm and leg on the same side of his body conformed to cerebral palsy. 'I felt it was important to make his condition specific rather than attempting some generalised cripple thing,' he explained. 'To me that is kind of offensive to say, "Oh well, I'll just do something a bit weird" without looking into it at all. That's not doing justice to people who are disabled or to the character.'

Daniel's choice of voice coach was able to explain the mechanics of the condition to him, as well as teaching him how to walk and pick things up and move around as if he was heavily disabled on one side. It was, he said 'one of the odder skills I've had to learn. It has very few practical applications, besides doing a play.'

There was one time, however, when Daniel's independent rehearsal for the role left him squirming. He decided to get in part one night while walking to his corner shop. Thinking there was no one around, he put up his hood and shuffled along –

only to realise a mystified woman was walking behind him! He faced the dilemma of either carrying on his cripple's walk or reverting to normal. 'I waited for her to pass me but she went into the shop too! I had to wait for her to come out. That was my experience of preparing for the part.' But it was no wonder that Martin Grandage was later to comment that Daniel had done more research for the part than he had himself.

The specific local Irish accent came from sheer hard work – with a little influence from his Belfast-born father – including intently listening to recordings of Aran Islands' inhabitants. Daniel knew that if he didn't get this right no one would take his role as Billy seriously. He has admitted that he is paranoid about mastering accents but that luckily he is blessed with a good ear for them: 'I just kept thinking, "Well, even if you don't have it now, that accent is somewhere inside of you. It's going back a while but it's in there somewhere."'

His diligence won praise from Michael Grandage. 'Dan is a huge preparer … he has not got a mass of theatre credits yet he approaches the work as if he's been acting for twenty or thirty years … I was very aware I was talking to someone with a very good knowledge of themselves. This is quite rare – self-knowledge in actors – and it's a wonderful quality.'

Among the cast of *The Cripple of Inishmaan* were Padraic Delaney (who appeared in Ken Loach's 2006 Palme d'Or winner *The Wind That Shakes the Barley*), Gary Lilburn (of TV's *Mrs Brown's Boys* and *EastEnders*), Pat Shortt (winner of Best Actor Award for his part in the 2007 film *Garage*) and established film actor Conor MacNeill. Sarah Green was the village girl and object of Billy's unrequited love.

Daniel's character was the target of some violent tormenting and he had to take several choreographed falls. 'I've learned that I really enjoy stage violence!' he said. 'I was lucky enough to spend a lot of my lunchtimes as a child choreographing fight scenes on Potter. So I'm quite proud about it. The stunt department always said that I bounce.' At the end of the play Daniel's character gets blood on his face – a sight that, together with the fatigue of having just come offstage, waiting photographers outside took delight in. 'It stained a bit but I wasn't going to spend extra time removing it. I just wanted to go home. I know I look a mess when I come offstage but it does annoy me when you've just done a show and newspaper reports comment about my appearance. I am just pale and this is what my face looks like.'

For Daniel, this latest venture naturally brought with it renewed concern that he would not prove himself. Although by now well adapted to being onstage, he had to admit, 'It was tricky and horribly intimidating thinking everyone is going to think it is terrible.' He was aware he was still learning his craft, he told interviewers. As usual, there were press conferences on the *Inishmaan* publicity tour.

There was the expected Daniel Radcliffe/Harry Potter frenzy surrounding the opening of *The Cripple of Inishmaan*. Some of the audience even screamed at the close of the opening performance. Daniel shrugged it off. 'Hysteria is fine. It is always welcome. People might have come to see Harry Potter but ten minutes in they realised they were seeing a play too.' Daniel not only had to face a patient crowd of fans outside the theatre door every night, but he also had to run the gauntlet of paparazzi photographers who followed him home. 'It got a bit tiresome ... at least two or three nights a week they'd follow us and I'd be like, "I'm going home to bed! I've done a show. I'm not going anywhere.'" Another trick Daniel developed was to drive 'for miles' if he was being followed by photographers in a car. 'It would just take some time out of their day.'

Yet again, despite his fears of presenting another persona to his Harry Potter followers – 'There is still in many, many people's minds the notion that I'll never be able to escape Harry Potter' – Daniel won excellent reviews. He was praised for his 'gift in playing social outsiders' and for his 'melancholy intensity and resolve'.

Charles Spencer wrote in *The Telegraph*: 'Radcliffe brings a touching stoicism and simplicity to his performance as cripple Billy, all the more moving because it is so understated.' Spencer added that, unlike many child stars, Daniel had 'grown up gracefully'.

While critical of Daniel's attempts at an Irish accent, Paul Taylor in *The Independent* praised his 'honest, sensitive, unshowy performance ... Radcliffe comes across as the genuine article'.

Kate Bassett of the *Independent on Sunday* commented: 'The good news is that Radcliffe's acting has substantially improved since his merely proficient performance in *Equus* some years back. His Billy is quietly stalwart. The Irish accent is surprisingly OK, and the disabilities (involving a clenched hand and a stiff leg) aren't hammed up.'

The Guardian's Michael Billington said that, although Daniel was not the obvious first name for the part, 'He is the undoubted star ... [he] proves, as he did in *Equus*, that he is a fine stage actor with a gift for playing social outsiders.'

But the highest acclaim came from the *Sunday Telegraph*'s Tim Walker who described Daniel's performance as 'stupendous ... the finest piece of acting I have seen all year'.

Only a handful of critics gave a lukewarm review of the play, such as The Arts Desk's Veronica Lee who wrote: 'Although it's an ensemble piece, Radcliffe – not yet free of Harry Potter references despite his West End and Broadway successes, but he's getting there – is the marquee attraction here, yet turns in a lacklustre performance in a play brimful with deliberately showy characters.'

Daniel was named Best Leading Actor in a New Production of a Play – West End, in the 2013 Broadway World UK Awards. He was shortlisted for his role as Billy in the Best Actor category of the WhatsOnStage Awards to be announced in February 2014. He was up against some illustrious competition: in the same category was *Skyfall* actor Ben Whishaw for his part in *Mojo*, set in London gangland of the 1950s, and *Peter and Alice* (telling the story of those who inspired *Peter Pan* and *Alice in Wonderland*); James McAvoy for *Macbeth*; Lenny Henry for the African-American themed *Fences*; and Rory Kinnear for Iago in the National Theatre's production of *Othello*. Fellow Harry Potter star Rupert Grint (who had made his stage debut as Sweets in *Mojo*) was nominated as London Newcomer of the Year.

Perhaps in an intentional reference to his success in the horse-blinding play *Equus*, Daniel had said he wanted to prove 'I'm not a one-trick pony' and also, now aged twenty-three, he was 'too old to be running around in a school boy's cape' anyway. 'I am getting an impression that I'm starting to be seen as a young man, which is lovely. I thought that would take longer, to be honest, but it hasn't.'

The Cripple of Inishmaan finished its run on 31 August 2013. Daniel said he had found the whole experience amazing – but he was mentally and physically exhausted. It had been another long run in a generally frenetic working life. During the three-month run, he had celebrated his twenty-fourth birthday in July. Pictures taken as he left the theatre that night showed him looking gaunt and tired. It was only one occasion when observers noted how his determination to embark on a non-stop work schedule looked to be taking its toll. Daniel himself had admitted, 'I just didn't want to take an easy way out of this. I wanted to really try and take risks and make a career for myself.'

For once, Daniel admitted he felt like a rest and had arranged for three weeks off that October 'to bum around New York and see some shows'. It was one of the rare occasions he actually needed some proper downtime. But the self-confessed workaholic was not to be away from acting for long. Not long after playing a tortured soul of someone disabled onstage he now had to prepare to play a hunchback on the big screen. 'It was the most exciting script coming out of the big studios I have ever read,' he said of the role of Igor, servant to legendary figure Frankenstein.

CHAPTER 12

DARLING DAN

He had somehow survived the hysteria surrounding his full-frontal and simulated-sex stage appearance, had won over critics and audiences for his portrayal of an outcast, and *still* had millions of adoring fans for whom Harry Potter was now a part of life. In the midst of this was to come another Potter shocker. Our lovely boy wizard was to play homosexual poet Allen Ginsberg. And there would be a sex scene from an age when such acts were illegal: in one scene, Ginsberg loses his virginity to a man he picks up in a bar.

The film *Kill Your Darlings* saw twenty-four-year-old Daniel playing beat generation poet Ginsberg as a seventeen-year-old student at Columbia University. It was to make all the furore over *Equus* five or six years earlier seem pretty mild. Or, as one critic noted: 'Daniel is certainly going a long way to distance himself from Harry Potter.'

It was while appearing in the 2008 Broadway run of *Equus* that Daniel had auditioned and won the part of Ginsberg. But at one point it looked like his longed-for project would fall through. For he was committed to working on the last two Harry Potter films, which meant he could not be available for *Kill Your Darlings*, and an alternative actor, Jesse Eisenberg, was found. It was only when the film was postponed that director John Krokidas approached him again and he could finally get involved. Having made the decision, hot on the heels of *The Woman in Black*, Daniel was thrown straight away into another project, or in his words it was a case of 'kick bollocks; scramble'.

In the end, the film was completed in just twenty-four days, with Daniel getting through nine pages of script a day. It may have been demanding but he loved it. 'You've got no time to slow down … I wish all my films could be done at that pace.' He said the low budget for the film was an asset rather than a hindrance and commented, 'If we had shot this film on a bigger scale for $10 million over ten weeks, it wouldn't be as good a film. I used to get asked how much the film cost and John eventually came over to me and said, "Dan, can you stop telling people how much it cost because people will always expect me to make films for that amount of money," which is right. If you can do it quick and fast, they'll want it quick and cheap. I do think the chaotic way we shot it somehow correlated with the beat generation and bled through.'

The film focused on Ginsberg's infatuation with fellow 'beat' writer Lucien Carr (played by Dane DeHaan) who, together with the rest of the circle, including Jack Kerouac (Jack Huston) and William S Burroughs (Ben Foster), broke most of the boundaries that existed in New York in the late 1940s and early 1950s. Carr was later to murder fellow homosexual, David Kammerer, and dispose of his body in the Hudson River. Kerouac was arrested as an accessory.

Daniel scoured Ginsberg's diaries and read his works in preparation for the role. Krokidas commented: 'In his journals and inside his own head, Ginsberg believed he had much more to offer the world than people assumed. I thought that Daniel Radcliffe the person might identify with that.'

Daniel also tracked down some who had been around at the time, and to capture the mood of the time he did what he always does when preparing for a role and sought inspiration from music. On this occasion, he listened to songs by Jo Stafford, with two, in particular – 'You Belong to Me' and 'No Other Love' and their theme of unrequited love – setting his mood. 'Music has always been a huge part of my preparation. It is a very powerful and emotional thing,' he said. Krokidas said he and Daniel had 'borrowed' a method used by established actress Zoë Wanamaker, which was using music that was relevant to a scene to get into the character's mind.

Daniel had had to use an American accent before but now he had to put a different slant on it. 'Nailing Ginsberg's accent was a huge thing for me,' he said. 'I enjoyed learning how to speak in a New Jersey accent. On set, I just did it all the time. I listened to a lot of Allen Ginsberg at various stages of his life and Jersey accents of varying degrees on the Internet. I didn't want to go too far with this because Allen didn't have a terribly strong Jersey accent ... I'd talk in the accent and read a lot of his poems and diaries out loud by myself and with my dialect coach.'

Daniel also steeled himself for a homosexual kiss and other

intimacy between himself and DeHaan, scenes he said were surreal: 'But to be honest, there is no time to be awkward. We just had to get in and do it and that was probably for the best.'

DeHaan was also asked about the intimate scene. 'Everybody asks me what it's like to kiss Daniel Radcliffe! That kiss has been sensationalised in a really strange way. I'm an actor. I make-believe what is happening in the movie is actually happening in real life. So it wasn't me kissing Daniel Radcliffe, it was Lucien Carr finally kissing Allen Ginsberg, the person he's been wanting to kiss since they met. And that's a beautiful moment.'

There were absolutely no qualms about the whole gay thing for Daniel. To him, it was just another acting job and negative comments riled him. 'To me it's the acceptable face of homophobia. People say, "So how was your gay sex scene?" and you think, "Just call it a sex scene. There's only one, I won't confuse it with another one." But I'm not surprised. I had the same with *Equus*. If people can write a headline with the words "Harry Potter" and "naked" or "gay sex", they will. But hopefully people will want to see a film about the beat poets and not just a lurid sex scene they've been led to believe there is, when there isn't.'

Daniel spoke quite graphically to *Flaunt* magazine and referred to Krokidas being gay. 'I don't think there's any difference between how one falls in love. People express love differently, person to person, but it's not gender or sexuality related. The only difference it made was obviously the actual sex scene, of course … Basically, gay sex, especially for the first time, is really fucking painful according to John … he said he had never seen that portrayed accurately on film before. He wanted it to look like an authentic loss of virginity.' Ginsberg loses his virginity to a sailor after being picked up in a bar and Krokidas enlisted the help of his female director of photography, Reed Morano, to help. Daniel said, 'Reed got on to the bed. I think she played the man and they sort of showed me the position we were going to be in initially. That's the thing, it's a sex scene in the film, but the filming of it is very perfunctory: you do this, then you do this, and then you do this.'

Daniel recalled how the homophobia issue got out of hand when he was touring round the university where *Kill Your Darlings* was to be shot. 'We were looking round this room for locations and stuff and this guy rushed out to me and said, "Oh hi! I'm so-and-so from such-and-such", some fairly prestigious magazine. He was attending a conference there and asked me for a comment on homophobia, in Uganda, I think. I told him I didn't have one because that wasn't why I was there and that upstairs there was a room full of people gathered specifically to talk about that.' Daniel added that he couldn't understand why anyone would want his opinion because he wasn't informed enough to give it. 'Actors spouting their political views is fine if they want to talk about that stuff, but don't expect people to take your opinion seriously.' He said that everything that's wrong about being a celebrity was summed up in that encounter.

One of Daniel's favourite recollections about 'that' scene was when Krokidas was giving him step-by-step instructions for it and then stopped the two actors mid-embrace shouting, 'Not like that. Crazy sex kissing!' That was the moment, Daniel said, that after ten years in a kids' franchise he felt he was really moving on! And he defended the scenes against any criticism. 'John said he'd never really seen a very authentic loss-of-virginity scene for gay men on screen, and he wanted to get it right. So it's not necessarily a steamy scene, as it's being portrayed in some articles. It's about vulnerability as much as anything else, and the fear and excitement that goes along with your first time.'

Daniel put his faith in the director when it came to the much-talked-about scene. He said: 'I trusted John that it was going to be the vulnerable, slightly afraid, and sweet tender scene that we all wanted it to be. And it comes at such a great point in the film, as part of a really powerful montage sequence. So, no, I never doubted that it would be anything but what it needed to be in the film. It's explicit in terms of the emotions that are being dealt with, the fear and excitement of one's first time, so I think we definitely achieved our goal in that sense … I certainly knew going in that the naked same-sex love scene would attract attention because it's slightly salacious and it's an easy headline.'

And again Daniel faced the anxiety of bearing his body to an audience. 'I remember thinking at the time that I was in quite good nick. And then I saw the scene and thought, "Oh, Jesus, I look like a whippet." I was not in any way lean – but I guess it would have been inappropriate for Allen Ginsberg to look like he'd been going to the gym.'

This new role demanded a new look and Daniel wore brown contact lenses, sported a perm and his lips were outlined to make them a bit fuller like Ginsberg's. But there were comments about how his spectacles made him resemble an older version of Harry Potter.

Yet again, Daniel worked with a dialect coach. He enjoys the challenge of changing accents, which is just as well, as packing in several diverse projects each year means equally varied voice tuition. Of his need to diversify, Daniel has said, 'I've always said it's a long process and, in a way, it might be a lifelong one. It's about proving to people that I'm in this for the long haul and that I wasn't looking to get as famous as I could for as long as I could and ride that out.'

There was a lot of focus on the Jewishness of the film – especially from those who watched with a particularly interested eye. Daniel himself was born Daniel Jacob Radcliffe, and the *Jewish Journal* noted how proud Daniel was to be Jewish, that he had a Jewish humour book and loved Jewish jokes. In short, playing the gay Jewish Ginsberg was Daniel's 'first major Jewish role'.

The *Jewish Chronicle* reported how delighted John Krokidas had been when Daniel was able to tell him that his mother was Jewish, as he was concerned about a non-Jew playing Ginsberg. Daniel, who admitted he was not religious and was 'Jewish by race rather than faith', told the *Chronicle*: 'We've had plenty of non-Jewish actors play Jewish characters and vice versa. But I think John was aware that there was a certain part of the Jewish community in America that might baulk at the idea of me playing Allen Ginsberg. So I think he was relieved that I have Jewish blood and he could say, "No, no, no, he's Jewish!"'

But there were other rather more delicate concerns voiced by director John Krokidas. He had been intent on casting a Jewish actor for the role: a *real* Jewish actor. And there was only one way to find out if Daniel would bring realism to the naked scenes. Krokidas admitted he panicked when he realised the sharp-eyed would see straight away if Daniel was not totally in character. He recalled: 'I wondered how I was going to have him take his clothes off if he's uncircumcised. It is so mortifying but I actually texted Dan and he confirmed that he is indeed Jewish from the waist down.'

On a deeper level, Krokidas – who was directing his first feature film – said he had chosen Daniel for the role because he felt the young actor would have good insight into Ginsberg's relationship with his mother. He was right with Daniel telling the *Jewish Journal*: 'The mother was such a strong figurehead in Jewish homes at the time and presumably must have been in the homes of Ginsberg's friends. And for him not to have had that was one of the aspects that made him feel different from everyone else around him.'

Daniel had used the name Jacob Gershon (Gershon being the Jewish version of Gresham, his mother's maiden name) when he wrote more than a hundred poems in idle moments on the Harry Potter set, and he had also had a few published under that name. 'I got really into it when I was about fifteen. I would always use form and metre and rhyme. I love that stuff … Unfortunately I mentioned this in an interview and it didn't take long for people to realise it was me.'

Daniel did, however, send some of his works to luvvie Stephen Fry and Leeds-born poet Tony Harrison, whom he said gave him great responses. A lot of his early writing was about love and being a teenager and four appeared in *Rubbish* magazine (yes, that really is its name) in November 2007. The magazine's Jenny Dyson said: 'Dan's one request was that his identity be kept secret, hence the birth of "exciting and dynamic young poet" Jacob Gershon. The idea of publishing four works for their own merit appealed to *Rubbish* greatly, especially as each of Dan's poems hold unique charm and demonstrate an exemplary grasp on metre and rhyme.'

One poem was about junkie rock star Pete Doherty, another about deluded fans who queue up for TV talent contests and another about a man's attempts to seduce women. The fourth of Jacob Gershon's poems was called 'Away Days' about a man cheating on his wife with prostitutes. It now appears on the Internet and begins:

Beside these verdurous and wind-blown fronds
I lie with two-legged, glistening blonds.

Ms Dyson praised Daniel's efforts, saying: 'The transitory years between childhood and adulthood hold a special type of awareness for a seventeen-year-old poet. The sensibility of that particular age in a writer or artist shares equal measures of knowingness and innocence unique to the teenage years. Dan conjures up the zeitgeist, touching on celebrity, fame and relationships in a knowing, playful way. Poetry has the ability to vividly evoke the essence of the era it is born into. Jacob Gershon's poetry will capture this time for future generations.'

Daniel summed it up simply by saying that he had to write in form and metre otherwise he became 'unbearably self-indulgent', adding, 'It's what Robert Frost said: "Free verse is like playing tennis with the net down." Looking back on this early work, he is still quite pleased with some of his poems – but by no means all of them. 'I used to think I was very good at poetry but they're not as good as I thought. There are about five of them I still look at, and think, "That's OK." You've just got to be your own version of rock'n'roll. Just be your fucking self. There is nothing less cool than pretending to be someone you're not.'

Discussion about his Jewishness aside, *Kill Your Darlings* was, to the rest of the world, a controversial biopic in which Daniel had yet again to prove himself. He was to learn a lot from Krokidas, one lesson being how he could shake off some of the self-consciousness that still took a grip when he was in very un-Harry-Potter-like roles. This was the technique devised by 1930s actor Sanford Meisner involving an actor's response to a situation rather than that of the character he was playing. It was a major acting breakthrough for Daniel. 'Until I was twenty-one, working on Potter, I was really just going on my instincts. I didn't have any kind of acting technique or process or anything like that,' he said. 'Nobody had ever really talked to me about different methods and things you should do … it [the Meisner technique] just completely changed something in me and gave me freedom.' Daniel said Krokidas had taught him more about the craft of acting than probably any other director he had worked with.

He said that Krokidas had given him 'a huge amount of space' and introduced him into a new way of acting that he never knew existed. It was another personal landmark in Daniel's career and had come at a time when he was suffering some self-doubt about his abilities. 'John placed an amount of faith in me and saw something in me that I hoped was there, but John had more faith in me than I had at the time,' he told Film3SixtyMagazine.com. 'When I first started working with John, I'd lost a lot of confidence in myself and my acting, but John showed me a technique that I never had because I'd always been running on instinct and he gave me some really good tools to work with. Along with just growing up a few more years, [they] have made me into a much better actor. I think that there are people out there who are starting to see me as an actor and not the guy who played Harry Potter. There are people when I'll be 90, and they'll say he is still Harry Potter to me, but I can't think about those people going forward. I can think about all those people out there that saw *The Woman in Black* and didn't think about Harry Potter or have seen *Kill Your Darlings* and definitely didn't think about Harry Potter, and I have to keep going. I really like the choices I'm making and where I'm going in life, and the people I'm getting to learn from, and I'm very happy in what I'm doing.'

In turn, Krokidas praised Daniel's commitment to the role of Ginsberg: 'I knew he was an incredibly hard worker and I had heard what a sensitive and smart person he was.' He also said that the young actor had taught *him* a few things too: 'Dan said to me, and it was a good lesson, that when the shit hits the fan during production and everyone is falling apart or nervous or worried they won't get the scene.'

Daniel also won praise from Ben Foster who played William Burroughs. 'I admire him so much. He is a tremendously courageous human being, great mind. He's done some work in this film which I think is going to shock and impress and put to bed so many doubting minds. Everyone seems to be ready to cut the man down and he's going to prove them wrong. He's a hell of a talent.'

One good friend Daniel made among the cast was Michael C Hall from America's *Dexter* series, who played David Kammerer. 'Michael and I hung out a bit, and when we were together, it definitely freaked people out, because we didn't have trailers on this film set, so we were just hanging out on sidewalks and stuff. People were walking by and going, "Is that

that Harry Potter guy and Dexter chatting over there?" He has a huge amount of attention and probably gets called Dexter as much as I get called Harry Potter, so it's nice to just talk to him about that and see how he handles it, which is quite similar to mine. It doesn't really bother him. He's obviously very proud of Dexter, and I'm very proud of Harry Potter.'

Another good friend Daniel made was twenty-seven-year-old co-star Dane DeHaan. The two had gelled when they first met and shared a love of American football. 'On our first day, me and Dane got beauty treatments together,' recalled Daniel. 'I got a perm and he got highlights. I looked like one of the scousers from Harry Enfield.'

DeHaan and his wife Anna Wood also spent a short break with Daniel and his girlfriend Erin Darke in his apartment. 'Anna was working on this TV show in New York,' said DeHaan, 'and we were living in LA at the time, so she was couch surfing, pretty much. So I contacted Dan and I was like, "Hey, don't mean to put you out but, if this is possible, that would be really cool."'

The two actors spent the waiting time on set playing Scrabble, a game that made them both fiercely competitive. 'Dane said only his wife and dad had beaten him before!' said Daniel.

But, as well as the friendship, Daniel respected Dane greatly; they had been through a pretty testing time with *Kill Your Darlings*, after all. 'We've got a very similar approach to acting,' said Daniel. 'But we also have a huge amount of respect for everyone on set, not just the actors. I don't think I could ever be friends with somebody who didn't have that. That's the one thing I can't stand. But also Dane and I have both got quite stupid, silly senses of humour. We also talk football a lot as well…'

And as far as DeHaan was concerned the thought he was kissing a famous boy wizard on a film set never crossed his mind. 'I never had that moment, ever. It was always that I was Lucien Carr and I got to kiss Allen Ginsberg. That was a wonderful thing.'

The two also shared a scene when they were half-naked in the Hudson River – at four o'clock in the morning. Daniel recalled: 'I'd been in the water for only about forty minutes but Dane had been in there for about four hours. A police car pulled up and one of the officers asked, "What are you guys doing in there?" We told them we were filming and they wanted to know if someone was in the water. We told them there was and they were like "Rather you than me" and just went off. As we were shivering away, we realised that, if the New York Police Department doesn't want to do our job, maybe we shouldn't be in the Hudson.'

Another scene had Daniel as Ginsberg arriving on the Columbia University campus: 'The scene was one of those weird moments when the entire college had turned out to watch us film it. In the film, it's this shot of Allen walking up on his own with nobody paying him any notice, and just outside the frame are five hundred people on either side of the camera who'd turned out to watch that day – and then literally they would cheer after every take. So I'd be running down the steps of Columbia like Rocky.'

At one point, the crew were forcibly ejected from the university at four o'clock in the morning. 'We were running through the campus trying to knock off one last shot before we got expelled from the premises. These drunk college kids were just like, "What the fuck?" And I was in Ginsberg gear with a perm.' But it all added to the fun of filming as far as Daniel was concerned. 'As someone who grew up on film sets, those are the moments you love because there's so much urgency … It is those slightly chaotic mad-dash moments that I live for.'

Daniel was back on the round of interviews both in America and Britain to promote *Kill Your Darlings*. The challenge this time he said was playing someone 'real', he knew the pressure was on; yes, there was some awkwardness doing certain scenes, and yes, it did seem that sometimes he took on roles that Harry Potter fans might consider 'weird' but the resulting intense interest would not influence him: 'I don't think I'll ever let that inform my choices. As much as anything else, it's about showing people you've got good taste. If a Brad Pitt or George Clooney film comes out, I'll go and see it because I know they've got good taste. So I want to be one of those actors where people go, "I don't know what this film's about but he's in it and he normally picks good things, so it must be good."'

Daniel joked that people were now thinking he looked through scripts and, if they didn't include nudity or sex, he didn't accept them. 'But in the end it just came down to a fascinating story.' Daniel was also seen on the sofa of numerous chat shows, and he took part in a video interview to promote *Kill Your Darlings* for *The Guardian*, puffing away on a large rolled-up cigarette, in which he said that his decision about taking a project was asking himself, 'Would Michael Fassbender [the German-Irish actor] do it? It's the Fassbender Test. It first applied to me when I was asked to do something that was, shall we say, a little bit corporate.'

The film also gave Daniel the chance to attend his first Sundance Festival in Utah in January 2013. '[It] was,' he reported, 'full of people trying to look cool all the time – and looking like they haven't made the effort.'

John Krokidas was also there for the debut showing. One Sundance review of *Kill Your Darlings* said Radcliffe not only pulled off a convincing young Ginsberg but as well as all the early preparation for the role and the long stints on the film set he had also been involved in a behind-the-scenes deal to get financial backing.

But Daniel wanted it known that he had still had to prove he was equipped for the part. 'They still need convincing … it's more than just my name being attached. I'm not a producer, I never produced anything in my life and I don't claim to be but if there is a situation where my name association with a film helps get that film attention or money, I'm happy with that. I don't particularly see that as a pressure. The pressure is doing a good job. That's the part I have to get right.'

In September 2013, Venice Film Festival was the centre of a teenage stampede when Daniel arrived to publicise *Kill Your Darlings*. Fellow actors such as George Clooney and Nicholas Cage were virtually left ignored as girls thumped on walls, making the building vibrate, and shook windows in a bid to get into Daniel's press conference. None of it rattled the now, dearly departed Harry Potter who had put away his wand for the very last time two years earlier. 'I've been dealing with it in various ways since I was eleven,' he said. 'I'm incredibly grateful for the swirl of support behind me. My fans seem excited by the unconventional path I am taking…'

Behind the scenes, however, the frenzy was no doubt taking its toll on Daniel who had a punishing schedule. Apart from promoting the film, he was giving countless interviews, talking to hundreds of fans and signing hundreds of autographs. A very incisive and detailed account of Daniel's gruelling itinerary was given by Susan Dominus in the *New York Times* in which she wrote of all his commitments there. Daniel fulfilled a request to publicise a department store, reached after a twenty-five-minute boat ride along the Grand Canal in Venice. Describing just one day, Dominus wrote: 'Radcliffe looked, on tiny side streets opening out to the water, on lacy balconies overhead, people were crammed in close, screaming his name – "Donyell! Donyell!" – and blowing kisses. From the deck, a manager with the film's Italian distributor called to Radcliffe, "Come up top!" The day was beautiful, with that warm Venetian light bouncing off the water. "I've been told not to – sorry!" Radcliffe called back. Radcliffe, who is 24, looked mortified by this precaution, which was not to protect his safety but someone else's labour. "I'm sorry I'm acting like I care about my hair," he told me, but my hairstylist gave me strict instructions not to make him look like an ass.'"

By the time Daniel reached the store around fifteen hundred people were waiting for him. He was asked to sit on a sofa behind a barrier and with girls pressed up to get as close to him as they could. It must have been overwhelming but Daniel cheerfully autographed everything from mobile phones to books and T-shirts. Dominus continued: 'Once an orderly queue was formed Radcliffe stood and signed autographs, as one of the 12 security guards hired for the event pushed the girls along to keep things moving. "Can I get a hug?" one girl asked. "No, but it's lovely meeting you!" Radcliffe said. Another young woman was shaking with emotion. "Are you OK?" he nervously asked. ("It only makes it worse if you're nice," he later observed, miserably.) At one point, he scrawled an autograph on a piece of paper, then threw it away quickly. "That one's no good." A vein in his forehead had become more visible than usual.'

Daniel signed his name around five hundred times but still took a moment to apologise, via a video camera, to all those fans still waiting outside to meet him – and whom he would have to disappoint. The wails grew loud and it was no wonder Daniel nipped into a corner and lit a much-needed cigarette. But he still did not hesitate when his driver asked for yet another autograph on the way back to the Lido.

Daniel and John Krokidas gave a number of interviews from a platform on a plaza overlooking the beach on the Lido. Daniel spoke to at least a hundred different reporters during his time at the Venice festival. After two whirlwind days in Venice, Notorious Pictures, the Italian film distributor, hosted a dinner for the film at the Centurion Palace, a lavish hotel on the Grand Canal. Arriving in the lobby, Radcliffe and Sam (his bodyguard) pushed their way through a hot, close crowd so he could do yet another interview, as a bright light shone in his eyes: 'The hosts had invited a mixed crowd to the dinner that followed: there was a Venetian prince wandering around and some aspiring filmmakers and a woman known for being an Italian showgirl, hugely tall and pneumatic. A young Italian woman, who had sprinkled some of the glitter from a centrepiece onto her face, asked what the English word for "*mago*" was, and someone answered, "Wizard." "Hello, wizard," she said to Radcliffe when she got close enough. Radcliffe posed for photos, again and again.'

At one point, Daniel sought sanctuary with his parents who

were sitting in another room. Explaining the need to escape, he said, 'I did finally hit a point at which I needed to be somewhere where no one was asking me for anything. For just this one occasion, Dominus noted, there had been no less than twelve security men guarding him.

On another occasion, some fans were so excited they accosted him in a toilet. 'I had a *Life of Brian* moment when I opened the toilet door and there were thousands of people standing outside waiting. It was all very surreal and mad as always.' He also needed two bodyguards and had been mobbed when walking along the seafront earlier in the day. There *had* been some pretty hairy moments.

Italian photographer Luca Locatelli reported how Daniel had said he was delighted by such a huge crowd when he had to leave the protection of the viewing theatre to get to his car, but was also scared in case it all got out of control. Locatelli said: 'After a few minutes people started to scream and the craziness started. Daniel's bodyguard covered him completely before grabbing him to get into the car. In that moment I saw the fame of Daniel full of happiness but fright at the same time.' So desperate were the paparazzi to get pictures of Daniel that they offered money to 'official' photographers to take a shot for them.

Things had been quieter earlier in the day when Daniel posed alongside John Krokadis on the red carpet wearing, the *Daily Mail* reported, the 'slick premiere look' of crisp white shirt, skinny black tie and handmade George Cleverley double monk shoes, 'while wearing his dark locks groomed to perfection'. And Daniel's personal take on the madness of premieres? 'The one piece of advice I would give to anybody getting into any sort of situation where they're recognised is at all costs retain your sense of humour. Have fun even if you're in a very mad situation. Premieres and stuff, having people scream at you, it's quite overwhelming; lovely in one way but at the same time intimidating.'

He needed to muster all this reserve when he attended the screening of *Kill Your Darlings* at the Odeon West End as part of the 57th BFI London Film Festival the following month. Daniel was again swamped by fans, but it must have been a little dispiriting to see all the Harry Potter posters waved at him with requests for him to sign them.

There had been no less than seven premieres for *Kill Your Darlings* and Daniel had coped with them all, even though attending them was not his favourite way to pass an evening. 'I feel like I should sing a song or something,' he commented. 'I don't know what to do. The parties afterward, I'm always nervously saying, "Nice to see you", and there is a procession of people meeting people, some you're excited to meet, some breathe their vol-au-vent breath all over you. So at the moment I just keep thinking that in six weeks I'll be back on a film set. And my life will be simple again.'

The following month, Daniel showed how far he had come from the boy Potter by appearing on the cover of Canadian men's magazine *Sharpe*. He looked dapper in a suit and tie. In an interview with the magazine, he also again rebuffed suggestions he was gay: 'I honestly have no desire to play with people's idea of my sexuality, you know. I'm straight.'

Kill Your Darlings opened on 6 December 2013. Some critics hailed it as Daniel's 'best post-Potter performance', and in the *Express*, Henry Fitzherbert said he had given 'his most assured performance to date'. Robbie Collin in *The Telegraph* wrote: 'Radcliffe embraces the chance to stretch himself on screen here in the same way he did onstage in *Equus*, and he makes a fine job of it. In spite of his character's owlish spectacles and bookish natural habitat, thoughts of Potter never enter your head.' *The Guardian*'s Peter Bradshaw praised Daniel for his 'forthright and candid performance as Ginsberg', adding, 'he is evolving into a formidable and potent screen presence'. Kate Muir in *The Times* said Daniel had given 'the most complex and interesting performance of his career to date'. Writing for *Empire* magazine, Damon Wise agreed, saying the film featured Daniel's 'best post-Potter performance'.

Although Daniel says he never reads reviews, there was one that friends drew his attention to – and which he said made him laugh. The *Hollywood Reporter* commented: 'The boy wizard never pinned his knees behind his ears…'

CHAPTER 13

END OF AN ERA

Daniel scouted around to find a special memento. Finally, he found the perfect souvenirs and popped into his pocket two pairs of trademark Harry Potter spectacles: one from his very first Potter film, the second from his very last. He wasn't alone in wanting something to treasure after it was all over. Rupert Grint took home with him a sign from the Weasleys' house in Privet Drive and Emma Watson was now the proud owner of a wand and cloak.

That last day of shooting the last ever Harry Potter film had been almost surreal and there was no major fuss made, despite the finale of such a history-making franchise. The cast just got on with it. All the celebrating had been done the night before. But today would be very poignant for all the cast. Daniel summed it up: 'There was a line written by – not sounding pretentious – but there's a line written by Chekhov in a letter to his last love, and he writes something like "Hello, the last page of my life." And when I started reading the last *Harry Potter* book, I thought that, this is really it, this is the last time I will take a journey with this character. And that was a really special experience to me, and I can't wait to do that movie, and that last scene.'

That very last scene of the very last Potter involved Daniel, Emma and Rupert diving on to the floor – special effect flames would be added later. 'It was an enormous moment,' said producer David Barron. 'We deliberately made it the last shot as we knew it would be very difficult for the three of them.' In fact, it had taken a lot for the three young stars to get through that last shot. Daniel had been able to hold it together during the day until Barron and David Heyman asked him how he was coping. Daniel said: 'I couldn't find any words. I just said, "I want you to know I've had a really nice time." I caught myself off guard. That was the moment I had a lump in my throat.' Daniel's answer when asked so many, many times about how he felt varied. Sometimes he said he didn't get too emotional; sometimes he admitted he had, at one time, wept like a child and been 'inconsolable for two hours or so'.

Somewhat poignantly, the Potter story closed with Harry and Ginny married and parents, and, likewise, Ron and Hermione. They stood on the magical platform and watched as their children rode away on the Hogwarts Express. There were obviously mixed emotions about walking away from the role that had been his life for ten years. As Daniel said: 'I've been working every day since I was eleven. I don't know how to not work, it's what I love doing. In fact, my identity is so wrapped up in who I am when I'm on set that I kind of need to work on that.' He had been shot to stardom overnight, become famous the world over and had had to contend with all that it brought with it.

They had, said producer David Heyman, been like a family. 'We had worked together for so long. Each person's last day was quite emotional.'

A short film was made of that last day, with most of the cast taking a bow in front of the people who had become close friends. There were hugs and kisses and it ended with the words 'It's a wrap' on screen as Daniel walked through wooden doors that closed behind him. 'What will I do with my day-to-day life now?' he asked the gathering on set. 'It was quite upsetting at the time. It felt pretty bleak at the time. I was crying, and everyone was crying. In fact, me and Rupert and all the crew were all in floods of tears. It felt very, very sad, and kind of hopeless on that day. And the next day I woke up and went, "Hold on, I've got two jobs I'm going on to. This is fine, this is not so bad." But at the time it was very sad and it was very weird, particularly seeing Rupert cry. It was kind of wrong. It was like seeing your dad cry or something.'

With everyone aware this would be their last time together, the 250 or so days' filming, too, became particularly poignant. 'You can relish every moment,' said Daniel. He had been away from Potter for about a year but the enthusiasm had not waned. Although the day's filming might wrap up at 4pm, he would still be hanging around for another couple of hours. 'It has become a running joke how long I stay here but I just love my job. And anyway the most interesting part for me is when I am not on camera because then I can watch everyone else doing their stuff and you can really learn from it.' The set still held some wonder for him. 'I think it is important to still be amazed by some parts of it because otherwise it is just a routine and you have to remember that this won't last for ever.'

There would be many happy memories – much reflection. David Heyman, one of those instrumental in getting Daniel on to the Potter production line, commented: 'He was endlessly curious and he was ambitious for his craft. One of the things I most respect about him is he pushed himself to get the most out of every moment in his life.'

Heyman remains a close friend of Daniel, together with William Steggle who worked in the Potter wardrobe department. Of Steggle, Daniel said, 'Because he is a cynical man he has put me off pretension at every stage. It is totally possible for an actor to be involved with the crew and have a chat with everyone and be really good friends with them, then go and do a scene. That should be your job.'

Parting gifts were exchanged, with Daniel handing out presents to all the crew. Gifts were also exchanged between the cast. Rupert Grint gave Daniel a trumpet, which bemused him as he can't play one. The instrument was inscribed with what Daniel described as jokey abuse, 'because that is what Rupert does. He's slightly mad. And I still have no intention of learning to play the trumpet…'

So Daniel had made it through to the end of Harry Potter. Sadly for him, there would be no partying with the rest of them. Four hours after the final scene was shot, he had to get on a plane to New York to take to the stage as a presenter at the Tony Awards. During the flight, he read through the script for *The Woman in Black*. Harry Potter might have come to an end but the rest of Daniel's life was just beginning.

Daniel said he didn't want to ever sound ungrateful for those ten magical and life-changing years, which had seen him mature from a shy eleven-year-old to a confident twenty-one-year-old – and also have his famous scar applied around two thousand times by the make-up department and get through around a hundred and sixty pairs of spectacles. In the entire time he had played Harry Potter, Daniel had only ever taken two days off sick when he had gastric flu. The boy wizard would always remain with him: 'I know that Potter is going to be with me for the rest of my life,' he said, 'so to try to set a goal where nobody talks about that any more is stupid. It would be like Paul McCartney might have gone on to do a lot of other things, but people are always going to want to talk about the Beatles. It's just a fact of your life, so you can't get annoyed by it or resent it. You have to embrace the fact that you were involved in this incredibly cool thing that did wonders for the British film industry and, though you might not always be happy with the work you did on it, the opportunity it has given you to forge a career for yourself is amazing.'

But he knew full well that, in the eyes of the world, no matter what diverse acting project he took on in the future, he would always, always be Harry Potter. 'There will be some people who will always see me as this character. I know that and understand that. That's fine as long as they are not casting directors and film-makers. Hopefully, it won't hold me back.'

Even co-star Tom Felton was to admit: 'It's hard to see Daniel and not think of anyone but Harry. Even I've called him Harry for a couple of years. It's odd. It's what you know him as. It doesn't make it any easier that he looks just like Harry.'

Despite their professional and happy façade, all three

young Harry Potter actors were to admit that the challenge of expectation, and everything else that went with their fame, took its toll. Emma Watson admitted that, in latter days, the Potter experience was 'horrible' and that she felt she was in a controlled routine. 'I get told what time I get picked up. I get told what time I can eat, when I have time to go to the bathroom. Every single second of my day is not in my power.'

Rupert Grint had found it all 'quite suffocating'. Daniel, no doubt feeling pretty much the same, was more reticent, however. David Yates, who directed the last four Potter films, said the young actor, even if he felt 'good, bad, indifferent or terrible' on set, still carried on even under intense pressure.

Daniel himself commented, 'The second you seem down, everyone's very concerned. It affects the set.' Yates once told Daniel that he was 'conditioned' to work. The young star said, 'I don't mind that. If that's the flaw I have, that I'm impossible to stop working, that's fine with me.'

Nonetheless, being eternally known as the famous boy wizard was to cause problems, not only when he was starting out, but also well after the last film was finished. Daniel was sometimes subjected to verbal abuse and unwanted attention. Some of the worst took place when he was seventeen and eighteen. There would be the occasional encounter with a guy who wanted to beat him up just for being Harry Potter. 'You get a few people, or drunks who'd want to pick a fight with me, but again, I didn't want to give them the satisfaction … I'm not a fighter. I believe I'm articulate enough to talk myself out of most things.'

Then there were the wags who would approach Daniel when he was having a cigarette outside and ask him to cast a spell to stop the rain. 'They've taken their brave pills, so they think they're going to be really witty and tell a Harry Potter joke and I just stare at them, thinking, "Are they really doing this?" I've heard every single one and they don't make me laugh.'

He was also still very much aware that his massively successful career was deemed to be good fortune as well as anything else and he always felt he had to justify it. 'It's as much to myself, as to anyone else. People always say, "Oh he's got a chip on his shoulder" like it's a bad thing. I think it's a perfectly good thing if you let it motivate you. When you fall into a position when you're eleven years old, you do tend to think that, you know, everyone, you were lucky to get there. And I was lucky to get there. And I think there's a sense that you just fell into it and that you rode the wave and carried on. And that's not what I'm about. I don't know how many people think like that – there may be none, there may be millions, but it doesn't matter. It fires you up.'

There would never be a role like Harry Potter. Daniel had been announced as the boy wizard shortly after his tenth birthday and he had, he had to admit, had a ball. 'I got to do some really cool stuff and I probably won't get to do so much anymore,' he said rather ruefully. It was also a time to reflect: 'You can argue about the best way to come into the industry and you can say there's people that can slug it out for years and have to work a long time for shit money, and then eventually get somewhere. Now, that's a very fucking frustrating part of acting that 90 per cent of actors are on, unless they get lucky at a very young age. But the trade-off in that is, when they are young and starting off and doing that sort of work, the pressure on them to be amazing isn't high; you're allowed to make mistakes and you're allowed to learn on the job.'

235

And, as Daniel went on to say, his life had been very different: 'I had amazing success incredibly young and starred at the forefront of this huge franchise. You get the chance to learn from the best people in the industry, but at the same time, I will forever have a lot of shit acting that I did when I was a kid on screen that I hate, and you have to learn that people will latch on to that and some people won't be able to see you as another character. So, you know, you're definitely aware that that's out there. But I think one of the best things to do is to accept it.'

In the background throughout it all, of course, were Daniel's parents. Even though he became so famous, they still monitored his reactions to it all, asking regularly whether he wanted to continue in the Potter franchise. 'After each year my mum and dad would say, "Are you still enjoying it? Do you still want to go back?" I would be like "yes" and that was it right up until film number five when I just signed up for six and seven, because at that point there was no way I was not going to do the last two.'

The premiere for *Harry Potter and the Deathly Hallows: Part 2* took place on 7 July 2011. Fans had travelled across the world to stake their place at the heart of the action. Many were dressed in Hogwarts robes and had lightning flashes on their foreheads. There was much placard waving with messages ranging from sad goodbyes to the more cynical 'Harry Potter is over. See you in therapy'. It was estimated that around eight thousand fans were there. Said one: 'You kind of live it because you grow up with them. You feel everything they feel and you just want to see the end. You want to see them triumph.'

There had been Harry Potter red-carpet nights before, of

course, but this was so much more poignant – and so much longer! For on this occasion, the carpet spread three-quarters of a mile from Trafalgar Square to the viewing theatre in Leicester Square. It was rumoured to have been the longest there had ever been. Around 6.45pm, Daniel arrived and walked along it, as did fellow cast members, including Rupert Grint, Emma Watson (who openly wept), Michael Gambon, Robbie Coltrane and Julie Walters. In all, twenty-two Harry Potter actors had gathered. Speaking from a stage near Nelson's Column, Potter creator J. K. Rowling thanked past and present cast members for 'the amazing things they did for my favourite characters'.

Following the premiere event, many of the cast went on to a party at London's Old Billingsgate Market. Daniel was notable for his absence but there was good reason. He had introduced the film on two different screens and then gone off to appear on *The Graham Norton Show*. 'By that time it was 10.30pm, and if I was going to go to the party I'd be the first one there. Then I'll be there signing autographs all night and doing photos. And I thought, "You know what, this year…"' So Daniel got a reasonably early night at home, took off his Nick Tentis suit, donned his tracksuit bottoms and watched the Discovery Channel with a bowl of Sugar Puffs. 'That was my rock'n'roll premiere night,' he said.

Daniel's commitment to *How to Succeed in Business Without Really Trying* also meant he could not attend the London press conference of *Deathly Hallows: Part 2*. The American premiere took place at the Lincoln Center in New York on 11 July. Again, thousands of people turned up with police having to clear the streets as crowds swarmed to get a glimpse of what must have now been a very exhausted Daniel and co-stars. What had been a major part of all their lives was now drawing to a close and they were to move on as people and actors. 'If I can make it out the other side of this and forge a career for myself for the next, however long,' Daniel said, 'then any other child actor who comes after me will hopefully not have to deal with all those irritating questions, because if me, Rupert and Emma can do it after the most successful franchise ever, then that puts the argument about failed child actors to bed.'

He told the *Hollywood Reporter* at the time: 'I think my feelings are that the series is, kind of, its own commemoration – I mean, to me at least. I won't be able to look at any of these films without remembering what they did for the British film industry at a time when it wasn't doing great. It's now flourishing, but in the early half of the decade, you know, there was nothing happening, and films were closing, and Potter was the only, kind of, sure thing happening in England. And, you know, my memories of it are incredibly nostalgic, and romantic, and, I think, how everybody views their teenage years, you know, with complete idealism, having forgotten that there was ever any, you know, hormonal rage or any of that kind of stuff. You know, I had a moment the other day of actually really missing it for the first time since, of going, "God, I miss those people!" But, yeah, I mean, it's been over a year now, and I've been having this amazing year here [in America], so it's been a great first year away – may they all be this good!'

The last ever Harry Potter film reviews were bound to be pretty emotional. Peter Bradshaw in *The Guardian* wrote: '"It all ends," says the poster slogan. A potentially grim statement of the obvious, of course, yet the Potter saga could hardly have ended on a better note. With one miraculous flourish of its wand, the franchise has restored the essential magic to the Potter legend.' The *New York Times* said: 'Mr Radcliffe, button cute, capable, opaque, was tougher to warm up to. But it's pointless to think of anyone else. He became Harry, Harry is him, and Mr Radcliffe's depthless quality now seems right for a character who, in the books and movies, was never as interesting as the magical world he revealed to us.'

The film went on general worldwide release later that month, opening on a record-breaking 11,000 screens. It was a fitting tribute for Daniel as he took his last Harry Potter bow. 'The most wonderful thing I hear is people coming up and saying, "Thank you for my childhood", which still blows my mind but is very sweet. When people say, "What's it like to be associated with such a big franchise?" I say, "It's very easy when your franchise is something that is so loved."'

There was talk that Daniel was now going to quit acting for good and perhaps take an Open University course in archaeology, a subject he had become interested in from his intense watching of TV such as the Discovery Channel. But, of course, he would never really abandon his acting life. It was too much fun he said, he loved it too much to want to stop and it was what he had grown up doing. 'There's an assumption that people make where, if you've grown up on a set, surely you must be tired of that or want to go somewhere else. But actually I've never known anything but being on film sets and I love them. They are places of immense comfort and familiarity. I hope I get to die on one. Honestly. Later rather than sooner.'

On 21 November 2011, Warner Bros. held a luncheon in New York to mark the end of the Harry Potter series. Daniel was among the guests, along with director David Yates, producer David Heyman and Alan Rickman. Heyman said it had all been an amazing 'odyssey' and Yates that it had been an 'incredible journey'. Daniel had said earlier how 'devastated' he would be when it was all over. 'There is nothing I watch without it triggering a series of memories. Everything about the films is so linked to my life. At the same time it is exciting. It is the end.'

Earlier that month, as he had been for several years, Daniel was listed in the *London Evening Standard*'s 1,000 most influential people – 'A veteran at the age of 22, Radcliffe polished off the Harry Potter series in style (*Deathly Hallows Part 2* was probably Radcliffe's best performance to date) and now the challenge for the wealthy young man is to build a career away from Hogwarts.'

Harry Potter and The Deathly Hallows: Part 2 earned Daniel the Choice Summer Male Movie Star Award and the MTV award for Best Hero. He also won nominations for Favourite Movie Actor, Favourite Movie Star under 25, Nickelodeon Kids' Choice for Favourite Movie Actor, MTV Movie Awards for Best Male Performance and the Teen Choice Award for Male Star. The film won awards for Favourite Movie Ensemble and Best Cast. Neither Daniel nor Rupert was there to receive the Best Cast Award but it was accepted by Emma Watson who said: 'I don't think I will ever accept an award on behalf of so many people. From Ralph Fiennes to Helena Bonham Carter to Hedwig and Dobby and all of them, this is amazing. We had over two hundred cast members and I wish they could all be up here with me now. Sadly they can't. Obviously I share this award in particular with Dan and Rupert. Wherever you are,

I hope you're watching and I miss you both dearly. Just thank you. I really, really appreciate it.'

Daniel had said he felt the final Harry Potter instalment was 'light years' ahead of the previous ones and that he felt enormous pride about it – which is why he felt he had to speak out at what he saw as a snub towards the film by the movie industry. It was at the 2012 Academy Awards that Daniel felt the final Potter film was ignored when it came to getting an Oscar or two: 'I don't think the Oscars like commercial films or kids' films unless they're directed by Martin Scorsese … I was slightly miffed. There's a certain amount of snobbery. It's kind of disheartening. I never thought I'd care. But it would've been nice to have some recognition just for the hours put in.' It is hard to believe with all its worldwide success, but Harry Potter *had* missed out on the all-important Oscar awards.

In all, the franchise had received Oscar nominations for six of the eight films – but they were all in the technical categories and none resulted in an award. *Harry Potter and the Deathly Hallows: Part 2* received three nominations for Art Direction, Makeup and Visual Effects. Some critics agreed that there was something wrong when such a global phenomenon was not recognised. They described as 'tragic' the fact that Alan Rickman was 'dismissed' for his portrayal of Severus Snape in the Best Supporting Actor category. All this was despite reported efforts by Warner Bros. who had set up a website to push *Deathly Hallows: Part 2* in the Oscar stakes that year. The site called for this final film to be rewarded in a dozen categories including Best Picture, Best Adapted Screenplay and Best Director for David Yates – and Best Supporting Actor for Rickman. Daniel commented in support of his co-star: 'I don't think there is going to be another performance from an actor in a supporting role that is so powerful.'

On premiere night, David Yates was philosophical about the lack of Oscars: 'I think we've all made peace with that. There are so many things to enjoy being part of in this whole series of films – most of all, the affection of the fans and the fact that there's a global community who follow these stories with great passion. If you go down to Trafalgar Square right now, you'll see a mini-Glastonbury of people from all over the world who've been camping out in the rain for the last three nights. And that's more compensation than lots of trophies. So I think we're cool about that. That's somehow more important, I'd say.'

Jo Rowling was later to cause great upset among devoted Harry Potter fans when she dared to suggest that it should have been Harry who ended up with Hermione and not Ron at the end of the saga. Completely taken aback about the ensuing outcry, Rowling was forced to remark: 'Maybe she and Ron will be all right with a bit of counselling, you know. I wonder what happens at wizard marriage counselling? They'll probably be fine. He needs to work on his self-esteem issues and she needs to work on being a little less critical.'

But the magic continued with the announcement that a Warner Bros. Studio Tour London was in the pipeline at Leavesden for the following year. The tour, proudly boasting that it had the backing of Daniel, Emma and Rupert, was to include some of the franchise's most iconic sets such as the Great Hall, Dumbledore's office, the Ministry of Magic and Harry's famous cupboard under the stairs. The idea was to offer 'muggles and movie fans the first opportunity to journey behind the scenes'. Daniel said: 'It was such a magical place to grow up. People will be amazed to see the incredible sets that we've worked in all these years.'

And so the Harry Potter era for Daniel was over. Even though it had had a huge effect on his life, he sometimes felt the worldwide reaction was misplaced. 'For me I'm done, I'm finished. People have to remember, we are not mourning the death of an actual person. There is not an appropriate grieving period which I have to observe.'

He would always be aware of the impact it had all had on the film industry as well as his life: 'I'm still very proud of Potter. Even though it was *the* most commercial series in the world – in terms of the money it made and the appeal it had – we always did try to make them as challenging as possible. I think the reason I'm so proud of it, still, is that we made eight films that got *better* and better and better until the last one. *That's* not very often achieved in film and the fact we achieved it is a testament to the amount of care and love put into it by everyone who was involved on that set, all the time.

'So, yeah, I still think we did a remarkable thing and even if we were very mainstream – which, of course, we were – we brought a lot of integrity and sort of a boldness to the franchise. Because, when I was growing up, I don't remember people talking about franchises before I was in one. I remember people talking about how *Lord of the Rings* and Potter would be like "franchises", that's the first time I remember…'

Daniel was brave enough to admit that he was not totally satisfied with his performance for the whole run, but now he wanted to improve professionally and move on personally. 'People can say I'm successful – I've had a very charmed life and I've been very lucky to have done the things that I've done – but at the same time, I was never 100 per cent happy with the work I did during Potter. My definition of success is about making a transition out of Potter and forging a long-term career for myself with longevity. Define success on your own terms and don't give up until you get there.'

But he could never dismiss the phenomenon that he had been such a major part of. 'I'm sure that in another twenty or thirty years' time there will be a new phenomenon. And I will at some point be saying dismissively to my children, "Huh, Harry Potter was bigger than this ... This is nothing compared to Harry Potter ... You think that's fans? That's not fans!"'

CHAPTER 14

WILD ABOUT HARRY

It was one of the questions Daniel always dreaded in interviews. It went from the downright patronising when he first started out in Potter at such a tender age, to the more intrusive as he got older: 'Have you got a girlfriend?' Daniel always found it awkward to answer, either because there was no one special in his life – or because there was but he wanted to keep it private. He was to admit that he was economical with the truth whenever he was asked in interviews whether he had a girlfriend.

Despite all the opportunities, he was never one for routinely taking a random girl fan to bed. It was important to him that he knew someone first. 'I was always nervous about the groupie thing. I like to like somebody before I sleep with them. You know you're going to have to talk to them afterwards, even if it is a one-night stand.' But he would rather be in a proper relationship. 'I love coming home to somebody,' he said, adding that to go to a stage door to pick a girl 'you have to be some kind of dick'.

Daniel has said that he had his first 'proper girlfriend' when he was fourteen, and they were together for six months. It obviously ended badly because he said, 'I was just a really messed-up person after that. At the time it feels like the most important thing in the entire world, but I promise you it won't be the problem you're having tomorrow.'

One of Daniel's first public admissions that he was now really taking an interest in girls came when he was eighteen. He had just got back from a publicity tour of Australia and had been smitten by a mysterious young woman backstage at the Australian Film Industry Awards ceremony. The *Sydney Daily Telegraph* reported that it was trying to wave its magic wand and locate the object of Daniel's interest after he'd confessed his lovelorn state: 'There was one girl there, oh my God, she had these eyes that just looked at me like she wanted to pounce on me. She stared at me the whole night and I was going to get her number and then I couldn't find her. I must have walked around that party for an hour trying to look for this girl, like some sad pathetic dweeb, but it would have been so worth it.' When asked if the newspaper could help find her, Daniel was said to have 'blushed' and regretfully shaken his head, saying, 'I don't know, I don't know her name, I can't remember her name. It was one of those things but she was stunning.'

One woman, twenty-year-old trumpet player Cassi McKay, later came forward to suggest it might have been her who caught Daniel's eye. 'He was looking at me a bit, and I guess I was batting my eyelids back. We said hello and had a quick chat.' The two had posed for a photograph together but Cassi said that, although she would like to meet up with Daniel again, she already had a boyfriend…

A couple of days later twenty-three-year-old saxophonist Savannah Blount told the press that *she* might be the mystery woman too. She said, 'He was quite lovely. He was very charming, very polite. Maybe if I was working over there or touring, you never know.'

Daniel's publicist played it all down, saying Daniel's comments were 'meant in jest, but sadly have been blown out of all proportion'.

Daniel had also been linked to singer Lily Allen after the two were seen dining out at a London restaurant, and, of course, to Emma Watson whenever they were in each other's company.

One of Daniel's serious girlfriends was twenty-six-year-old Irish actress Laura O'Toole, whom he met when appearing in *Equus*. He said at the time: 'She's just a normal person and she's not out for anything else, which is very, very good. I seem to be a long-term relationship kinda guy. In my head I'm Byron spreading failed romance…' When the two separated Daniel said it was all very amicable and that he was now 'just being single and running around chasing girls. I'm not getting too many responses but, yes, I'm having a go.' He was, he said, going on dates for the first time with girls he had not met through work. At one time he was linked with Olive Uniacke, stepdaughter of Potter producer David Heyman. A former set PA on the *Deathly Hallows* films, she was said to have accompanied him on his twenty-first birthday trip to Moscow. Daniel was not her usual sort of partner, a friend commented: 'She has usually gone for bad boys and Dan is quite preppy.'

A colleague was quoted as saying: 'Olive is a very lovely young lady. She and Dan have been close for a long time. She was always in and out of his dressing room during filming and she has always been really protective of him.' Known for holding some of the best parties around, Olive, it was pointed out, had money in her own right and 'so is certainly not a gold-digger'. There were rumours that Daniel and Olive rekindled their relationship a few years after their break-up.

All of Daniel's associations with girls have a Harry Potter or work link; he said he had his first kiss with a girl he met on set, lost his virginity to a girl he met on set, and then dated several more he had met in the same way. 'All my girlfriends that I've ever met have been through work. So we got to know each other really well and then kind of ended up going out. It's quite nerve-wracking dating outside of that because it's not something I'm used to.'

And for a young man whose life and work revolve around words, he admitted he sometimes had trouble keeping the conversation going with new girlfriends. 'Not that I struggle with talking but I have this incredible anxiety about awkward silences and pauses and all that stuff, which I think everybody worries about. But I get quite wound up about that beforehand. I do actually manage to be quite chatty in the end – and probably a bit boring. I just try to make the girls laugh. That's the only thing I'm particularly good at on dates.'

And he scotched any idea that his fame made it easy to find a girlfriend. 'It's weird, you know, because people sometimes ask, "Does being Harry Potter help you get girls?" I was nine before I did Harry Potter, so I don't know what it's like to get girls without the aid of being Harry.'

But his most important relationship was with production assistant Rosanne Coker, a 'wonderful, wonderful girl', whom he said was too good for him. Although he had noticed her on the set of the sixth Potter film, he finally mustered the courage to ask her out at the wrap party of the last film. 'I started looking at Rosie and going, "Jesus, I quite fancy you!"' Rosie's father Malcolm was quoted as saying: 'They are a really nice couple, but only got together after the latest film had finished filming, because they thought it might cause problems. They worried it might be unprofessional, because he was playing the main character in the Harry Potter film, and they both decided it was best to wait.'

For a while, the two were happy with Daniel declaring, 'When Rosie's here, every day seems better. Ultimately, I think it comes down to that – having someone in your life who makes you happier than you thought you could be. However, he admitted, 'I'm not an easy person to love … there are lots of times when I'm a very good boyfriend but there are times when I'm useless. I'm a mess around the house. I talk nonstop. I become obsessed with things.' He said Rosie listened to him and loved his oddness and awkwardness and found it all cute. So carried away with Rosie was Daniel that he even told journalists about the first time he tried to kiss her – missing her lips and ending up catching her neck. 'I texted her afterwards to tell her I was sorry. Fortunately, she found it really funny.'

It was telling of Daniel's fame that, within hours of it becoming public knowledge that he and Rosie were an item, her name suddenly became the third most popular name on Google. Daniel and Rosie became very close and she made regular trips to see him while he was working in New York, often staying with him at his Manhattan apartment. Her visits – and public appearances – with Daniel sometimes provoked unwanted attention. Once, when the couple were eating in a New York restaurant, a girl started taking pictures. A greatly annoyed Daniel said, 'This girl didn't even look and was carrying on talking to her friend while she pointed a camera phone. This huge flash from two tables went off. I was in such disbelief. I waited until the end of the meal, getting angrier and angrier. At the end I went up to them and said, "If you had asked, it would've been fine. What you did was rude – just for future reference!"' Daniel spoke glowingly about Rosanne and happily told reporters that he had even met her parents. 'It was pretty nerve-wracking but I think I passed. But we are a little way off calling them in-laws.'

But despite rumours of a possible proposal, and having the approval of Rosie's parents, it was announced that the relationship was over in October 2012. Daniel said he had 'screwed up' because he had talked about his 'wonderful, wonderful' girlfriend too openly. He had previously spoken about how Rosie had given him a two-year deadline 'to be a fully functioning human being'. The break-up sadly came shortly after Daniel had talked about marriage in obvious reference to Rosie: 'When growing up I thought of marriage as being very official, drawing up a contract. It seemed slightly clinical to me. But then you meet somebody that you really love and you think, "Actually I wouldn't mind standing up in front of my friends and family and telling them how much I love you and that I want to be with you forever."'

Despite once declaring how happy his daughter was and

what a 'lovely guy' Daniel was, Rosie's father now said she was out of the country and trying to move on.

There was speculation that the main reason behind the split was Daniel's closeness to twenty-eight-year-old American actress Erin Darke, five years his senior, whom he had met on the set of *Kill Your Darlings*. There were reports he 'wooed' her with trips to London. This affair, too, was to end, however. One magazine reported: 'Erin thought it was a real relationship, going as far as introducing Daniel as her boyfriend. He's flown the route to London and taken her on dates and spent plenty of time with her in NYC, but Daniel just up and left New York without a second thought. Erin was devastated.'

It seemed a very out-of-character way for Daniel to behave, as he had always shown a lot of respect for women, especially strong, clever ones: 'I never understand men who are threatened by intelligent women. Maybe it's that Freudian thing. My mum is a really intelligent, smart woman, and feisty as well, so that's always the basis of my comparison. Whenever I meet girls who don't stand up for themselves or don't have a bit of chutzpah about them, it does nothing for me.'

However, the relationship between Daniel and Erin was to pick up again. The smiling couple were photographed out shopping in New York in April 2014 during Daniel's Broadway appearance of *The Cripple of Inishmaan*. Some publications also claimed that the two had got engaged, quoting one source as saying: 'They're trying to keep it low key. But they're both bursting with excitement. It's the happiest we've seen him in years!'

Any engagement was strongly denied by Daniel. He told *The Daily Beast*: 'No! Absolute bollocks. *Absolute* bollocks. It was funny. I got a text from my English teacher saying, "Is it true? Congratulations!" and I had to text her back, "I'm afraid not! We're very happy, but we're not getting married." Marriage is not a thought that is even *remotely* close to me at the moment.'

In between all the attention paid to his heterosexual love life – he has had to repeatedly refute any suggestions there were feelings between him and Emma Watson – Daniel had, at one time, to fend off speculation that he was gay – not that the accusation really bothered him as he is a gay rights supporter. On his twenty-third birthday, gay website, The Backlot, provided '23 reasons we love Daniel Radcliffe', in which they included his honesty and his response to gay rumours. There were also several pictures of a topless Daniel from *Equus*.

One of the most surreal interviews Daniel gave was an interview with Judd Apatow on the Funny or Die website in which, while Apatow seemed to be playing it straight, Daniel was giving pretty wacky answers. Asked about his ten years as Harry Potter, he said that it was around the fourth film that he realised he *was* Harry. 'There was a time when I used to think I was an actor playing a wizard when in fact I was a wizard playing an actor,' he said. Then, 'When I left Harry I became Dan and he is a pretty fantastic character … that's how I was received and I discovered that's how the world works.' Daniel is then asked what he does when he leaves Harry behind and he answers, 'I chill out. I talk to women and tell them I am Harry and see where it gets me.' Apatow might have been confused when Daniel insisted the flying broomstick game of Quidditch was not fantasy, and that he had spoken to several professional Quidditch players who 'all said they would be proud to have me in their team'. Daniel then offered to show the interviewer his Quidditch scars and his 'broom burns' and left the sofa where he'd been talking and Apatow is heard saying, 'No, put your trousers back on.'

On a more serious note, Daniel has admitted that playing the Quidditch scenes *was* perhaps 'one of the least fun things'. It wasn't a pleasant experience, he said, and 'it does hurt quite a lot'.

In the December issue of *Out* magazine, it was reported Daniel had been close friends with a transsexual singer called Lady J and was earning himself 'major points in tranny heaven' for allowing Lady J to interview him. The two had met in 2008 when Daniel attended a party with his parents. Lady J said: 'He's really down to earth. I was surprised at how normal he is. You hear about these child stars who are crazed with fame. He's just really interested in his craft.' Apparently they bonded over a conversation about religion and American politics. 'He seems to be really interested in learning about new things. He's like a sponge.'

Daniel was also reported as saying, 'I'd love to play a drag queen or transvestite but not because of the costumes. Wait, what am I saying? Yes, because of the costumes.' Any such quotes, no matter how tongue in cheek, sometimes prompted the wrong sort of attention. At one time, a young lad was sending Daniel photographs of himself, which Daniel said were 'so not appropriate'. Apparently the lad 'circled my crotch on all these photos with an arrow pointing to it, which just said, "Did you have a boner here?" He didn't get a signed photo like most people do…'

Daniel has said that he tries to answer his fan mail 'as much as is humanly possible' but does not always get the time to deal with it as well as he would like. He has also been sent weird gifts such as Freddy Krueger masks and ears and scrapbooks containing pictures of him. 'I also got sent a photograph of a milk bottle and door. It was my house! There were two people in front of it. There was only a door between us. That was very strange.' He has received letters asking for bits of his hair and, spookily, baby pictures, as well as pictures of himself at various film premieres. Accompanying notes have included one that read: 'Did you have an erection in this picture?'

Fortunately, the majority of Daniel's fans are normal and he knows that meeting his adoring public is something that comes with the job. 'I know there are people who are slightly obsessed, but it doesn't really worry me too much. As long as it stays at the pitch it is now. Occasionally, you meet someone slightly worrying, but I never really feel in danger.'

Thus, whenever he is out and about he takes it all in his stride, even on the occasion fans cried and screamed at him when he was enjoying a quiet meal at a restaurant in Leigh, Essex back in 2012. One staff member said: 'Some fans came running into the bar asking for autographs but our boss asked them to leave. Daniel was really nice and friendly. It was so exciting and there were even girls standing outside the bar screaming and crying.' It proves once again that Daniel goes out of his way to always be polite, receptive and friendly.

But there are pitfalls when Daniel does try to lead a normal life, like the time he stood in the wings at a Red Hot Chili Peppers concert in London's Hyde Park. The word spread among the crowd that he was there. Then came the chants: 'There's only one Harry Potter'. The most unusual place he has been recognised was at the top of a roller coaster in Paris.

'It was just about to go down. I heard someone behind me shout, "It's him!" I was wearing a snood and just my eyes were showing, so that person deserves a medal.' He has also had someone try to shake his hand at a urinal.

Sometimes it just all gets too much for girl fans, especially in Japan where they get the most excited and hysterical. 'The Japanese fans are probably the most aggressive and at the same time the most restrained. They will charge towards you and then suddenly stop as if there is an invisible barrier,' Daniel said.

One time he appeared in a Japanese programme called *Let's Go To School* after two girls wrote to the programme makers and said they wanted Daniel to pay a visit. 'These two young Japanese guys in tuxes who presented the show told me that no one knew I was going and that it was going to be a big surprise. We got round the corner and there were hundreds of girls leaning out of the windows to a dangerous degree. Normally, it's kind of like big Japanese celebrities so they're not used to other famous people coming around.' Daniel joked that he had to leave one girl 'for dead' at the school after she fainted the moment he spoke to her to apologise for accidentally brushing against her in a corridor.

Another time Daniel was mistaken for *Lord of the Rings* star Elijah Wood and was asked to sign a photograph of him. 'I couldn't say it in Japanese so I wrote, "I'm not Elijah Wood but thanks anyway." If I was a bit more puerile I would have written, "*The Lord of the Rings* is Rubbish."'

There are videos around of other Japanese fans meeting Daniel who are either struck dumb or scream. 'Japanese fans are the most enthusiastic without doubt,' explains Daniel. 'I find it all a bit strange but it is there [Japan] that I had my own kind of Beatlemania.' At one Japanese press conference, Daniel mentioned how he had been sent a giant ear. 'The whole conference collapsed. They loved it.'

There is, too, the occasional British fan who finds it all too overwhelming. 'This fourteen-year-old girl came into my dressing room with her dad – he was clearly not a Potter fan, barely knew who I was – and she started freaking out. You have to address that situation very early on, otherwise she'll spend the next ten minutes crying ... that could be the only interaction they have with you and you know if they do end up crying they will walk away thinking they have missed an opportunity.'

Daniel has also had to deal with proposals of marriage and now has a readymade tactic: 'Try and make it funny. Like if somebody shouts, "I love you", I normally shout, "I love you too, but I think we should see other people." John Larroquette, who did *How to Succeed in Business Without Really Trying* with me in New York, suggested that I say, "I love you too, I'm so glad I don't know you", which is kind of great. Generally speaking, it's always very sweet and I doubt many of them expect they're going to get a yes, so you're not really disappointing people too much. Just say, "I'm flattered but spoken for."'

As Susan Dominus noted in her article in the *New York Times* when she followed Daniel on his Venice Film Festival publicity rounds, he always worked a crowd in a friendly and professional manner: 'Radcliffe's manners were unfailingly polite as he fielded questions; he moves through the world like a royal who not only embraces his responsibility to his public but also obsesses about it. "I meet hundreds of people, and I'm not going to remember them," he said. "But every single one of them will remember their interaction with me.'"

His way with the public impressed one particular American group. The National League of Junior Cotillion students and directors voted Daniel one of the Ten Best-Mannered People of 2012 'for the kindness extended to his Harry Potter fans'. The annual selections are based on 'the demonstration of dignity, honor and respect'.

Daniel has said he just doesn't understand why girls see him as a sex symbol, 'but if that's how they want to see me that's fine. I certainly won't be doing anything to dissuade them.' The worldwide hysteria is for 'a different type of me, the me that's on red carpets and stuff. That's who a lot of people seem to be attracted to. But the me who sits in a dark room for eight hours watching TV with a big bowl of pasta, in my socks and underwear isn't as appealing to women.'

For the cricket-loving and music-obsessed young man (he has some pretty diverse tastes) who soaks up general knowledge and facts from books and television, his allure is mystifying. 'I'm happy in my own company; I'm not particularly what people want when they meet a movie star, which I'm quite happy about.'

The only time that Daniel ever lost it when questioned about his personal life was when he, Emma and Rupert attended a charity event, Festival Carols of Christmas, in December 2012. He had suffered the inevitable questions about a relationship between him and Emma, answering politely, 'I have absolutely no feelings for her whatsoever. She's like a sister to me.' But somewhere along the line, something snapped and Rupert had to calm Daniel down after a very uncharacteristic outburst from him. 'I have not been thinking, hoping, wishing, fuck, dreaming of having sex with Emma and her perfectly sweet, delicious bum and perky tits since the first day I saw her, when we were eleven!'

He once made another rather graphic comment to *Heat* magazine – and one wonders what sparked it. 'This is way too much information, but I don't like girls with nothing down there either. It freaks me out. You have to have something, otherwise it's fucking creepy.'

In another interview, Daniel said he had a 'massive crush' on singer Katy Perry. 'I've been in a room with her and couldn't say anything. I thought she had probably seen an interview with me when I admitted my crush and knew these thoughts are in my head. I couldn't even look at her because she might think I was just this weird boy fan.'

He was, on reflection, possibly too open about how he had lost his virginity as well. He had said how the woman in question was older than him and that, although the age difference 'wasn't ridiculous, it would freak some people out'. In 2008, *US Weekly* claimed the 'older woman' Daniel had talked about was his ex-girlfriend assistant hairdresser Amy Byrne who was twenty-three when the two met on the set of *Harry Potter and the Goblet of Fire* in 2005 when Daniel was sixteen. There were reports that Daniel visited her rented home and that Amy did his hair and make-up before publicity events in London. Daniel's publicist Vanessa Davies said the two were just 'good friends'.

Despite the inevitable interest in his love life, Daniel has said that he likes the idea of being a young parent and would like to meet someone before he reaches the age of thirty and do the normal thing of settling down with a wife and family. It is one of Daniel's hopes that, when he eventually marries, the union will be as enduring as his parents who have been happily married since 1984. 'My mum is the only girlfriend my dad has ever had,' he said. 'I look at them and I see how they've built their own mythology together. That's what I want, to build a universe with someone. Everything that happens prior to finding that one person is kind of rubbish. You've got to find somebody who you love and who loves you, and then cling onto them … I really want to have kids. I've grown up around lots of people who were having kids when I knew them, because a lot of them were a lot older than me. And I saw the wonderful change in them. A lot more tired, a lot more happy.'

Daniel was back as a cover star in *Fiasco* magazine in November 2013, and his comments about wanting to be in an action film were picked up by the world's press: 'I would love to do an action film but I need to find the Simon Pegg [the English actor, writer and comedian most famous for the 2004 film *Shaun of the Dead*] role. I kind of fancy playing nerdy computer guy in something.'

CHAPTER 15

MOVING ON

Daniel's appearance on *The Graham Norton Show* on 7 December 2013 caused something of a stir. Gone was his usual short-haired clean-cut look and in its place was a very long-haired young actor – Daniel was sporting hair extensions for his new role as hunchbacked assistant Igor in his upcoming film *Frankenstein* and, despite his determination to talk seriously about the project, it was his dramatically different image that caught everyone's attention. Although he had made a public appearance shortly before at a screening of *Kill Your Darlings* at Cineworld Haymarket, this was the first time television viewers had seen the shoulder-length hair.

Of course, as expected, Norton was to josh twenty-four-year-old Daniel about it – 'This is the price you pay,' he said of the young actor's weird new look. Fellow guest, TV cookery show star Mary Berry couldn't get over the new image. She stroked his hair and commented how soft it was. 'Is it yours?' she asked.

Daniel replied: 'It's from, I assume, a dead person or a person that donated their hair.' He added that the first time he looked in the mirror he thought he looked like American killer Charles Manson: 'I don't mind how it looks but I mind dealing with it. I don't know why any man would have it voluntarily. The amount of work it takes, having to dry it – doing anything to it is a fucking nightmare. I do have a whole new sympathy for women. I wouldn't be growing my hair this long in my own time.' The dramatically different look was fun, Daniel said, but it would not be a permanent change. The one positive thing about his scruffy look was that he was not so easily recognisable in public!

His TV appearance prompted a flurry of social network comments:

'My first thought was ewww, but it's for a Frankenstein movie. Freaky is appropriate in this case…that is definitely not a good look for him…'

'I'm actually not fond of Daniel's longer looks, but he surely looks better than another long-haired celebrity, Chord Overstreet of *Glee*. At least Daniel's looks clean and taken care of…'

'Looks like weirdo. That's just not right…'

'…Ewww is right! And what is it with those eyebrows. I don't think anything would make him look good.'

But it was early days for *Frankenstein* with rehearsals just started. Daniel said his character of Igor 'is given a lot more depth than we've seen him allowed in any other incarnations of the story'. He was drawn to the 'wild script' by Max Landis because 'it constantly surprises you and it's great, great fun as well'. He added: 'The relationship between Igor and Victor is one of two young men at the absolute forefront of the technology of the day. Plus it's a story about them pushing each other further, eventually having to make decisions about their relationship and their mortality.' He was, he said, 'very excited' to be working with James McAvoy as the title character. The main cast was completed by Adam Scott and Jessica Brown Findlay. It was scheduled to be released in October 2014.

In the lead-up to its release, Daniel was regularly photographed on set, including in what looked like a particularly tough scene when his hands were tied and in the wet and the cold he had to stumble around in mud at Greenwich in London. He also had to run frantically wearing a purple striped waistcoat and baggy trousers and dash alongside a moving car. It was all watched by curious onlookers, who also noted how Daniel still took time out to chat to some of the child actors working with him.

It had been another hard-working year for Daniel. Also scheduled for release in May that year was *The F Word*, a romantic comedy, one of three of his films to have been shown at the Toronto International Film Festival the previous year. 'It's that rarest of things,' he said of the film. 'It's a really cheerful, happy film without being sentimental.' Daniel took the role of Wallace, trying to find love again after the end of a relationship. He meets Chantry (Zoe Kazan) at a party who has a boyfriend, so she and Wallace decided to be just good friends (the 'F' in the title stands for friends).

'Wallace is a character very close to myself,' said Daniel. 'When I got to the second page of the script and Wallace was correcting some guy's grammar, I realised I am that irritating person.' He and Zoe hit it off straight away. 'She was fantastic to work with. So much fun. I am very enthusiastic and it is nice to meet someone who matches that level. She is super smart and really funny, a great actress.'

The high regard was mutual, with Zoe saying, 'Dan Radcliffe is someone who I think is just immensely talented. I'd heard nothing but amazing things about him and I had met him once. We had a drink and I had just sort of thought how smart and funny he was, and that those qualities, the kind of lighter qualities, we hadn't really seen on screen before. So I was excited to play with him and draw some of that out.'

The film was shot in Canada, where Daniel now felt quite comfortable after his long stay there. *The F Word* was, he said, the first contemporary project he'd done since Potter 'but it was in another world. It was nice to be able to say words I might say.'

As the *Hollywood Reporter* was to say: 'Hitting all the rom-com notes with wit and some charm, it'll be a crowd-pleaser in theatres and help moviegoers move on from seeing co-star Daniel Radcliffe only as the world's favourite wizard.'

The film was directed by Michael Dowse, who had sent the script to Daniel before getting a speedy agreement from him to do the film. 'First of all we were on Skype and then I came to London,' recalled Dowse. 'The minute I met Daniel I knew he was right for the part.'

The screenplay was by Elan Mastai and the rest of the cast included Mackenzie Davis, Adam Driver, Jordan Hayes, Oona Chaplin, Rafe Spall and Megan Park.

The Toronto International Film Festival was a huge deal for Daniel with not only *The F Word*, his first romantic comedy, but also *Horns* and *Kill Your Darlings* being shown. 'It was nice to do a film where at no point did I have to get covered in blood or break down or have a massive fight,' he said – testimony to just how intense his workload had been over the last year or so.

There had been a pretty tortuous press conference for Daniel at the festival, where he sat alongside Dowse and Mastai, and Zoe, Adam and Megan. The conference lasted nearly an hour and many of the questions were directed at Daniel. He looked bemused when he was asked about the 'loopy' Canadian sense of humour, and no doubt wondered where this sense of humour was when he commented on how, apart from rehearsals, he just wanted to get on the set 'and take the piss out of Zoe' and was met with total silence. He gamely fielded awkward questions about love and sex including one about whether he thought men and women could be friends. 'Yes. Have I slept with all of them? No.' And he said yes, he was in favour of monogamy: 'Hooking up is not fun. Sex is a lot more fun if you're actually enjoying the company of the person you're with.' There was reference to how Zoe and Daniel had to swim in Lake Ontario for one scene, only finding out later that it was potentially poisonous – 'it would have been nice to know before'.

Daniel then painstakingly described how to make the Fool's Gold sandwich featured in the film: 'It's a loaf of Italian white bread coated in butter, baked, hollowed out then spread with an entire jar of peanut butter, an entire jar of jam, and then you stuff it with a pound of crispy bacon. I ate it and it tastes exactly like you would think it tastes: It's fantastic ... But it's not like anyone is going to be tempted to eat that at home.'

There were other questions about how he handled fame and

if he thought love had changed over the years. To one question about how he felt about his previous work, Daniel replied, 'I wouldn't be sitting here talking to you if it wasn't for Harry Potter. I'm under no illusions.' One got the impression he was relieved when it was all over. But with not one but three films of his on show, he had to survive all the promotional events. And he was delighted that, although not planned that way, he had a showcase for three vastly different performances. 'To come to Toronto with three totally different films and three totally different roles – I felt very lucky to be able to show them all at once to people so hopefully, if they went into the festival asking that question, they got their answer.'

There were mixed reviews from the film festival for *The F Word* – the title of which was later changed to *What If* and for which a general release date was given as August 2014. Tim Robey in *The Telegraph* wrote: 'As a chance for Radcliffe to take baby-steps as a romantic lead, it's more successful than not – he's a polite Brit to whom the star brings his natural diffidence. By now Radcliffe's very obviously a lovely chap, and his persona here is appealingly, straightforwardly, close to the real one … Radcliffe has had three films at the festival this year – the black comedy *Horns*, Beat biopic *Kill Your Darlings*, and this. Though it seems the least prepossessing, it actually needs him – his stolid decency – or it would just be all T'ronno scenesters at ping-pong bars, and their hard-to-care-about love lives. Lively and promising though Kazan is, her character's a bit of a shambles, claiming betrayal when Wallace tries to be honest, as if she hasn't been making goo-goo eyes herself. On the girlfriend front – and, frankly, the rom-com front – our boy wizard can do better, but you've got to start somewhere.'

The Guardian's Henry Barnes said: 'It's pulled this way and that by a hiddly-fiddly soundtrack, spun senseless by scene after scene of Radcliffe and Kazan trading flirtatious banter. "A pickle jar is like a tomb for cucumbers," muses Kazan. Radcliffe, actually rather good in the role of a deadpan Brit, looks at her like she's truly screwy, before remembering he's in a rom-com and therefore the line's endearing … There's little meat, loads of fat and way too much sugar. It's really hard to finish. It's liable to leave you queasy.'

In January 2014, it was announced that *The F Word* was nominated by the Canadian Screen Awards for Best Motion Picture and Best Adapted Screenplay, with Michael Dowse nominated for best Achievement in Direction and Mackenzie Davis for Best Performance by an Actress in a Supporting Role. More crucially for Daniel, he was nominated for Best Performance by an Actor in a Leading Role. Screenplay writer Elan Mastai commented: 'For all his fame and success I don't think Daniel has ever been nominated for an acting award, so I think it's really amazing that Canadians have recognised the actor that he's become.'

What If had its London premiere in Leicester Square on 12 August 2014. It was hailed as the 'feelgood film' that summer but was not the massive smash anticipated and its opening box-office takings were to rank among the bottom three of Daniel's film departures from Harry Potter. The *Daily Mirror* was lukewarm in its review saying: '… Meanwhile Radcliffe's limitations are again thrown into sharp relief. His performance is so flat – and his character so dull – you wonder why Chantry is wasting her time on him.'

Supernatural thriller *Horns* was based on the book by Joe

Hill, son of supernatural author Stephen King. The screenplay was by Keith Bunin, the director was Alexandre Aja, and the cast included Juno Temple, Max Minghella, Joe Anderson and Kelli Garner. *Horns* premiered at the Toronto International Film Festival on 6 September 2013 and like *What If* was filmed in Canada.

After the widespread publicity about Daniel's personal drinking problems, there was an ironic theme to the story, with Daniel's character Ig Perrish awaking one morning after a heavy night. Luckily, the similarity ends there, as Perrish realises horns are starting to grow on his head. The story gets even darker when he becomes the main suspect for the rape and murder of his girlfriend (played by Juno Temple).

On the obligatory round of interviews to publicise the film, Daniel once again talked about this role being 'very, very different' to all previous ones. He said the part was 'deeply emotional and also incredibly outrageous in some ways ... Ig is going to be one of the biggest challenges I've had to date. He's in the grip of mourning his girlfriend, who has been murdered and raped, and in the middle of that he has to deal with the small town he grew up in where they have all turned on him.'

Completing the film was not without its problems with rumours that its visual-effects studio, Montreal-based Newbreed, was experiencing a 'severe cash crunch' and that a new company would have to be brought in to complete the shots. The original delivery date of the film was put back from May to July 2013. The dark role, with Daniel having to act drunk throughout – one scene took twenty-five takes – and long sessions in the prosthetics make-up department, took its toll on Daniel. 'There were some days when I got in and

I just didn't really want to talk to anyone else. I just wanted to go to bed. It's gruelling because every scene is somebody confessing something to me or somebody confessing something to someone.'

The horror film also featured a hundred snakes, one of which escaped and went missing for hours. It was finally found in a warm hiding place. Said Daniel: 'It did get a bit tense at one point. We had brought a hundred snakes into Canada and let them all loose. But we had to leave with the same number.'

Director Aja described Daniel as 'a very interesting actor' and praised the young star for his bravery in breaking away from the Potter franchise. 'I really appreciate the fact he took that risk because a lot of actors in the same position would have chosen not to expose themselves in such a daring character.' He added: 'I think people will see that Daniel Radcliffe's character fits with the continuity of everything he's done before. I feel that people who grew up watching him in Harry Potter will also identify with his character in *Horns*. There is a dark side, but it's very humane. He's the one who's turning into the devil, but he's the most human character.'

For Daniel, it was another role far removed from the one that had taken up so much of his early life, the character he would forever be associated with. 'I think one of the challenges will be to get people to see me as an actor rather than just one character,' he said. 'And to a certain extent, some people will always see me as this character. But the minute you accept that, it frees you slightly. As long as the people that see me forever as Harry aren't casting directors, other actors and directors, I should be fine in getting other jobs. So far I've been all right.'

There were mixed reviews. One critic stated it was worth

watching 'for the way it liberates Radcliffe from the Potter franchise…' Another said that unfortunately the film 'never manages to figure out the right outlet for Radcliffe's performance'. It was described as 'certainly the weirdest movie' of his career. On this occasion, Daniel's optimism about a drastic role change was a little misplaced. 'It's a risk in as much as any film is a risk, but all I can do ultimately is trust my instincts and my judgement and find the work that excites me and make the kind of films I want to see … I don't think of it as a huge risk but I am not in the business of saying what about my life is risky and what's not. I just have to keep doing it.'

A good review did come from website Movie Pit, however. 'The real revelation in *Horns* and most likely the main reason for its success has got to be Daniel Radcliffe's strong performance. If any role can help shed away the Harry Potter label thus far, this is it. His focus and commitment scene after scene is a marvel to behold. He definitely anchors the picture at its most venerable state especially during the violent, over-stuffed third act.'

There was also *Gold*, the film it was announced in October 2013 that Daniel would be starring in. Directed by James Watkins who had worked with Daniel in *The Woman in Black*, the film is based on *The Perfect Distance*, an account of the Sebastian Coe–Steve Ovett rivalry in the 1980 Olympics. Daniel would be playing Coe. 'I will be wearing very short shorts over the coming months,' Daniel commented. He certainly cut a bizarre figure when practising his running for the film as he still had the Frankenstein hair extensions! The film was shot in Britain and Russia in April 2014.

In November 2013, Daniel made a mean and moody

black-and-white film to advertise the 300th issue of *ShortList* magazine. He is seen chain smoking at an old typewriter with words such as 'Excited' and 'Excessive Smoking' flashed on screen. Top crime authors were invited to pen 300-word stories for the magazine and Daniel's trailer was used 'to whet your appetite' … 'one of the biggest actors on the planet'. Those involved with the filming were impressed by Daniel's willingness to do what was asked of him: 'When we asked if we can make him look "rained on" for the final shot, Radcliffe, notoriously up for a challenge suggested we tip a bottle of water over his head. There's a sense that he isn't simply a canny young upstart trying to shrug off Potter pigeonholing with a couple of well-placed "leftfield" and grown-up roles. Radcliffe is leftfield. He's an eccentric, somewhat intense oddity, unafraid to test the boundaries and probably get it wrong here and there.'

Again, managing time in between his other projects, Daniel was a guest star in the first episode of the TV series *The Kumars* which was returning to SKY1 on 15 January 2014 after a seven-year break. Also starring with him were Chevy Chase and Olivia Colman. Meera Syal reprised her role as the risqué grandmother Ummi, at one point explaining to Daniel: 'The Weasleys are just like an Indian family; boy, boy, boy, then they have a girl and they stop having sex.' Daniel was introduced as 'Master Radcliffe' and described as a 'marketable young man'. It was another example of how Daniel was slowly changing his image and making a name for himself in so many different ways. 'A lot of people will be generous and open-minded enough to see me as other people,' he said of moving on from Harry Potter. 'But I think that to a lot of people I will always be Harry. However, there's one thing that might work in my favour, and that's that I'm still going to change so much, I hope. I'm not going to grow – that's tough luck – but hopefully the change in me physically will help people disassociate me from Potter. But I would never want to dismiss it because it has given me every opportunity. You know, people say to me, "Are you worried about being typecast?" – I've got to say no. I haven't been so far, so I don't know why I should in the future.'

On *The Kumars*, Daniel also got the chance to perform his party trick – playing the signature tune of *Match of the Day* on his cheeks. (Another party trick of his is being able to 'count' to three with his tongue, rolling it into weird shapes – a knack displayed on TV a couple of times including on the Spanish show *El Hormiguero* in February 2012 and the Ellen DeGeneres talk show in the States.)

In early 2014 came the big announcement that Daniel was to return to Broadway, this time in his hit play *The Cripple of Inishmaan*, and with the full British cast. The New York run was to preview on 12 April and officially open on 20 April at the Cort Theatre. For Daniel this was a wish come true. 'We were fortunate enough that we got a great reaction from London crowds, but I remember at the time really thinking, "God, this play I really think it would go down so well in New York, and I really hope we get the chance to do it there."' Speaking to the American press, Daniel said he was more than ready once again to play a physically challenging role. 'Potter was a very physical role and I got to do so many stunts and so many different types of getting hit or falling or climbing up something. There are a couple of very physical moments in *Cripple* for Billy – one is at the end of the show, and one, a moment early on, where he has to climb down a wall in our production.'

Daniel was once again to become the darling of Broadway. In the *New York Times*, Ben Brantley wrote: 'Mr Radcliffe's Billy embodies the essence of this beautifully ambivalent play without dominating it, which would throw the production off balance. Despite Billy's gnarled form, which makes even walking an agonizing process, he often registers as just one of many vivid portraits in a gallery of oddballs. But then he turns his sea-blue stare outward, and the loss and loneliness in his eyes lance right through you.' David Rooney of the *Hollywood Reporter* said, 'the Harry Potter star has never been better, more than measuring up in this flawless ensemble'. The *Chicago Tribune*'s Chris Jones said Daniel's performance was the best of all three of his Broadway appearances, adding: 'It really breathes as it hobbles along, and yet it's never showy nor overly optimistic.' 'Radcliffe plays Billy with a crafty mix of guile and vulnerability,' wrote Thom Geier in *Entertainment Weekly*. 'His Irish accent is more than passable and while he doesn't stint from the role's physicality – curling his left hand and stiffening his left leg throughout the show – he refrains from milking the disability for easy sympathy.'

After the opening night *The Guardian* stated that, as much as the critics loved Daniel's 'warm, sympathetic performance', they were also impressed with the play itself and suggested both cast and the production were likely to win Tony nominations that May. In fact, shortly after it was announced that Daniel was to return to Broadway and six weeks before rehearsals for *The Cripple of Inishmaan* were even due to begin, there was an outcry at the news that lobbying to get Daniel a Tony nomination for the play was already underway. Imogen Lloyd Webber (daughter of Lord Lloyd Webber), news editor of Broadway.com, was behind the ploy to get the young star nominated for award, New York theatre's equivalent of the Oscars. She told Fox TV: 'Good for him! It's great that a young person of his stature wants to come to Broadway, so I do hope the Tony Committee nominates him because he deserves it.' This rallying was, commented one critic, 'unprecedented' before the actor 'has even set foot on the stage'. But Daniel's supporters noted how the official opening of *The Cripple of Inishmaan* on 20 April meant it was in good time for the cut-off date for Tony nominations on 24 April.

In February that year, Daniel won the prize for Best Actor in a Play at the WhatsOnStage Awards voted by the public for his role in the play, which bode well for his getting this ultimate acclaim for his performance. Still sporting his hair extensions for his role as Igor, Daniel cut a dramatic figure at the Prince of Wales Theatre. ('You would have been forgiven for thinking Daniel Radcliffe wasn't in attendance at last night's WhatsOnStage Awards ... Mainly because he strolled in with LONG hair. Not quite Rapunzel-long, but still significantly lengthy,' commented *Tatler* magazine.) Event host Mel Giedroyc exclaimed, 'Oh my days, it's Oliver Cromwell as I live and breathe!'

Accepting the trophy, Daniel said, 'I am deeply honoured to receive this prestigious award. I accept it on behalf of the whole cast who together helped make this production of *The Cripple of Inishmaan* a truly joyous experience for me as an actor ... It's very lovely to win. We were blessed with amazing audiences all the way through the run.' Also nominated for the award was

James McAvoy, who takes the lead role alongside Daniel's Igor in the film *Frankenstein*.

It was 'kind of crazy' to be nominated against James as well as Ben Whishaw (nominated for his role as club owner's son Bay in *Mojo*), he said, and added: 'Watching them was very formative in my experience of theatre … They were just amazing so to be in a category alongside them is just surreal.' He also thanked director Michael Grandage 'for his leadership and inspirational direction'. Daniel said he was 'absolutely thrilled to now be given the opportunity to take Martin McDonagh's "achingly witty and poignant play" to Broadway'.

The director also won an award, among four he had scooped for his sell-out seasons at the Noel Coward Theatre, this time around for Best Director.

To Daniel's delight, his old Potter chum Rupert Grint was named Newcomer of the Year (the same award Daniel had won in 2008 for *Equus*) for his portrayal of a 1950s drug dealer in *Mojo*. And Rupert said he had Daniel to thank after his encouragement to make the stage debut. 'Dan has always said it's a great thing to do and he absolutely loves it. Just watching him enjoy it told me it must be quite fun,' said Rupert.

But there was to be a bitter blow for Daniel. For he was *not* among those prestigious Tony nominations for *The Cripple*, which comprised Sarah Greene for Best Performance by an Actress in a Featured Role, Best Revival of a Play, Best Direction of a Play (Michael Grandage), Best Scenic Design (Christopher Oram), Best Lighting Design (Paule Constable) and Best Sound Design (Alex Baranowski). There were two categories in which Daniel could have been nominated –

Best Performance by an Actor in a Featured Role in a Play (the nominees were Reed Birney in *Casa Valentina*, Paul Chahidi, Mark Rylance and Stephen Fry in *Twelfth Night*, and Brian J Smith in *The Glass Menagerie*) and Best Performance by an Actor in a Leading Role in a Play (the nominees were Samuel Barnett in *Twelfth Night*, Bryan Cranston in *All the Way*, Chris O'Dowd in *Of Mice and Men*, Mark Rylance in *Richard III* and Tony Shalhoub in *Act One*). Even Daniel's old foe the *Daily Mail* offered its condolences to the young actor saying: 'The 24-year-old was snubbed in the nominations for the 68th Tony Awards – which recognise achievement in Broadway Theatre – when they were announced on Tuesday despite receiving excellent reviews for his role in *The Cripple of Inishmaan*. He previously lost out for his role in *Equus* back in 2008 and *How to Succeed in Business Without Really Trying* in 2011 – roles which many believed he deserved nominations for.' *The Cripple of Inishmaan* finished its run on 20 July 2014.

Daniel was gallant and gentlemanly over his not getting a Tony. Any disappointment was hidden by his delight that the roles were pouring in as proof there would always be life after Harry Potter for him: 'The fact that I get to do so many different things is one of the parts of my job that make it incredibly fun. Maybe the fact of playing one character in one environment for quite a long time built up an energy to want to get out after Potter and grab as many different things as possible; you are constantly learning something new, so you are always in a very receptive state.'

Among these new roles was as civil engineer Washington Roebling, the main designer of New York's Brooklyn Bridge.

Backing for the film came from Goldcrest Films and, said managing director Pascal Degove, 'Having Daniel's involvement is a massive coup for the film; not only is he perfect for the role, but he's consistently proved himself to be one of the very few actors who is genuinely a massive draw for audiences of all ages.'

It was also announced that shooting was to start soon for a Japan-set crime thriller called *Tokyo Vice* in which Daniel was playing real-life American crime reporter Jake Adelstein of the *Yomiuri Shimbun* newspaper who investigated notorious gangster Tadamasa Goto. It would be a debut film-directing role for Anthony Mandler who said of Daniel: 'I think he's absolutely ready to go to the next level. We sat down a couple of times and had some incredible meetings. His take on the work and on the book is right in line with mine, and I think it's all about the next phase after Mr Potter.'

In May 2014 came the news that Daniel was in talks about the lead role in the film adaptation of Dave Eggers' comic novel *You Shall Know Our Velocity*. He was mooted for the role of 'bookish' Will and friend of ladies' man Hand. The story tells of how, after their friend Jack is killed in a car crash, the two set out to scatter his ashes at the Pyramids, taking with them his insurance pay-out to give away to those in need along the way. Director for the project was to be Peter Sollett. Quoted in the *Hollywood Reporter*, Christian de Gallegos of the International Film Trust behind the project said: 'Playing the lead character in the biggest film franchise of all time, Daniel Radcliffe has managed to establish himself as one of the most versatile actors of his generation and he is perfect to play Will.' Filming was scheduled to start early in 2015.

But Daniel's determination to embark on – and stay with – a totally new acting life away from Harry Potter was sometimes hindered when he was constantly linked with Jo Rowling's new spin-off Potter projects. In November 2013, it had been reported that a play based on her Harry Potter tales was expected to open in the West End 'within two years'. Rowling would not be doing the writing but she was to co-produce. Baz Bamigboye in the *Daily Mail* said that the play would be steered by prominent London and New York producers Sonia Friedman and Colin Callender and would focus on 'the previously untold story of Harry Potter's early years as an orphan and outcast'. Warner Bros. were also said to be involved. Rowling was quoted as saying that 'Sonia and Colin's vision was the only one that made sense to me, and which had the sensitivity, intensity and intimacy I thought appropriate for bringing Harry's story to the stage'.

Then there was Rowling's proposed film, *Fantastic Beasts and Where to Find Them*. Daniel had stressed that he would not be involved but there was regular speculation. 'You don't want to say no,' he said, 'because it just sounds like you're being dismissive and then that sort of gets taken out of context on the Internet and people start going, "Oh, he's turned his back on it, and it's this and that", and it's not any of that, but the reality is I will have worked for some time on that stage to get people to see me as an actor rather than just that character. So I'm not sure what the benefits would necessarily be of stepping back to it.'

It didn't help quell the rumours when Rowling joked that she would love him, Emma and Rupert to make some 'heavily camouflaged cameos' in the film, based around Newt Scamander, the fictional author of *Fantastic Beasts*, the textbook used by Hogwarts students. In an interview with Emma, Rowling said, 'I want you and Dan and Rupert in really heavy make-up in the background of a scene in *Fantastic Beasts*, and I'll join you and we'll sit in a bar room having a laugh for an afternoon. Do you not think that would be fantastic? We can mess around as extras in the background. And then we can see if anyone can spot us. I personally would like to be in drag, just to make sure no one can spot me at all.'

But, although he said maybe, just maybe, there could be a slight chance to link up with Warner Bros. again, Daniel remarked: 'I don't think I'm going to be coming back. We can't be doing these characters when we're forty, so there has to be a line drawn.' *Fantastic Beasts* is set seventy years before the arrival of Harry, Ron and Hermione at Hogwarts and, added Daniel, with an air of never say never, 'I might just return if time travel rears its head again…'

He wasn't enamoured of the idea of there being a Harry Potter musical, either, despite his Broadway success and despite the fact the idea had been mooted some time ago, although not seriously. 'I do like musicals,' he said. 'I do love Broadway. And I do love Harry Potter. Do I want those things to be combined though? My instinct is that I don't.'

One early false rumour of early 2014 was that Daniel was to play Prince Eric in a film adaptation of Disney's animated classic *The Little Mermaid* and that Emma Watson would play Ariel.

It has been an incredible journey for Daniel. He has had to deal with mega-stardom at such a young age, battle through the angst of his teenage years, fight his own demons and live his life on the public world stage – all before reaching thirty. As he himself said, 'There was some part of me as a kid that thought I was not allowed to express anything negative about my life. The expectation of me is that I should just be delighted all the time. I do have a wonderful life and I've been very fortunate, but in the last few years I've been going, "You do have a wonderful life, but you also have a very weird life at times and you are allowed to have feelings about that." I am generally upbeat though.'

Perhaps it is fitting at this point to repeat the words Daniel said at the premiere of the final Harry Potter film: 'I don't think the end of the story happens tonight because each and every person who will see this film will carry this story with them through the rest of their lives. A huge thank you to all of you, first of all for giving me the job and to Jo for letting me have the job. Every opportunity I get from now on goes down to the fact I got very, very lucky when I was eleven.'